Cleopa

Although there are many books written about the most famous Cleopatra, this is the only study in English devoted to her less well-known but equally illustrious namesakes.

Cleopatras traces the turbulent lives and careers of these historically important women, examining in particular the earlier Macedonian and Ptolemaic Cleopatras, and the impact of their dynastic marriages on the history of the Hellenistic World. John Whitehorne also evaluates current views of Cleopatra VII's dramatic suicide, and considers the evolving political significance of royal women in the last three centuries BC.

Clearly and engagingly written, *Cleopatras* reveals the true significance to the ruling dynasties of the 34 known Cleopatras who were not Cleopatra the Great, and illuminates some fascinating but little-known aspects of ancient Greek and Egyptian history along the way.

John Whitehorne is Reader in Classics and Ancient History at the University of Queensland, Australia.

Cleopatras

John Whitehorne

London and New York

First published 1994
by Routledge
11 New Fetter Lane, London EC4P 4EE

Simultaneously published in the USA and Canada
by Routledge
29 West 35th Street, New York, NY 10001

First published in paperback 2001

Routledge is an imprint of the Taylor & Francis Group

© 1994, 2001 John Whitehorne

Printed and bound in Great Britain by
TJ International Ltd, Padstow, Cornwall

British Library Cataloguing in Publication Data
A catalogue record for this book is available from the British Library

Library of Congress Cataloging in Publication Data
Whitehorne, J E G (John Edwin George)
Cleopatras/John Whitehorne
p. cm
Includes bibliographical references and index.
1. Queens-Middle East-Biography. 2. Queens-Macedonia-
Biography. 3. Middle East-History-To 622.
4. Macedonia-History-To 168 BC   I. Title
DS62.23.W47   1994
939′.3-dc20   93-5583

ISBN 0-415-05806-6 (hbk)
ISBN 0-415-26132-5 (pbk)

CONTENTS

CONTENTS

ILLUSTRATIONS

between pages 102 and 103

All are reproduced courtesy of the Trustees of the British Museum.

PREFACE

'Guaranteed 100 per cent true.' That is what a learned Oxford don is said to have written jokingly (one hopes) on an offprint of a scholarly article which he was sending to an equally erudite colleague.

No such guarantee is offered or implied for what follows. Ancient history is somewhat like theoretical physics in as much as the evidence is never complete and never can be, and consequently the full truth is ultimately unknowable. The best we can do is to observe and record the evidence as accurately and fully as possible and make our hypotheses fit as closely as we can. That is what I have tried to do here.

In a general work like this one relies very heavily upon the more scholarly labours of many others. Even so, because this book was written with the general reader in mind rather than the specialist, I have resisted the temptation to append a vast bibliography and have confined myself to citing only what I thought was most important, up-to-date, or convincing. No doubt therefore I have cited references which I ought not to have cited and left uncited those which I ought to have cited.

This book had its origins in an invitation to write the article on Cleopatra for the *Anchor Bible Dictionary*. At that stage, like most classical scholars I knew that the famous Cleopatra was Cleopatra VII and I had enough maths to work out that there must therefore have been at least six others. But I never expected to find so many, or that their lives would turn out to be so varied and complex. Later, when I began to write, I naively expected to find a theme common to all of them, which could be used to draw their lives together. But despite my best efforts a common theme has obstinately refused to emerge. If there is one, it is only that power corrupts women as surely and nastily as it does men. I am sorry that this is not very profound or original. None the less I hope you will enjoy finding out about these Cleopatras as much as I did.

ACKNOWLEDGEMENTS

I am grateful to my colleague Kate Mortensen who was a mine of information about Macedonian history; Professor P. W. Pestman for kindly providing me with copies of references from his forth-coming work on the Theban choachytes; The University of Queensland for the grant of a Special Studies Program which allowed me an uninterrupted period of time for writing; the Librarian and her staff at the Institute of Classical Studies, London, where most of my writing was done.

Translations of demotic are those of the editors of the texts, except that in the interests of clarity I have occasionally taken the liberty of making a slight modification without, I hope, losing anything of the sense. All translations from Latin or Greek are my own. The illustrations are reproduced by the courtesy of the Trustees of the British Museum and I am indebted to Janet Larkin of the Department of Coins and Medals for arranging the photographs for me.

Finally my grateful thanks go to all the members of my family and others for their good-natured toleration of what must have seemed a strange obsession with the Cleopatras.

1

FROM MYTH TO LEGEND
The Earliest Cleopatras

What's in a name? Perhaps a great deal. Or perhaps not so much after all if the name in question happens to be an ancient Greek feminine name. The meaning of Cleopatra, 'famous in her father' or 'renowned in her ancestry', is clear enough. What is not so clear is what weight, if any, we should attach to the meaning of the name.

It would certainly be accurate to describe most of the earliest known Cleopatras (mythological as well as historical) as renowned in their lineage. Furthermore what inscriptional evidence there is suggests that as a name Cleopatra did not become either common or widespread until the third century BC. For example there are no more than a handful of Cleopatras known from Attic inscriptions, and none is dated to earlier than the fourth century BC. Yet neither of these facts is enough in itself to allow us to claim that the name must have been confined originally to an aristocratic elite, or to imagine that parents must always have had the meaning of Cleopatra in mind whenever they bestowed the name on one of their daughters.

A salutary warning about the dangers of using etymology to read too much into an ancient Greek name is provided by the well-known case of Myrrhine, which means 'myrtle wreath'. Myrrhine was a popular name for freeborn girls in classical Athens of the fifth and fourth centuries BC and in the New Comedy of Menander we often find it as the name of older married women.[1] Characters of this type could hardly be regarded as sex objects, of which there is a notable dearth in this style of comedy. Yet 'myrtle wreath' could also be used as a contemporary slang term for the female sex organs.[2] As a result the name could well be used in an obscene sense to give us a clue about its bearer's character (as

1

could our own name Dick, for example, if spoken in a meaningful way).

The climax of Aristophanes' famous play *Lysistrata* is a sex strike as Athenian and Spartan women get together to compel their husbands to make peace by withholding their sexual favours. In that play the Athenian housewife whose comical teasing brings her despairing and ludicrously tumescent husband almost to bursting point as the strike is put into effect is called Myrrhine. In the context the name has obviously been chosen with an eye to its sexual connotations and the name of Myrrhine's husband makes this quite clear. He is called Kinesias, a real Athenian name which shares its initial syllable with what is probably the most common ancient Greek equivalent for our own most common four-letter word. And in case anyone in the audience was still too dense to see what he was getting at, Aristophanes deliberately coupled it with a suggestive deme name Paionides – based on *paio*, 'beat', in the same way as Kinesias is based on *kineo*, 'move', and meaning the same thing. The result is that there can be no possible doubt at all about what sort of 'myrtle wreath' it is that 'Mr Farquhar' of 'Bangor' is particularly interested in.

In a particular context therefore a name can be loaded with a great deal of meaning. But it can tell us little on its own once it is stripped of its context. So too with Cleopatra. But the geographical spread of a name may be slightly more informative. The massive German classical encyclopedia of Pauly-Wissowa has entries on thirty-three Cleopatras.[3] Some of them are mythological. There is at least one who, as we shall see, might better be described as legendary, a creature of that ill-defined half-light which exists between the truly mythical and the recognisably historical. Some are definitely historical. But the only feature, apart from the name, which most of these early Cleopatras seem to share is what might loosely be called their northern connections. Like the first mythological Cleopatra,[4] they come not from the mainland of Greece, but from those exotic lands on the edges of their own small world which held such a great fascination for the early Greeks.

Although she is never explicitly named in the play, it is the best known of the mythological Cleopatras who provides a large part of the subject matter for the fourth choral ode of Sophocles' *Antigone*. By that point in the drama Antigone's role in the illicit burial of her brother Polyneices has been discovered and she has just been condemned by Creon to be entombed alive as punishment for her defiance of his edict forbidding the burial. After she has been led away under guard, the chorus stands and sings of several mythological figures who have suffered a fate similar to hers. There was Danae, walled up by her own father in his palace in Argos in response to a Delphic oracle that he would be slain by his own grandson. Yet all his precautions came to nothing when Zeus visited Danae in a shower of golden rain and got her pregnant with the hero Perseus. Then there was king Lycurgus, punished for opposing the introduction of the worship of Dionysus into Thrace. Driven mad by the god he was finally imprisoned by his own subjects in a cave on Mount Pangaeus. Finally there was Cleopatra:

> By the waters of the Black Rocks, the cleft sea,
> the Thracian Salmydessus looks to Bosporus' shore
> where once, not far from home, Ares saw
> dealt to the twin boys of Phineus
> a ruinous blow,
> a blinding from a savage wife,
> sightlessness for their eyes' orbs as they cried for vengeance,
> smitten by the shuttle points in her blood-smeared hands.
>
> Pining away, they wept in bitterness for their bitter fate,
> those sons of a mother whose marriage was no marriage.
> But by her lineage she shared in
> the ancient stock of Erechtheus,
> and in faraway caverns was she reared
> by Boreas among her father's storms,
> a wind-rider over the steep rocks,
> a child of the gods. Yet even on her
> the long-living Fates had their grip, my child.
>
> (Sophocles, *Antigone* 966–87)

Sophocles does not name Cleopatra here for he had no need to. His Athenian audience was already more than familiar with the story. The sorry tale of Cleopatra and her barbarous husband Phineus had already provided the material for several Attic tragedies. In 472 BC Aeschylus had presented a *Phineus* along with his extant play *Persians*. At some later date Sophocles himself had also written two plays called *Phineus* as well as a third on the topic called the *Tympanistae* (The Tambourine Players) about which even less is known. All these plays are now lost, but in them the

3

myth of Cleopatra would obviously have been elaborated much more fully than it is in the *Antigone*.

Cleopatra was the child of Boreas, wind-god of the North, and Oreithyia, a daughter of the legendary Athenian king Erechtheus, whom Boreas had carried off to the wilds of Thrace. When Cleopatra came of age Boreas had married her to a local ruler Phineus, king of Salmydessus, a town on the Bosporus which in later times was to become a by-word for the murderous savagery of its inhabitants. Although she bore him two sons, Phineus had Cleopatra put aside in order to take a new wife. The latter, like all evil stepmothers, soon turned against her predecessor's children. In the version of the myth used in the *Antigone* it was she who blinded them by striking out their eyes with the shuttle from her loom. In another version she accused them to Phineus, who blinded them himself only to be afflicted with blindness in his turn as a punishment from Zeus.

It is easy to see the connection between the fates of both Danae and Lycurgus and what awaits Antigone. All three got walled up alive. But apart from having been brought up in a cave herself as a young girl (*Antigone* 983), it is not entirely clear what the exact link is between what happened to Cleopatra and the fate which looms over Antigone in Sophocles' play. Perhaps the connection is with what subsequently happened to Cleopatra's two sons. In one version of the myth their evil stepmother, after she had put out their eyes, had them incarcerated, perhaps along with their mother in her tomb, and left them to starve to death; Sophocles' reference to them 'pining away' may be an allusion to this. Certainly a later up-beat ending to the myth has all three victims still alive and grateful to be rescued by the Argonauts who were travelling through the Bosporus *en route* to Colchis in search of the Golden Fleece. On the other hand another version has Cleopatra put to death by Phineus even before the children have been blinded. As so often, different writers chose to emphasise different aspects of the story with the result that the mythical details are ultimately irreconcilable if not downright contradictory.[5] All we can say for sure is that the blinding of Cleopatra's sons was a favourite incident of the Attic stage and one which must have combined the infanticidal pathos of Euripides' *Heracles* with the ever-popular theme of blindness (Sophocles' *Oedipus* plays of course, but also Euripides' *Hecuba* among the extant dramas).

The Athenians probably liked the story not only for its blood and guts but also because of the link it had with their own legendary king, Erechtheus. It was an object lesson too for any contemporary Athenian girl silly enough to think about turning her back on Athens' high civilisation in order to marry a foreigner from the ends of the earth. For what is striking to a modern observer about the variant versions of the myth is not the contradictions between them but the emphasis which all the different versions place upon the myth's connection with the peripheries of the Greek world. In this case the badlands in question are the wilds of Thrace. Yet the stories about all the other mythological heroines called Cleopatra also have in common the fact that they too are set on the fringes of the civilised world.

Homer tells a tale of another mythical Cleopatra and thereby also gives us some clue about how long the name itself must have been around the ancient world. The Cleopatra who appears in the *Iliad* (9.555–605) in the episode which Phoenix recounts to Achilles in his unsuccessful attempt to persuade the sulking warrior to return to the battlefield was the wife of Meleager, the hero of the Calydonian boar hunt. In this story the exotic location is not north-eastern Greece, but Aetolia in the North-West. Phoenix tells Achilles of a time when the city of Calydon itself had been under siege. Meleager was supposed to be fighting in the city's defence but, like Achilles, he had gone into a sulk and had refused to return to the battle which was raging for control of Calydon. As a result the attackers were on the verge of storming the city and it was only Cleopatra's tears and entreaties which finally prevailed upon her husband to set aside his wounded pride and rally to the aid of her kinsmen. For Cleopatra's own origins were partly Aetolian. It was from there that her father Idas had originally abducted her mother Marpessa, snatching her away from out of a band of dancers and carrying her off to Messene.

Then there was the Cleopatra who was the daughter of king Tros, who gave his name to Troy, and the nymph Callirhoe, the 'fair-flowing', so called because she was the daughter of Troy's river, the Scamander. It was her brother who was Ganymede, carried off to heaven by Zeus to be his cup-bearer (Apollodorus 3.12.2). And there was the Cleopatra who, along with her sister Periboia, is said to have been the first of the virgins which the people of Locris were obliged to send to Troy every year after the end of the Trojan War. This was in expiation for the crime committed by Ajax when he had dragged the suppliant Cassandra away from Athena's altar and raped her. Finally there was the Cleopatra who is said to have been the sister of king Midas, he of the ass's ears and the touch that turned all to gold.

We shall have more to say of this Cleopatra later on. But first we need to establish her background by looking briefly at the early history of Macedonia,[6] for although according to one legend Midas was king of Phrygia in Asia Minor, a strong tradition also associated him with Thrace and Macedonia. Indeed the name of Cleopatra is recorded in connection with an expedition Midas had made against Thrace and Macedonia in order to avenge the invasion of Asia Minor by the Greeks. Furthermore Macedonia is the earliest location given for the so-called Gardens of Midas, an immensely fertile region where wonderful roses with sixty petals each grew wild and where Midas is said to have captured the satyr Silenus by luring him to a spring whose waters he had laced with strong wine (Herodotus 8.138). It was in this region too, under the shadow of Mount Bermium, that according to Herodotus the earliest kings of Macedon had first established themselves. It was here that they had founded their royal capital of Aegae, which was to be the burial place of all the Macedonian kings down to the time of Alexander the Great.

Such was the atmosphere of legend surrounding the beginnings of Macedon's drive to power in the mid-seventh century BC. That drive was to culminate some three centuries later in Philip II's enforced unification of Greece and the subsequent creation by his son Alexander the Great of a Greek-speaking empire which extended right across Asia. Those achievements have been the subject of countless books and scholarly articles, but far less is known of the kingdom's early history. Indeed even during the classical period the Macedonians were always something of an unknown quantity as far as the city-states of Greece itself were concerned.

Throughout most of the sixth century BC the Macedonian kings had been on friendly enough terms with their southern neighbours. But during much of the next century relations between the kingdom of Macedon and the Greek city-states were characterised by a deep sense of mistrust, which was only occasionally set aside when the needs of self-interest became paramount. Much of the problem between them was economic in origin. When the Persians under their king Darius had expanded across the Hellespont (c. 512 BC), their occupation of the Thraco-Macedonian region had been a boon for the Macedonians. In return for an oath of fealty sworn by their king Amyntas I to the Macedonians' new Persian overlord, they had not only been permitted to extend their own territorial interests. They had also found themselves ideally situated to obtain a major share of the region's increased trade with both Greeks and Persians.

The following years saw the consolidation of both territory and trade. Persia's new European subjects, including Macedon, were hardly affected by the disturbances of the Ionian Revolt. There is little reason to believe Herodotus' (6.44) assertion that a few years after the turn of the century the Macedonians rebelled under their new king Alexander I and needed to be put down by the army of Mardonius on its way through the region towards mainland Greece on the first Persian invasion of the Greek homeland.[7] But the retreat of Xerxes' forces in 479 BC after the failure of the second Persian invasion, while initially it offered the Macedonians further opportunities for local territorial gains, inevitably led to a confrontation with the new player on the scene as the victorious Athenians attempted to extend their own influence in the region.

This brought the Macedonians face to face with a rival who was not content simply to trade. Instead the Athenians seemed intent on seizing control of the whole of the region's valuable resources of shipbuilding timber, slaves, and silver mines and diverting them to their own use. It is here that we find the origins of later Athenian suspicions of Macedon and their subsequent, mainly unsuccessful attempts to meddle in Macedonian royal politics. Yet these untrustworthy semi-barbarians (as the Athenians saw them) – a people who had actively assisted Xerxes' designs upon Greece itself by providing garrisons for the medizing cities of Boeotia (Herodotus 8.34), and who, unlike the Thracians, had been conspicuous in their failure to attack the retreating Persian armies as they passed through their territory – were in fact just as Greek in their origins as the Athenians themselves were.

In 500 BC, flush with his country's new-found wealth and importance, the young Macedonian prince Alexander I had presented himself at the Olympic Games as a contestant in the men's foot race. His Greek competitors had tried to have him excluded on the grounds that as a Macedonian he was a non-Greek and therefore ineligible under the rules to enter any panhellenic contest. Alexander, however, proved to the satisfaction of the games' marshals that he was of Argive descent and he was accordingly accepted by them as a bona fide competitor. In the race itself he came in equal first (Herodotus 5.22), making one suspect that the original protest by his rivals may well have a claim to be regarded as one of the earliest recorded examples of those 'dirty tricks' which so beset modern sport.

What Alexander had been able to demonstrate was something which, if not unique in Greek history, must nevertheless be regarded as extremely unusual. He was an Argive Greek ruling over non-Greek Macedonians. His descent, he claimed, could be traced back to Temenus, a legendary king of Argos who was himself a descendant of Heracles, the son of Zeus. Herodotus (8.137–8) tells a charming folktale of how three brothers of that line, who had been exiled from Argos, had ended up in Lebaea in Upper Macedonia. There they worked as thralls for the local king, tending his flocks and herds. Whenever the king's wife baked bread for them, the loaf intended for the youngest brother, Perdiccas, rose to twice the size of the others. Alarmed by this the king called the brothers to him and dismissed them from his service. Attempting to trick them when they demanded what was owed to them, he pointed to a shaft of sunlight falling on the floor through the smoke-hole in the roof and told them to take the wages they deserved. While the two older brothers stood there too stunned to answer, the youngest scratched a line around the patch of sunlight with the dagger from his belt and, thanking the king, symbolically collected up the sunlight three times into his tunic before all three brothers set out once more on their wanderings.

Of course the brothers were long gone by the time that the king, even more alarmed by the boy's action in gathering up the sunlight than he had been by the incident of the loaf, decided to have them pursued and killed. They had crossed a river, which then arose behind them, like the Red Sea behind the Israelites, so cutting off all pursuit, and had travelled onwards to the Gardens of Midas. From there on the slopes of Mount Bermium the three brothers set out to conquer the land of Macedonia.

It was from the youngest brother of this tale, Perdiccas, that Alexander claimed to be able to trace his descent, and it is at this point that we may be able to take our first tentative step from the Cleopatras of myth to the Cleopatras of history. When Alexander made his claim at the Olympic Games, the Argive branch of the Temenidae was presumably able to confirm to the satisfaction of the games' marshals that there had indeed been an early member of the family called Perdiccas who, along with his brothers, had been sent into exile. Whether the family had also been able to guarantee all the links in the genealogical chain which Alexander claimed connected him with Perdiccas is far less certain.[8] Nevertheless, despite later variations in the name and number of Alexander's ancestors, an official genealogy for the Macedonian royal house was certainly in place by the middle of the fifth century BC when Herodotus came to visit Macedonia. He was perhaps followed there later by Thucydides for both historians agree as to the names of the Macedonian kings down to their own time. Perdiccas I had been succeeded by his son Argaeus, from whom the royal line, the Argeadae, took its name. He in turn was followed by Philip I, Aëropus (the name also of one of the three original brothers from Argos), Alcetas, Amyntas I, Alexander I, Perdiccas II, and Archelaus.

At this stage there is no female side given for the genealogy. For that we have to wait until the hellenistic period and a biographer and antiquarian writing in Alexandria in the third century BC. In his work on the demes of Alexandria, many of which were named after the early kings of Macedon, Satyrus gives the canonical version of the royal line, beginning with Dionysus and Zeus and continuing down to the kings of his own day.[9] More importantly he also gives us the names of the mothers of some of the kings, including a Cleopatra who was the wife of Perdiccas and mother of Argaeus. She may well be the first historical Cleopatra of whom we have any knowledge.

Hammond was inclined to regard these early Macedonian queens as anachronistic projections back into the archaic period of names in common use in the royal house in the fifth and fourth centuries BC.[10] This perhaps does an injustice to Satyrus. After all Satyrus was a writer who not only had all the resources of the great Library of Alexandria at his disposal but is also generally acknowledged to have known how to use them. Admittedly it looks suspicious when we find that Cleopatra is also the name of one of the wives of the later king Perdiccas II, who ruled Macedon in the last quarter of the fifth century BC. Nevertheless it is noteworthy that Satyrus does not give names for the mothers of all the kings in his list. The list of queen mothers is complete for the first section, down to and including the mother of Ceius, the successor of Temenus as king of Argos. Most of this part of the list is mythological in character. It is complete also for the Macedonian section, from the time of Perdiccas' own mother. But in the middle, Argive section of the royal line the information is patchy, with the mothers of only a few of the kings being named.

One explanation for this might be that Satyrus was putting this information together for himself from different sources and had neither the means nor the inclination to assemble the full genealogy of the Argive Temenidae. Another explanation, which is equally plausible, might be that Satyrus was drawing on a single source, presumably of Macedonian origin, and that source genuinely did not know the names of some of the earlier queens of the line. Had it done so, it surely would have given them. Furthermore its failure to give them strongly suggests that those names which are given ought to be treated as genuine. If the later names had been invented at some time in the fifth or fourth century BC then why not go the whole hog and invent names right the way through the list?

An additional argument in favour of the historicity of these early Macedonian queens can perhaps be found in the tradition mentioned earlier, which made one of the mythical Cleopatras the sister of king Midas. Alexandrian poetry in its heyday produced many strange hybrids in the course of its search for new forms of literary expression, but few are stranger than the work to which a later scholiast was to attach a unique and tantalising note which links the names of Cleopatra and Midas. The *Alexandra* of Lycophron, written *c.* 280 BC, is a narrative poem in the form of a messenger speech from tragedy. It runs for almost 1,500 lines (about the length of a complete Greek drama) and recounts the prophecies made in the course of a single night by Cassandra, the most beautiful of the daughters of Priam of Troy. Cassandra, it will be recalled, had made a pact with Apollo. In return for a promise to accept him as her lover the god had granted her the gift of prophecy. But after she had subsequently broken her side of the bargain by refusing his advances, Apollo in anger at her deceit had let her keep his gift but withheld all belief in whatever she foretold. In the *Alexandra* the utterances of the deranged princess are reported in detail to the king the next morning by the prison guard who has been set to watch over her. One can only be amazed at his prodigious memory, given the obscurity of the language which Lycophron uses and the wealth of mythological allusion with which he weighs down his poem!

The burden of Cassandra's prophesying is that the Trojan War, soon to end in disaster for Priam and his people, is but one episode in a continuing vendetta between East and West. This will only be resolved finally when the two are united by a hero yet to be born, presumably Alexander the Great. Towards the end of the poem Cassandra foretells of the vengeance to be taken by king Midas on behalf of Asia for the Dorian invasion and colonisation of Asia Minor:

> The Phrygian, avenging the blood of his kin,
> Will sack in turn the land which was nurse to
> The Corpse-Lord, who implacable in mien
> Gives flattery-proof judgements upon the dead.
> Having once cut off his ass's ears from their
> Uttermost roots, he will bedeck his brows
> And strike fear into the bloodthirsty flies.
> (Lycophron, *Alexandra* 1397–1403)

The reference to 'ass's ears' makes it clear that 'the Phrygian' is king Midas. 'The blood of his kin', which Midas was to avenge, was most likely intended by Lycophron to refer to the Trojans as a group since they were traditionally considered to be a part of the Phrygian race. Yet in his comment on this line Tzetzes, a twelfth-century Byzantine scholiast, interpreted the word *adelphos*, which is used by Lycophron, as meaning not 'kin' in a generic sense but quite literally as 'brother/sister' and said that what the poet meant by it was the blood of Midas' sister Cleopatra.

Tzetzes may be a late writer but that is no reason to dismiss this statement out of hand. Although he gives us no further information about who this Cleopatra was, or how or why she had been killed, there seems little cause to doubt that like much else in Tzetzes' commentary this isolated piece of information goes back to an early source in the Alexandrian Library. But it seems to be too much of a coincidence that Tzetzes should record that Midas had a sister named Cleopatra; then that, according to Herodotus, the Gardens of Midas had been the starting point for Perdiccas' conquest of the rest of the land of Macedon; and finally that, according to the information given by Satyrus, the wife of Perdiccas and mother of Argaeus, the first truly Macedonian king, should also have been called Cleopatra.

Should these three different traditions be taken together and interpreted as a reflection of a real historical event? Perhaps behind them all lies a dim memory of an early dynastic alliance, only partially comprehended but none the less genuine for all that. There is a variant version of the origins of the Macedonian royal line (Justin 7.1.7–12), which inserts another king called Caranus (a name which simply means 'headman' in Doric Greek) immediately before Perdiccas and attaches most of the latter's achievements to his name. But it then goes on to tell how the Argive newcomer, after he had founded the royal capital of Aegae, 'next drove out Midas, for Midas held a part of Macedonia'. There need be no contradiction between this account and the version given by Herodotus if we see Midas' attempted vengeance for Cleopatra, 'the blood of his kin', and his subsequent expulsion as interrelated.

What I suggest is that on his first arrival in Macedonia Perdiccas probably secured his position by marrying into the family of a local ruler. Herodotus says nothing about it, having typically lost interest in the story by this time. Yet in folktales of this type it is traditionally the youngest son, the cleverest of the brothers, who eventually wins the hand of the king's daughter. Furthermore commonsense suggests that, even with divine backing, Perdiccas would have needed something more persuasive than an aristocratic pedigree from Argos and a pocketful of sunlight to achieve the takeover of a tract of prime agricultural land whose original inhabitants apparently had no intention of moving. So perhaps the name of Perdiccas' new wife was indeed Cleopatra, and perhaps she was indeed the sister of a local king called 'Midas'. Midas is a Phrygian dynastic name and although there may be some reason for doubting its authenticity in this context, since most of the Phrygian inhabitants of the region had migrated to Asia Minor some 150 years before, the name of Cleopatra may well be genuine given its other northern connections.

My guess is that at some later time, secure enough in his power to do so, Perdiccas may have disposed of this wife, perhaps under questionable circumstances. Or perhaps he merely set her aside in favour of a more advantageous alliance. King 'Midas' had objected, as well he might at this slight to his sister and therefore to himself, and had come to an armed confrontation with his erstwhile brother-in-law. The result was that the original king found himself ejected from his own native land and compelled to flee into exile with his supporters, and Perdiccas and his son and successor Argaeus were able to set up a truly Greek royal family in his place.

All this is hypothetical of course, and must remain so. But the making of such dynastic alliances was part of the very fabric and foundation of Macedonian royal power in the historical period. So too was the dangerous habit of setting them aside if anything better came along. When we consider our three different traditions together, it seems quite probable that this was the fate which also befell this early Cleopatra, the sister of king 'Midas'. Like her tragic namesake in Sophocles' plays, this Cleopatra probably found herself put aside after her sometime Prince Charming from mainland Greece had grown tired of her. Having got from her all that he needed and all that she could give him – her brother's kingdom and a son and heir to legitimise his claims and continue his line – Perdiccas doubtless moved on to consolidate and extend his authority over the rest of Macedonia by means of further dynastic marriages.

2

CLEOPATRA, PERDICCAS II, AND ARCHELAUS

The Perdiccas of the last chapter, first king of that name and legendary founder of the royal house of Macedon, must have had a happy time of it with his new kingdom. His successor as king was his own son Argaeus – something that was not always to be the case later in Macedon's turbulent history. That son, as we have seen, was most likely the result of his union with a woman who was a local princess, and probably the earliest historical Cleopatra whom we can identify with any certainty.

Although at first sight this Cleopatra appears to be a figure of legend rather than fact, as I have suggested she may well have been a member of the family already ruling the area when Perdiccas and his brothers first arrived on the scene from Argos. After first making a dynastic alliance with this family, headed at the time by a king 'Midas', Perdiccas was eventually able to displace them and drive them into exile in their turn. Such a reconstruction of events would certainly help to explain the seemingly contradictory traditions which we have about Midas, for while one source has him as a Phrygian king 'invading' Europe, another represents him as ruler of a Macedonian tribe called the Briges, who was subsequently forced to emigrate with his people to Phrygia where he became king by adoption. The detail that at the time of Perdiccas' arrival the Briges themselves may no longer have existed in the Macedonian area as a separate tribal group is not significant.[1] What is significant is that both traditions have preserved a common memory of an enmity between an indigenous people and a group of newcomers, which had arisen out of competition for the same fertile region of Macedonia.

More importantly, as far as we know, the first Perdiccas never had any trouble from his two brothers who had accompanied him

14

on his journey into exile. Presumably there was room enough in the new land for all three to carve out a decent living for themselves. Indeed it has been suggested that this story of three brothers reflects an original division of Macedonia between three different but related groups.[2] But whatever the exact historical details may have been, we hear no more about the other brothers.

Perdiccas' namesake was not to be so lucky. Perdiccas II was one of five sons of Alexander I, the king who had first proved the hellenic bona fides of the Argead house to the games marshals at Olympia. Despite a subsequent blot upon his record as a good Greek when he failed to join in immediate pursuit of the defeated Persians as they withdrew through his territories in 479/8 BC, Alexander was an astute politician who nevertheless managed to do extremely well for Macedon out of Xerxes' defeat. Initially he was able to use the Persian withdrawal from the Thraco-Macedonian region to gain yet more territory from his Thracian neighbours, thus confirming Macedon's position as the leading state in the area at this time. Then, after taking a couple of years to sniff the breeze and assure himself that it was now going to keep blowing steadily in the same direction, Alexander himself finally turned on the Persians. Out of the rich spoils of his victory over them he was able to dedicate solid gold statues of himself at the major Greek shrines of Delphi and Olympia (Herodotus 8.121, [Demosthenes] 12.21).

The inherent value of these splendid monuments (incidentally the earliest known portrait statues of a Greek ruler) has ensured that they have long since disappeared, but their dedication was enough to secure Alexander's hellenic status for all time. To later generations he would be known as 'the Philhellene' and it may have been this act of dedication that earned him that title. Paradoxically, however, the same victory over the Persians which brought him honour among the Greeks in general served to bring him nothing but trouble from one group in particular.

The success of Alexander's assault on the Persian base in the Thracian area led to his seizure of the Nine Ways, a strategically important point on the lower reaches of the great River Strymon where the city of Amphipolis was later to be founded by Athenian colonists. This in turn brought him into direct conflict with Athens. The Athenians too had designs on this area as is shown by the speedy arrival of an Athenian fleet under Cimon in 476 or

475 BC and their capture and occupation of Eion at the mouth of the Strymon.

After that life began to get a lot tougher for Alexander. The rare glimpses which we have of it show that the three-way tussle for control of the Strymon area which now developed between the Athenians, the Macedonians, and the resident Thracians lasted on and off for the rest of Alexander's lifetime. Despite the occasional Macedonian success, its cumulative effect was to leave the kingdom considerably weakened by the time of Alexander's death. Although Alexander must have been of a good age by the middle of the fifth century BC when he met his end,[3] his death none the less seems to have been violent and unexpected (Curtius 6.11.26). As a result the Macedonian succession was left uncertain and the kingdom was put up for grabs. While it has been disputed whether it had ever been Alexander's intention to divide up his kingdom,[4] the intrigues and struggles for control in the years following his death clearly show that this is what in fact happened. Apparently none of his sons had a strong enough following to command the total allegiance of the Assembly of the Macedonians, and ultimately it was they alone who had the right to acclaim a new king of Macedon.

The kingdom was therefore split up, no doubt to the intense satisfaction of the Athenians who had everything to gain if the region could be kept destabilised. Although modern scholarship recognises Perdiccas II as king of Macedon from c. 452 BC to the time of his death by natural causes c. 413 BC, his hold on the kingship was insecure for almost half of his reign. One of his brothers is said to have lived privately and therefore taken no part in the dynastic struggles. About another there is no evidence one way or the other. But the other two held principalities of their own and they were more than willing to challenge for the kingship.

What concerns us here are not the confusing and incomplete details of the feuding which ensued between Perdiccas and his brothers, nor the record of Perdiccas' shifting – not to say shifty – relations with Athens and Sparta during the period of the Peloponnesian War. It is rather to determine what part, if any, was played in the events of these years by our next Cleopatra. As the last of Perdiccas' wives and later the wife of his son (by another earlier wife) and eventual successor Archelaus, she is most definitely an historical figure and arguably one of some importance as we shall see.

We first hear of this Cleopatra in relation to the machinations surrounding the accession of Perdiccas' successor Archelaus in *c.* 413 BC. In the course of a lively discussion in Plato's *Gorgias* a Sicilian teacher of rhetoric called Polus is attempting to rebut Socrates' view that only the man who is just can also be called happy. He reminds him of the example of Archelaus, who at the time of the dramatic date of the dialogue had recently become king of Macedon by doing away with all other claimants to the throne:

POLUS   Then according to your argument this Archelaus is unhappy?

SOCRATES   Yes, my friend, if he's indeed unjust.

POLUS   Well of course he's unjust! He had no claim to the kingdom he now holds, seeing that he was born from a woman who was a slave of Alcetas, Perdiccas' brother. In all justice therefore he too was a slave of Alcetas and if he wanted to act justly, he would have stayed his slave. Had he done so, then, according to your argument, he would have been happy. But now he's become incredibly unhappy because of the immense crimes he's committed. First of all he sent for this very same master and uncle of his on the pretext of giving him back the kingship which Perdiccas had taken from him. After throwing open his house to him and his son Alexander – his own cousin and contemporary – he got them drunk, threw them in a cart and carried them off in the dead of night. Then he murdered them both and disposed of their bodies. And although he'd committed these crimes he failed to realise that he had become completely unhappy and make repentance. But a bit later he resisted becoming happy by doing what was just and bringing up his brother Perdiccas' legitimate son – a lad of about 7 years old who was the rightful heir – and handing the kingdom over to him. Instead he threw him down a well and drowned him and told his mother Cleopatra that he had fallen in and got himself killed while chasing a

17

goose. So now in so far as Archelaus is the most
unjust man in all Macedon he is the most
unhappy of all the Macedonians. Not the hap-
piest. Perhaps there are some Athenians – apart
from yourself, Socrates – who would prefer to
be any Macedonian at all rather than Archelaus!

(Plato, *Gorgias* 471a-d)

Polus is obviously the worst kind of contemporary 'talking head'
as far as Plato is concerned, and it is not surprising that Socrates
is shown to have no trouble in disposing of the intellectually
bankrupt argumentation behind this scurrilous piece of gossip. But
the gossip's content has proved a lot less tractable. Modern views
about its credibility range widely from total belief to total rejec-
tion. Some would believe all but the details. For others it is the
circumstantial nature of those same details that gives the tale its
veracity.

Whatever credence is given to items of embroidery like the
felicitous lie about the goose,[5] the basic outlines of Plato's account
are doubtless correct. After the death of his father, Archelaus'
ambition for the throne was so great that it led him to eliminate
any surviving males in the family whom he felt might challenge
his claim. His uncle Alcetas was probably well advanced in years
by this time. Yet he had to be murdered because, as a son of
Alexander I and the ruler of a principality in his own right, it
might be felt that he still had a legitimate claim to be king and,
more importantly, the means to enforce it. Alcetas' son Alexander
had to be disposed of because, as much as anything else, he was
the same age as Archelaus. Macedon was still a frontier society
where the king was required to be first in battle as well as counsel.
As an able-bodied royal contemporary whose bloodline was just
as good as that of Archelaus, Alexander would probably have been
equally acceptable to the Assembly of the Macedonians. Little
interested in the finer points of royal succession, their major
demand seems to have been that their rulers be proven warriors,
cast in the epic mould of their forebears. In addition Alexander
could presumably have counted on the support of that part of the
country once controlled by his father, had it come to a showdown
between the two cousins.

Finally there was Cleopatra's little boy. Only 7 years old, he
obviously constituted no threat personally to Archelaus. And his

18

age also meant that he did not pose any immediate danger of a challenge. Archelaus could therefore have let him live on in obscurity, as his father Perdiccas had let one, perhaps two of his own brothers live out their lives as private citizens. After all, as the boy's guardian, he could have had a close eye kept on the child and easily disposed of him later at any sign of trouble. So why did Archelaus kill him? And – perhaps just as strange – why did he not dispose of Cleopatra at the same time and obviate once and for all any possibility of revenge? The answers to these questions need to be sought in a tentative reconstruction of the position of Cleopatra at the Macedonian court.

The account which Plato puts into the mouth of Polus attempts an explanation for the murders in terms of Archelaus' supposed illegitimacy. Although his father was the king, as the child of a slave woman owned by Perdiccas' brother Alcetas, Archelaus should have taken his mother's status according to Plato. In the eyes of Athenians like Plato, coming from a state where citizen status depended upon one's father and mother both being citizens, Archelaus' birth should have made him a slave and so deprived him of any claim to the kingship, despite his royal blood on his father's side. His unnamed half-brother was born from a legitimate wife, and so for Plato it was he who should have been the rightful heir to the throne after the demise of Alcetas. Archelaus was only a bastard.

This question of legitimacy, however, is a red herring which seems to have been dragged in as a result of a mainland Greek misunderstanding of the marital customs of the Macedonian kings.[6] It has long been recognised that Macedon's two most famous kings, Philip II and his son Alexander the Great, practised polygamy. Philip had seven wives. Alexander had at least two, marrying Roxane in order to gain control of Bactria and Stateira, the daughter of the Persian king Darius, to increase his prestige among the Persian elite. It is also likely that the custom had been introduced well before Philip's time, probably as a result of contacts with neighbours like the Thracians, among whom the practice of polygamy is attested by Herodotus (5.5). The evidence for the earlier period is only circumstantial, but it has been argued that the dynastic crisis which followed the death of Philip's own father Amyntas III is to be explained as a consequence of the polygamous nature of Amyntas' union with his two wives Eurydice and Gygaea. That period saw Macedon ruled by three kings in the brief space of a decade before Philip succeeded in 359 BC and then in the 350s BC a series of challenges to the kingship of Philip himself. Like Philip, two of those three kings were Eurydice's sons, and the third was her son-in-law. The disaffected challengers were the three sons of Gygaea.[7]

Plato's comments about the lowly status of Archelaus' mother are likewise explicable in terms of a polygamous union. In societies which practise polygamy wives are commonly ranked according to status. So if Archelaus' mother was no longer considered to be the king's most prestigious wife because she had been displaced by a wife of higher status in the person of Cleopatra, then we can understand not only Plato's mistaken assumption that she was a concubine rather than a wife and his consequent social antipathy towards her, but also Archelaus' very real fears of Cleopatra's son.

The strength of polygamy is that it ensures the continuation of the line by providing many potential heirs. Its weakness is that it generally fails to give any clear indication of which heir is to be preferred. In a polygamous household all the children derive their standing from their father. All are legitimate since he is legitimately married to all their mothers. But the children's status derives from that of their mothers (which it also affects). The mother's status in turn will vary according to a number of factors, such as the standing of her family, the current political situation, her own age, attractiveness, ability to produce children, and so forth. But there can never be any fixed determination of status. Anyone's place in the family pecking order can always be changed by the arrival of a new wife, or the birth of another son and potential heir to continue the line.

This was the situation in which Archelaus is likely to have found himself after Perdiccas' marriage to Cleopatra. Up until that time he had enjoyed a position of high prestige at the Macedonian court, for whatever mainland Greeks like Plato may have thought, the Macedonians themselves clearly did not regard Archelaus as a social pariah. An undated Attic inscription,[8] which records a treaty between Athens and the Macedonians, begins the list of those signing for the Macedonians with 'Perdiccas son of Alexander, Alcetas son of Alexander, Archelaus son of P[erdiccas ...' (line 60). At that point the text is broken and it is disputed what names stood in the rest of the line. Nevertheless, as Hammond saw,[9] since the next line ends with a non-royal name we can assume that all those previously listed were members of the royal family and deduce that they were named in descending order of precedence at the Macedonian court. First came the acknowledged king Perdiccas, then his brother Alcetas (in recognition, no doubt, of his status as a powerful independent prince), then Archelaus, who was most probably the king's most important son at that time by virtue of a combination of his own seniority and the status of his mother and her family.

Sometime after the signature of this treaty, however, Archelaus found his prestige threatened when his father took Cleopatra as his new wife. As we shall see in the next chapter, the future Alexander the Great was to feel equally threatened by the marriage of his father Philip II to a later Cleopatra. Not surprisingly so, in view of the fact that at a drinking party held some time after the wedding the bride's uncle called publicly on the assembled guests to pray that the marriage would produce a legitimate heir to the throne. On that occasion the mere expression of this hope was enough to precipitate a drunken brawl. Later the fear that it might be realised was to contribute to the murder of Philip's young widow and her infant daughter, even though by that time Alexander was already secure in his position as king and there was apparently little danger to him from that source. Yet Alexander's position at Philip's court was actually much more secure than that of Archelaus at the court of Perdiccas since it seems that Philip and others may have already indicated that Alexander was the preferred heir at the time that Philip made his last marriage.

Archelaus, though, was already overshadowed by an uncle who had challenged his father's right to the kingship earlier in his reign. Now he saw his prestige not just threatened but actually eroded by Cleopatra's successful production of a son. Small wonder therefore that he should seek to do away with this Johnny-come-lately rival, if the high status of Cleopatra meant that her child was going to outrank him as heir when the throne fell vacant. Plato is therefore at least partly right when he has Polus in the *Gorgias* call the boy 'the rightful heir'. But he was the heir not because he was legitimate, while Archelaus was a bastard, but because his precedence was assured by the backing and influence of his mother's family.

An assumption of high status for Cleopatra may also help us to understand why Archelaus could not openly dispose of her son but had to tell such a far-fetched lie to account for his death. It also explains why he could not move against Cleopatra herself in the same way, for example, that Alexander the Great's mother Olympias quickly moved against Philip's last wife, eliminating that Cleopatra and her child soon after Philip's death. In the former case the power and influence of the woman's family must have precluded such a move. For reasons now lost to us it may have been politically necessary for Archelaus to retain their backing.

Accepting for a moment the hypothesis that Cleopatra's family was so powerful that Archelaus could antagonise them only at his peril, what was Archelaus to do with Cleopatra? Murder was out. Exile would have been taken as an unforgivable insult. Marrying her off to someone else was unthinkable; that would have involved making her new husband a free gift not only of her family's support but also of her own prestige as the dowager queen of Macedon. So Archelaus took her out of play in the only way he could. He married her himself.

It is Aristotle who gives us in passing the information that Archelaus also had a wife called Cleopatra (*Politics* 1311b.11). My suggestion, that this woman is to be identified with the Cleopatra who was the last wife of Archelaus' father Perdiccas, is by no means a new one. But it is one which seems to have fallen out of favour with recent historians of Macedonia. They prefer to dismiss the coincidence of names by remarking that Cleopatra was a favourite girl's name in that country.[10] Unfortunately there is little independent evidence to substantiate this claim. An article of faith, it rests on no more than the scattered occurrences of the name which are presently under discussion. Hammond also believed that a union between Archelaus and his stepmother would have been 'a pointless marriage'.[11] Yet under the prevailing circumstances the union was not only not pointless. It was unavoidable, for it was only by marrying his father's young widow that Archelaus could gain the support of her family and so secure his own grip upon the throne.

This reconstruction of the events surrounding the accession of Archelaus can only be tentative. Its credibility depends upon the acceptance of two propositions: that, like Philip II and Alexander the Great, the earlier kings of Macedon had practised polygamy; and that Perdiccas' original marriage to Cleopatra had been designed to win the support of a politically important group without whose backing his position as king would have been open to challenge. The first of these propositions has already been convincingly argued by Greenwalt.[12] The second is somewhat more tricky since there is no direct evidence about Cleopatra's family background. To find out something about it, we need to look at what had been happening in Macedonia around the time that Perdiccas took her as his last wife.

According to Plato, Cleopatra's son was about 7 years old when he met with his fatal 'accident' *c.* 413 BC. That would put Cleopatra's marriage back eight or more years to *c.* 421 BC at the latest (and confirm incidentally that she would still have been of an age to bear children to Archelaus after 413 BC, since a girl of her status would have been first given in marriage at about 18 or 19 years of age).[13] By that date Perdiccas was once more back in alliance with the Athenians. His relations with Athens had thereby come full circle because the first time that Thucydides mentions him (1.57.2) it is as someone who had once been a friend and ally of the Athenians. But that had been back in the mid-430s and there had been several fallings out since then.

The most recent tiff had been in 424 BC during the Peloponnesian War between Athens and Sparta when, for reasons of his own, Perdiccas had broken his treaty with Athens by supporting the efforts of the Spartan general Brasidas to open up a second front in the North of Greece. As is well known, Brasidas' efforts had met with sterling success when Amphipolis, the city which the Athenians had founded on the River Strymon to control the timber trade out of Thrace and Macedonia, was subverted by anti-Athenian elements in the population and surrendered to the Peloponnesians in the winter of 424/3 BC. Perdiccas does not seem to have been involved directly in this success, perhaps because he was busy whipping up anti-Athenian feeling elsewhere. Nevertheless it was not long before he showed up at Amphipolis, ready to extract an appropriate quid pro quo from Brasidas in return for the efforts he had already made on his behalf.

Perdiccas' asking price was that Brasidas and his Peloponnesian forces assist him in a further campaign against an old enemy of his own, the wily ruler of the neighbouring Lyncestians. Arrhabaeus, king of the Lyncestians, ruled the territory which bordered Perdiccas' kingdom on the West. Like the Argeads, the Lyncestae were another royal family of Greek birth, descended, so they claimed, from the Bacchiad clan which had been expelled from Corinth in the mid-seventh century BC.[14] They had settled the area around Lyncus in western Macedonia, having seized control there with the help probably of their eastern neighbours, the Illyrians. Their early history therefore was very similar to that of the Macedonian royal house but they were less well placed geographically than the Argeads, being sandwiched between an expanding Macedon on one side and assorted tribes of disorganised but ferocious Illyrians on the other.

In this position the Lyncestians not unnaturally often found themselves the object of unwelcome attentions from one side or the other. In fact it had been his desire to subdue the Lyncestians that had first led Perdiccas to make common cause with Brasidas. Thucydides (4.83) relates that as soon as Brasidas arrived in the area with his army, Perdiccas joined forces with him and the two commanders immediately set out against Arrhabaeus. But when they reached the mountain pass down to Lyncus, Brasidas suggested negotiations rather than fighting, hoping to win Arrhabaeus over as another ally for Sparta. Perdiccas retorted that he was not paying half of Brasidas' expenses to have him arbitrate. He was there to attack and destroy his enemies for him. Brasidas, however, persisted. He met with Arrhabaeus, who persuaded him to withdraw without a battle. Perdiccas was outraged but all he could do at the time was to make a token gesture, reducing his share of Brasidas' expenses from a half to a third.

In the spring of 423 BC, however, when Perdiccas met Brasidas at Amphipolis, both of them realised that the Macedonian king was now in a stronger position. They were both well aware that it was only a matter of time before the Athenians responded in force to the loss of Amphipolis and so, no doubt by threatening to withdraw his support, Perdiccas was able to get Brasidas to join him on another expedition against Arrhabaeus. This time the two armies, swollen by reinforcements which Perdiccas had gathered from the other Greek towns of Macedonia, descended the pass to Lyncus and defeated the Lyncestians with heavy loss. The victors then paused to await the arrival of Perdiccas' Illyrian allies and, while they were waiting, another wrangle broke out between them. Perdiccas was keen to follow up their victory by attacking the Lyncestian villages. Brasidas, on the other hand, was understandably nervous about the possible arrival of an Athenian fleet detailed to win back the cities which he had captured in Chalcidice, and was therefore eager to get back to the coast.

While they were arguing to and fro, news arrived that the crafty Arrhabaeus had managed to persuade the Illyrians to change sides and to stand with him against Perdiccas and Brasidas. Hearing this, the Macedonians and their local allies took panic and fled into the night, leaving Brasidas and his men to fight their way out. Having won through into Perdiccas' territory, the Peloponnesians vented their rage at this act of betrayal by looting the Macedonian baggage train and butchering the oxen which had pulled their carts (Thucydides 4.124–8). That was the last straw for Perdiccas. His new-found hatred for Brasidas and the Peloponnesians now far outweighed his ancient antipathy for the Athenians. Contacting the Athenian command in Chalcidice, he begged them to arrange a new alliance for him with Athens as soon as possible.

It is probably this alliance which survives, in part at least, on the Attic inscription mentioned earlier (IG I³ 89). The stone, which is terribly broken, records a treaty between Athens and Macedon to which the chief signatories on the Macedonian side were Perdiccas, his brother Alcetas, and his son Archelaus. It bears no date and attempts to date it using arguments based on letter forms or line length (which are imprecise criteria at the best of times) have produced suggestions ranging from c. 435 to c. 413 BC.[15] The provisions of the treaty itself, however, seem to fit best into the context of what we know of the events of 423/2 BC, which is the date to which the inscription was originally assigned.

In so far as they can be seen, the terms of the main part of the treaty provide for Perdiccas and the other Macedonian princes to swear an oath that they shall have the same friends and enemies as the Athenians (line 28), and they shall allow no one except Athenians to export oars from Macedon (line 31). In return the Athenians swear to recognise the right of Perdiccas and his children to rule over Macedon (lines 38–9) and promise that they will not attack any city controlled by Perdiccas (line 40).

For the most part these clauses are so general that they could fit virtually any period of Perdiccas' relations with Athens. Yet it can be argued that the clause guaranteeing the Athenians exclusive use of Macedonian timber for their oars rules out any date before the loss of Amphipolis. As long as Athens controlled Amphipolis, she had direct access to the timber supplies of the Thraco-Macedonian region. The loss of the city the previous year meant that her main source of shipbuilding timber was now threatened, if not lost entirely. It took a whole fir tree to make a single oar and each trireme in Athens' fleet of several hundred needed a supply of 200 oars.[16] The attractions to the Athenians of a guaranteed supply of oars are therefore obvious. But of course those attractions were just as strong in the mid–410s when the Peloponnesians were seeking to mount their own challenge to Athens' control of the sea ways and the Athenians were faced with the need to shut them out of the market for timber.

This clause may therefore exclude a date before 423 BC but not one after it. However the second part of the treaty seems to point more closely to 423 BC. To the provisions detailed above the Athenian assembly added as a rider (line 55) a second decree aimed at reconciling Perdiccas and Arrhabaeus. Arrhabaeus and his allies are to be guaranteed equal access with Perdiccas to Athenian markets (line 56). He is to make a treaty of friendship and alliance with Perdiccas (line 57) and when that is successfully concluded the Athenians are to make a similar treaty with him (line 59). Arrhabaeus himself must have approved these arrangements for his name too appears among the signatories to the treaty (line 67).

We do not know what relations had been like between Perdiccas and Arrhabaeus early in Perdiccas' reign, but there can be no doubt that in 423 BC they stood in dire need of normalisation. Perdiccas may have defeated Arrhabaeus in the field but that was only thanks to Brasidas' help. And as a result of Arrhabaeus' subversion of his Illyrian allies and the desertion of his own troops, he had failed to add Lyncus to his kingdom. Now he was faced by a coalition of two potentially hostile groups on his western borders. For his part Arrhabaeus may have managed to preserve his independence for the moment, but only by jumping out of the frying pan into the fire. In the long run his new allies, the Illyrians, might prove a greater threat than the Macedonians and, unlike his erstwhile 'ally' Brasidas, they were not going to return home and leave him in peace. At the same time he saw Perdiccas' hand strengthened by the new treaty with Athens.

Both kings therefore had an interest in ending what had become a Mexican stand-off and reaching a more lasting understanding. Perdiccas would thereby secure his kingdom's western border and exercise at least some control over a region which he had at last come to recognise was beyond his reach militarily. Arrhabaeus stood to gain a political counterweight to the power of his unpredictable Illyrian neighbours. He would also avoid the possibility of a combined attack by Perdiccas and the Athenians. Last but not least, he would gain access to Athens' markets for his country's resources.

How though to ensure that such an alliance would last? The obvious way was for the two royal families to join together in marriage, and this is where I believe that Cleopatra comes in. Although it is beyond proof, I suggest that if 423/2 BC is accepted as the date of the treaties between Athens and Perdiccas, Perdiccas and Arrhabaeus, and Arrhabaeus and Athens recorded or fore-shadowed in IG I³ 89, then all the factors fall into place. The likely date of Cleopatra's marriage (given that she had a 7-year-old in 413 BC), her high status at the Macedonian court as reflected in Archelaus' jealousy of her son, the Athenian attempt to mediate between Perdiccas and Arrhabaeus, and the presence of Arrhabaeus himself as a signatory to their treaty with Perdiccas all point to Cleopatra being a daughter or sister of Arrhabaeus whose marriage to Perdiccas was intended to guarantee their agreement.

Lest this sound too far-fetched, it should be remembered that we know of several other dynastic alliances of this type in which foreign marriages were born out of political necessity. Eurydice, the mother of Philip II of Macedon, was the offspring of another daughter of Arrhabaeus whom he had married to a chieftain called Sirras (Strabo 7.326C). Sirras himself was most probably an Illyrian, and the marriage, made c. 430 BC, probably represents an earlier accommodation that Arrhabaeus had been obliged to make at that time with his Illyrian neighbours to offset the power of Perdiccas.

Eurydice's own marriage was also politically motivated. Her wedding to the Macedonian king Amyntas III probably took place c. 393 BC. This was shortly after Amyntas had scrambled to the throne following several years of dynastic struggles between rival branches of the royal family, only to see his newly won kingdom invaded by a powerful group of Illyrian tribes led by Bardylis. Chased from Macedon and lacking the necessary strength to expel the Illyrians unaided, it is surely no coincidence that Amyntas should have chosen just that moment to marry a 'thrice barbarian Illyrian' as her detractors called Eurydice (Plutarch, *Moralia* 14B). Eurydice may have been a foreigner but Amyntas' marriage to her brought him welcome support against a powerful aggressor and helped him to win back his kingdom.[17]

Finally we should note that c. 400 BC, after trouble had once again flared up on the Lyncestian border, Archelaus himself gave his eldest daughter in marriage to Derdas, king of neighbouring Elimea. At the time Archelaus was engaged in another war against a coalition of Lyncestians and Illyrians and the marriage can be seen as an attempt to retain a balance of power in the western Macedonian area. In all these cases therefore we can see foreign marriages being dictated by the political needs of the times.

If Cleopatra was a Lyncestian princess, it is no wonder that, when Archelaus came to the throne, he could do nothing except marry her. By 413 BC the Lyncestians probably had a new king in Arrhabaeus' son and successor. Archelaus could be fairly confident that the new monarch would not be too concerned to learn that his sister's (or half-sister's) boy by Perdiccas had 'fallen down a well'. After all a male child with those bloodlines had the potential to unite both kingdoms and that would have meant the end of his own line as king of the Lyncestians. But Cleopatra's murder would have been a different matter. Such an affront would have been an open invitation to the family to retaliate. They might respond by putting up a pretender against Archelaus and attempting to overthrow him. Despite his outstanding efforts as a murderer, Archelaus would never have been able to dispose of all possible rivals thrown up by collateral branches of the Argeads. Or they could renew their Illyrian ties and combine with their highland allies to put pressure on Macedon's western borders while Archelaus, fully occupied with consolidating his succession, was most vulnerable.

Simply by taking his father's young widow as a wife of his own, Archelaus avoided all these potential problems. Once he had secured his western borders by means of this marriage, he was able to turn his attentions elsewhere. Within Macedon itself he reorganised and strengthened the Macedonian army. He moved the royal capital from Aegae to the more central and strategically important location of Pella, commanding what was to be the future route of the Via Egnatia in Roman times and the truck highway westwards from the modern Greek city of Thessaloniki. At Pella he established a splendid court to which he would later attract the leading lights of the Greek artistic and literary world, among them the famed painter Zeuxis and the tragedians Agathon and Euripides.

As for the Athenians, we find that after their defeat at Syracuse in 413 BC they needed Archelaus more than he needed them. He and his children were granted honorary Athenian citizenship for their services in making Macedonian materials and facilities available to Athens' shipwrights, but Athenian gratitude also took a more tangible form. In the South of his kingdom Archelaus was able to call on Athens' assistance to lay successful siege to Pydna, so ending the independence of what had been a Greek city existing as an enclave within Macedonian territory. Then in eastern Macedonia he regained Macedonian control over the valuable silver mines of Bisaltia, overlooking the River Strymon, which enabled him to replace the debased coinage of his father Perdiccas with a silver coinage of a fineness not seen in Macedon since the time of Alexander I.

None of this would have been possible without a guarantee of security from attack out of the West by a coalition of the Lyncestians with the Illyrians. Yet so successful was Archelaus in maintaining the balance of power in western Macedonia which his father had set up in 423/2 BC when he had accepted Arrhabaeus as his friend and ally and Arrhabaeus' daughter Cleopatra as his wife that we hear of no more trouble in that region before the century's end. For practically all of Archelaus' reign it was all quiet on the western front for Macedon. At least some of the credit for this has to be due to the success of the king's marriage to Cleopatra, his widowed stepmother. Hardly a pointless marriage when we consider the impressive strides which the Macedonian state was able to make during the unusually long period of peace which this diplomatic match ensured.

3

PHILIP II'S LAST WIFE

As we have seen, Archelaus' marriage to his father's young widow may have contributed substantially to ensuring the continued stability of Macedon's frontier in the West. That stability had been established by his father Perdiccas back in 423/2 BC when, at Athenian prompting, he had agreed to make up his differences with Arrhabaeus, the king of the Lyncestians, and had first accepted Cleopatra as wife as a pledge of his good faith. The kingdom of Macedon was thereby given a welcome respite, for a time at least, from incursions in that area. Unfortunately it did not last for ever. Cleopatra may have died. Or as she grew older she may have been sidelined in favour of another wife, despite her success in producing for Archelaus the only male offspring of whom we ever hear. At any rate, near the end of his reign, Archelaus once more found himself at daggers drawn with the Lyncestians. To make matters worse they were now back in alliance once more with Macedon's old enemies, the Illyrians.

With at least two other earlier wives in addition to Cleopatra, Archelaus had marriageable daughters of his own by this time whom he could use for political purposes and his response to the new threat from the West was typically diplomatic as well as military. A defensive alliance which he made with the king of Elimea, a region which lay to the South of Lyncus, was sealed with a political marriage between the Elimiote king and Archelaus' eldest daughter. At about the same time (c. 400 BC) another daughter was put to similar use in an attempt to stall the claims of a collateral branch of the Argeads. This was the line descended from Menelaus, a paternal uncle whom Archelaus had neglected to assassinate along with the others back in 413 BC – a rather grave error of omission as matters turned out. In a move obviously

30

designed to pave the way for the succession of his only son
Orestes, Archelaus gave this daughter to Amyntas 'the Little', the
son of Menelaus, 'thinking that in this way there would be least
possibility of a quarrel between the latter and his own son by
Cleopatra' (Aristotle, *Politics* 1311b.11).

It is likely, however, that one or the other of these marriages
backfired on the king. In 399 BC Archelaus was killed during a
hunting expedition by a stray spear thrown by a homosexual
companion called Craterus or Crateuas, who was probably one of
the Royal Pages. While one version of the story (Diodorus 14.37.6)
represents the death as an accident, another version found in
Aristotle (*Politics* 1311b.11–12) makes it deliberate and speaks of
a conspiracy which also involved two other youths from the court.
All three are said to have had different grudges against the king.
According to Aristotle, Crateuas was motivated not only by sexual
jealousy at the king's apparent neglect of him, but also by thwarted
ambition since Archelaus had promised him one of his daughters
but had then gone back on his word. We do not know whether
this was the girl who had been given to the ruler of Elimea or the
one married off to Amyntas 'the Little', but the timing of
the incident makes it appear almost certain that it must have been
one or other of them, and not a further unknown daughter.

Archelaus' efforts to use a political marriage to ensure the succession of his direct line may therefore have contributed directly
to his own death. Certainly they were only partially successful. It
is true that after the assassination (if that is what it was) Orestes,
his son by Cleopatra, was hailed as king by the Assembly of the
Macedonians. But he was still only a minor. Within a couple of
years his uncle and guardian Aëropus had disposed of him and
taken the throne for himself. There then followed a brief period
of intense instability as the crown passed in turn between the
line of Perdiccas, represented now only by Aëropus and his sons,
and that of Menelaus as these two branches of the royal family,
both descended from Alexander I, struggled with each other for
the kingship.

Ironically the crown finally came to rest with neither branch
but with the only other line of descent from Alexander I which
still survived. The king who came to the throne in 394/3 BC, after
a year which saw three kings of Macedon come and go in quick
succession, was Amyntas III, the grandson of Alexander I's fifth
and last son Amyntas. From that time onwards until the final

break-up of Alexander the Great's empire at the end of the fourth century BC, it was this branch of the family that would provide most, if not all, of Macedon's rulers, including her two greatest kings, Philip II (359–336 BC) and Alexander the Great (336–323 BC).

It is to the time of these two kings – the golden age of Macedonian history – that we now turn, for our next two Cleopatras are closely associated with them both. One was the last of Philip's seven wives and the only one he is said to have married for love. The other was Philip's daughter by his fifth wife Olympias and therefore the only full sister of Alexander the Great. Furthermore it was during the great durbar held to celebrate her marriage to her maternal uncle Alexander of Epirus that Philip met his own death, assassinated in the theatre at Aegae.

At the beginning of his reign Philip, like his predecessors, had more than his share of problems from the highlanders inhabiting the lands to the West of Macedonia. Like his predecessors he too sought diplomatic as well as military solutions to his difficulties. His policy in this regard is neatly summed up in the words which introduce the account of his wives given by the biographer Satyrus. 'Philip always made his marriages war by war', says Satyrus.[1] Every time that he won a war Philip followed it up by including a political marriage as part of the peace settlement, thereby extending and refining a policy which we have already seen used by earlier Macedonian rulers, albeit to a lesser extent.

Probably the first of these 'war brides' was Phila, a sister of king Derdas of Elimea. This alliance, contracted probably c. 360 BC shortly before Philip became king in his own right, renewed a marriage link which went back to the time of Alexander I. More importantly from Philip's point of view it secured a part of Macedon's vulnerable western border against any immediate incursion from Illyria. It also bought valuable time for Philip to clear away a couple of rival claimants to the Macedonian throne and to begin enlarging and reorganising the Macedonian army in readiness for the inevitable confrontation with the Illyrians under their leader Bardylis. That could now take place at a time and place of Philip's own choosing rather than his enemy's.

The time for action came in 358 BC with the news of the death of the king of Paeonia, to the North-East of Macedonia. After decisively defeating the Paeonians in a short campaign, Philip imposed an alliance on the new king. He thereby secured his north-eastern frontier, enabling him to turn to the North-West. There the Illyrians had occupied a number of Upper Macedonian towns in the Lyncestian area. At Philip's approach Bardylis, confident in the strength of his own forces, offered terms based upon the *status quo*. But Philip adamantly refused to cede what the Macedonians had come by now to regard as lands of their own. In the battle which followed the Illyrians were cut to pieces. The occupied territories were restored and as part of the peace settlement made with Bardylis Philip acquired the Illyrian princess Audata as his second wife. In fact it looks as though a face-saving arrangement may have been worked out. Under this the lands which Bardylis was compelled to vacate could be regarded as a voluntary gift by the Illyrian chieftain as part of Audata's dowry rather than as something taken by Philip as the spoils of war.

Through this second marriage Philip was able to incorporate Lyncus into his kingdom along with the other lands of western Macedonia. He next turned his attention southwards towards Thessaly, a region of northern Greece with which the Macedonians had long had much in common. Philip's involvement with the Thessalians was to yield him two more wives. His first marriage alliance with the area may have come as early as 358/7 BC when he married Philinna of Larissa. If so, it should be seen as part of Philip's diplomatic strategy, a continuation of the traditional Macedonian policy of securing the kingdom's southern border by supporting the Aleuad princes of Larissa against the power of Pherae. His second alliance with a Thessalian princess, Nicesipolis of Pherae, probably arose later when Philip was more concerned with extending his territories than securing what he already had, for although Satyrus makes this the King's fourth marriage, it is usually connected with his eventual military success against Pherae in 353 and 352 BC.

Little is known of any of these early wives. They obviously provided politically attractive matches at the time that Philip married them, but dynastically they all proved something of a failure. Accordingly it is no wonder that they are completely overshadowed in our sources, as no doubt they were at the court of Macedon, by Olympias, Philip's fifth wife by Satyrus' numeration. Olympias was a niece of the king of the Molossians in Epirus. This was an area which had also been tormented by Illyrian raiding parties and it was as part of a defensive pact against the Illyrians that Olympias came to Philip in 357 BC. As dowry she may have brought with her the region of Orestis, which lay between Elimea and Lyncus. If so, this was the last piece of the jigsaw puzzle to complete Philip's control of western Macedonia. More importantly, within a year of their marriage Olympias had borne Philip a male child – the future Alexander the Great.

Alexander was not Philip's first boy child. His first Thessalian wife, Philinna, had already produced a son for him. But Arrhidaeus, as the child was called, was to prove sickly and feeble-minded. Whatever his condition was, it eventually improved as Arrhidaeus grew to manhood.[2] But very little is heard of him during the lifetime of either Philip or Alexander, which suggests that he was never regarded as a serious contender for the succession. With Philip's other wives bearing only girls, it was Olympias' success in producing a healthy son and heir as much as her own strength of personality that led to her total dominance over Philip and his court.

That dominance is reflected in the language of Satyrus' account. When he jumps 20 years after mentioning Olympias and intro-duces Philip's sixth wife, the Thracian Meda, Satyrus presents her in such a way as to imply that right from the start she was regarded as inferior in status to Olympias: 'and when [Philip] conquered Thrace, the king of the Thracians Cotalus came to him bringing his daughter Meda and many gifts'. Meda, it is implied, was only one among many 'gifts' which the Thracian king paid over to Philip after his defeat. Clearly this was not a match between equals and Olympias knew well that she had nothing to fear from such a relationship.

This was not at all the case with Cleopatra, whom Philip took as his seventh and last wife, probably in the late summer of 337 BC.[3] The niece of Attalus, an ambitious Macedonian aristocrat, Cleopatra was still only a girl when Philip married her, and for once, according to Satyrus, his reason for the marriage was not political. It was because he had fallen passionately in love with her.

Cleopatra therefore appears to be the fatal exception to Satyrus' initial rule that all of Philip's marriages were politically motivated. This is not to imply, of course, that passion and political advantage have to be mutually exclusive. Plutarch (*Alexander* 2.2) also speaks of love in connection with Philip's earlier marriage to Olympias, even though we are aware that politically speaking that marriage was probably the most important alliance which the Macedonian king ever made. Yet with Cleopatra it is certainly much more difficult to see the same link between marriage and political advantage which is so patently obvious in the case of all Philip's other marriages. Although her uncle and guardian Attalus was an important Macedonian noble, we have no information about his position at Philip's court before the king's marriage to his niece. We therefore cannot judge what, if anything, Philip might have gained from making such a close alliance with him. Certainly though it cannot have been the acquisition of new lands and powerful external allies, which is what Philip had got from all his earlier matrimonial excursions.

Since all our sources are so emphatic about the role of *eros* in the formation of this final relationship with Cleopatra and there is no hint of any other motive for the marriage, it would be foolish to discount sexual jealousy entirely as a contributory factor in the reaction of Olympias to the match. There is no doubt, however, that the determining factor in her subsequent conduct, and that of her son, was something much more powerful. It was the overwhelming anxiety felt by both Olympias and the teenage Alexander about the threat which the latest bride presented to their place in the royal succession.

Alexander was now 18 or 19 years old. In the last few years he had grown more and more accustomed to being treated by Philip and those around him as the heir apparent. Yet the very nature of Macedonian royal polygamy meant that each and every new marriage made by the king profoundly affected the status and expectations of all his previous wives and children. Olympias may have produced a son, but her increased status as mother of the heir to the throne was once more being put under threat. Alexander himself may have been tacitly acknowledged by Philip and his courtiers as the likely heir and successor, but ancient Macedon recognised no such formal status as that of 'crown prince'. If he had another son, Philip could always change his mind.

If the new wife Cleopatra were to produce a male child, then everything would be thrown back into the melting-pot. Born in 383 or 382 BC, Philip himself was only 45. He was fit and active still. Indeed at the time of the marriage he was planning his greatest undertaking ever, the invasion of the Persian empire. So a generation's difference in age between Alexander and any new son by Cleopatra would have been much less of a problem in his eyes than those of Alexander or Olympias. Whichever way they chose to look at it, both of them had to acknowledge the unpalatable fact that any son born of the new wife would be likely to have the inside track. Cleopatra was a native Macedonian and her backers were physically present at court as she herself was physically present in Philip's bed. Olympias on the other hand was a non-Macedonian woman, now well into middle age, and her basis of support was far away in distant Epirus. Although a generation older, her son Alexander might hardly even be in the race.

This is the background against which we need to view what happened soon after the wedding of Philip and Cleopatra. It was at an all-male drinking bout held at some point after the marriage that matters came to a head. Macedonian males had a proud tradition of hard drinking at the symposia which formed a central feature of Macedonian court life. For them a symposium was not an occasion for making polite conversation about philosophy or singing archaic drinking songs celebrating the slayers of long-dead tyrants. Like the field of battle or the royal hunt, the symposium was a chance to parade their own machismo and to test that of their companions.[4] On this occasion the unstable mixture of alcohol and aristocratic *amour propre* which always characterised these events was to ignite in a particularly explosive manner. The story is told by Plutarch and Justin (9.7.3–7) as well as by Satyrus, but it is Plutarch's version in the *Life of Alexander* which is the fullest and most informative:

> The strife in Philip's household, arising from his marriages and love affairs, contaminated his whole kingdom from the women's quarters and gave rise to many accusations and great squabbles between father and son. These differences were aggravated by the malevolent nature of Olympias, a jealous and surly woman, who egged Alexander on. It was Attalus who gave rise to the most glaring breach between them at the time of Philip's marriage to Cleopatra, a young girl whom Philip had fallen in love with and took to wife, despite the difference in their ages. Attalus, who was her uncle, having had too much to drink called on the Macedonians to pray to the gods that Philip and Cleopatra might have a legitimate son, as an heir to the kingdom. Infuriated at this Alexander called out: 'Do you take me for a bastard then, you wretch?' and hurled a drinking cup at him. Philip rose up against his son, drawing his sword, but luckily for both of them in his drunken rage he slipped and fell over. With a

jeer Alexander called out: 'Look, men, this is the man who has been getting ready to cross from Europe into Asia, and he's fallen in a heap in crossing from one couch to another!' After this display of drunken boorishness Alexander removed Olympias and sent her to Epirus, and he himself went to live among the Illyrians.

(Plutarch, *Alexander* 9.5–11)

As Elizabeth Carney has observed,[5] this unseemly squabble had primarily to do with perceptions of male honour and the incident itself took place in an entirely male context. As a respectable married woman Olympias herself would not have been present at such a gathering. Yet she too chose to leave court as a result of what had happened. The implication of her withdrawal is surely that Olympias felt her own honour to have been as much impugned as Alexander's. Neither could overlook Philip's failure to do anything about the insult which Attalus had offered Alexander in front of all the Macedonian nobility. Furthermore the signifi-cance of the respective destinations chosen by Olympias and Alexander for their self-imposed exile will not have been lost on the king. Olympias went back to her own family in Epirus, where her younger brother Alexander now ruled as king. A subordinate ally of Philip, Alexander of Epirus found himself put in a difficult situation by his sister's return. Family honour more or less demanded that he take action against Philip. If not, he would himself lose face not only with the Macedonians but also with his own people. Indeed Justin (9.7.7) claims that Olympias actually urged her brother to declare war on Philip in order to avenge the slur upon their family's name.

Alexander went to dwell among the Illyrians. That sent a much more ominous message to Philip. The prospect of a war with the Molossians of Epirus would not have caused him undue alarm. It would have been inconvenient in the light of his plans to invade Asia, but there could never be any doubt who would emerge the eventual victor. However the threat of an offensive alliance between Epirus and Macedon's traditional enemies, the blood-thirsty and unpredictable Illyrians, was quite another matter. What Alexander and Olympias were doing therefore was to serve notice on Philip that he had better forget any ideas he had about cam-paigning in the East. As soon as his back was turned, he would find the whole of the West up in arms behind him.

For a moment Philip must have felt that in his infatuation for Cleopatra he had thrown away all the gains that he had laboured so hard over 20 years to achieve. His love for his young wife might indirectly end up costing him not merely his Asian invasion, but also an ally who was still of great value to him. If the worst came to the worst, it might even cost him the western half of his kingdom. Nevertheless Philip had extricated himself from worse scrapes than this in the past, often by the simple expedient of marrying the right person. At this stage in his own life, smitten as he was with Cleopatra, he may have eschewed the idea of another political marriage for himself. But that was not going to stop him trying the same trick again, using other members of his family.

We know of at least two marriage alliances arranged by Philip in the brief period between the break with Alexander and Olympias in late summer/early autumn 337 BC and his death by assassination in July (?) the following year. There may have been more.[6] The chronology of this period is very uncertain and so any connection made between these matches must remain hypothetical. Yet Plutarch, whose *Life of Alexander* is the only source for one of the marriages, places the earlier of them immediately after Alexander's return from Illyria following the quarrel at the party and just before the death of Philip himself.[7]

The bizarre tale which Plutarch tells has come to be known as 'the Pixodarus affair'. According to Plutarch (*Alexander* 10.1–5), Pixodarus, who was the satrap of Caria in Persian Asia Minor, wishing for an alliance with Philip sent an ambassador to propose a match between his eldest daughter and Philip's elder son Arrhidaeus. Alexander's friends and his mother Olympias egged Alexander on to believe that this proposal meant that Philip was now grooming Arrhidaeus for the throne. Alexander reacted accordingly. He sent a secret envoy of his own, a tragic actor called Thessalus, to persuade Pixodarus that his stepbrother was deranged and that he should therefore marry his daughter to Alexander himself instead. Well-known actors formed a sort of international jet set of the ancient world and as a result often found themselves entrusted with diplomatic missions. We can imagine Pixodarus' growing consternation as Thessalus told him of Arrhidaeus' mental instability and perhaps backed up his account with a cameo performance of one of his mad king roles from the tragic stage. At this point Pixodarus naturally enough withdrew his former offer.

It is apparent that he had known nothing of Arrhidaeus' mental condition, or perhaps he had mistakenly assumed that as the first-born Arrhidaeus would naturally inherit the crown regardless of his infirmities.

When Philip learned of his son's devious role in this affair he was beside himself with rage. Not only did he send a demand to Greece that Thessalus be sent to him in chains, and have four of Alexander's close friends and presumed associates banished from Macedon. He also went himself to Alexander's private quarters and gave him a severe dressing-down in the presence of one of his son's own companions, telling him that the marriage was unworthy of him. Hardly the sort of conduct to endear a father to even the most placid of teenagers, which Alexander surely was not.

No doubt all that Philip had to say to Alexander was true. But what had enraged him so much was not the prospect of having a 'barbarian' and a 'Persian slave' as an in-law. After all he had been quite ready to tolerate a match between his elder son Arrhidaeus and the Carian princess. It was that Alexander had gone behind his back and was starting to play the same sort of political games that Philip himself had played for so long – and with the same sort of success. An alliance with the satrap of Caria on the Turkish coast would have provided an ideal bridgehead for the upcoming assault on Asia. And if Alexander's plan had succeeded all the credit for it would have been his, not Philip's.

In the case of 'the Pixodarus affair' therefore Philip's plans for a political marriage were stymied by his son. But the king had much more success with the other alliance which he put together in this period. Plutarch's account of the drunken quarrel between Philip and Alexander concludes with the eventual return of Alexander to Macedon, probably fairly soon after the rift between father and son. Alexander's behaviour in the course of 'the Pixodarus affair' suggests that the reconciliation which he had worked out with his father may have been only superficial. But a public display of unanimity was probably all that Philip required.

We hear nothing, however, of Olympias or her whereabouts at this time. Despite her son's return, she may have continued to sit and sulk in her brother's palace in Epirus. Indeed Philip may have been quite relieved to be rid of her for a time. But it is irrelevant whether or not he personally wanted her to return. His main problem was how to placate her offended brother Alexander of Epirus and to honour him in such a way as to eliminate all possibility of any future threat from that area. Only by doing this could he ensure that his own son Alexander would never again be in a position to threaten his back as soon as it was turned.

Philip's solution to this problem was little short of brilliant. It was to arrange a wedding between Alexander of Epirus and his only other child by Olympias, his daughter Cleopatra who was therefore the full sister of the future Alexander the Great. Such a match between uncle and niece would instantly reconfirm the importance of the Epirote alliance with Macedon. It would also add immensely to the prestige of the Epirote king in the eyes of the mainland Greeks as well as his own subjects. For Philip it would also have the added bonus of taking all potential opponents out of play at a single stroke.

Once the marriage had been agreed, his son Alexander could hardly expect to enrol Alexander of Epirus in an offensive alliance against a king who was now his father-in-law as well as his brother-in-law. Nor would he get very far with the Illyrians as his only allies. If push came to shove, Alexander's Molossians would fall in behind Philip's Macedonians and leave the young prince well and truly out on a limb.

His wife Olympias for her part could hardly refuse to return to Macedon for the marriage celebrations of her own daughter and her own brother. Nor could she expect that brother to support her any longer against her husband, since he could now have no grounds of quarrel with a king who had honoured him so greatly. And with her son's plans for a pincer movement against Macedonia now effectively checkmated by Philip, any resistance would have meant her total isolation from both her families, leaving her completely powerless. Although we hear nothing of it, Olympias would have been left with no choice but to grit her teeth and return to her husband in Macedon.

While all this political manoeuvring was going on, Philip still found the time to get his new young wife pregnant. In the early months of 336 BC Cleopatra the wife was presumably confined to the women's quarters well out of reach of any of Olympias' sympathisers. When it arrived, the baby turned out to be yet another girl. The news must have been a bitter blow to Philip and a blessed relief to Alexander and Olympias. Try as he may, even the mightiest of monarchs cannot command that elusive Y chromosome. The child was named Europa, betraying Philip's vain hope that after his triumphant return from Asia he would beget a baby brother for her – a little 'Asianicus' or 'Asiaticus' perhaps – to be a symbol of his new domains and ruler in time over all his empire. As we know with the benefit of hindsight, that was never to be. Meanwhile there were the myriad arrangements to be made for the wedding of the new baby's stepsister, Cleopatra.

The celebration of the marriage of Philip's daughter Cleopatra to Alexander of Epirus, her maternal uncle, was designed not only to honour Philip's new son-in-law, but also to serve as the prelude to a lavish series of festivities which would focus all eyes upon Philip himself in his new role as leader of the Greeks in the long-awaited crusade of liberation against Persia. That great event was at last coming to pass, for even before the wedding invitations had gone out an advance party of the invasion force had already crossed over into Asia Minor. No doubt there were plans to regale the wedding guests with news of any early successes on the battlefield.

As part of the preparations for the expedition Philip had sent an emissary to the Delphic oracle to ascertain the attitude of the god Apollo to his undertaking. The reply which came back from the Pythian priestess was characteristically ambiguous:

> The bull is garlanded, his moment has come, the one who will sacrifice him is here.
>
> (Diodorus 16.91.2)

Naturally enough Philip understood this to mean that the bull was the Great King of Persia. He himself (so he thought) was the one who would be doing the sacrificing.

At the beginning of July 336 BC delegates and guests from all over the Greek world began to converge on Aegae, the former royal capital of Macedon. Many brought with them gold crowns and similar tokens of public esteem to confer upon the Macedonian king in the name of their city-states. These honours were graciously accepted by Philip in the course of the state banquet which followed the wedding. That part of the celebrations at least seems to have gone off without a hitch.

Early the next morning while it was still dark, the spectators packed into the theatre at Aegae eager to witness a dawn ceremony which would open the programme of athletic games set down for the second day of the festivities. A parade of glittering splendour made its way into the theatre. Included in the procession were magnificent statues of the twelve Olympian gods and along with them a thirteenth image, equally godlike, of the king himself. Then came the royal retinue, the members of the court and the king's most honoured allies and guests. Bringing up the rear was Philip himself, resplendent in a white cloak. At his own orders his body-guard of spearmen had dropped back a pace, leaving Philip flanked by the two Alexanders, his son and his latest son-in-law. Enveloped in the love and admiration of his fellow Greeks, what need had he now of bodyguards?

As the king entered the theatre erupted into applause. At that very moment a young man, one of his own bodyguards, thrust his way forward. Drawing a Celtic dagger from beneath his cloak he stabbed the king to the heart with a single blow. Philip collapsed, pouring out his spirit in a pool of blood.

4

A DOUBLE MYSTERY

The great king Philip II lay dead. Who had killed him and why? Despite the subsequent confusion the murderer himself was caught even before he could reach his getaway horses at the city gates. He was killed on the spot, conveniently ending any chance of a proper investigation of the crime even before one could begin. So there can be no certainty that his was the only hand upon the dagger. As a result the murder of Philip II has become a puzzle upon which modern scholarship has expended an inordinate amount of effort. Nevertheless if there is one thing that the ambiguous and incomplete nature of the ancient accounts of the event can tell us it is that even the dignitaries who were present on the day never knew for sure. Or if they did, they wisely chose to say nothing.

Like the assassination of John F. Kennedy, the more closely one looks at the murder of Philip II the more indistinct the picture becomes. The man who was caught and killed for the crime was a young Macedonian aristocrat called Pausanias. Yet it is unclear whether he was acting alone or with others (several getaway horses are mentioned for example) and the motive ascribed to him seems to modern eyes almost too far-fetched to command belief.

Although there are several versions of the story,[1] its main outlines are clear. Pausanias was a member of the royal guard who had earlier been one of Philip's lovers, for the king was as notorious for his many homosexual affairs as for the number of his wives and mistresses. But Philip had thrown him over in favour of another youth. He too was called Pausanias, a coincidence which straightaway gives the elastic band of our credulity a good stretch. Overcome with jealousy the first Pausanias began to torment his rival, spitefully accusing him of being half a woman and anyone's

43

for the asking. For a young Macedonian to be the object of a great king's affection was acceptable, even honourable. To be effeminate and promiscuous was not. Finally the taunts reached such a pitch that the second Pausanias was unable to bear them any longer. He determined to take his own life, but not before he had confided in his commander Attalus. Shortly afterwards he met his death in battle, heroically interposing his own body between that of his lover and king and a ravening band of Illyrians.

The nobility of Pausanias' death ensured that the whole matter immediately became something of a *cause célèbre* among the Macedonians, and the subject of intense gossip at court. Intent on avenging the young man's death, general Attalus hit upon a particularly nasty plan. He invited the first Pausanias to dinner, got him drunk, and turned him over to his stable boys to be gang-raped. Hurt and humiliated, Pausanias went to the king to accuse Attalus and demand justice, but Philip – although shocked by Attalus' barbaric conduct – refused to punish him. As the uncle and guardian of Cleopatra, Attalus was of course technically a member of Philip's family now. He had also just been selected by the king as one of the three generals to lead the advance party of the upcoming expedition into Asia. Unable therefore to dispense with Attalus' services, Philip instead tried to buy Pausanias off with expensive gifts and advancement in the royal guard. The result was that Pausanias determined to wreak vengeance not only on the man who had abused him, but also on Philip himself, who had betrayed him twice over, once by rejecting his love and then by turning a deaf ear to his pleas for justice.

Incidentally the name of Cleopatra is linked by Plutarch (*Alexander* 10.6) with that of her uncle as a partner in the crime which had triggered Pausanias' action. This is of course ridiculous. In the months immediately before the murder Cleopatra was still pregnant with the king's child and would therefore have been out of circulation. Had the assault on Pausanias taken place eight years earlier in 344 BC, as used to be believed,[2] she would have been no more than a child when she allegedly assisted her uncle in arranging this squalid act of savagery. The whole story of her involvement is much more convincingly explained as a calumny invented after the event to excuse Olympias' later mistreatment of the young widow and her infant daughter.

It is no wonder though that speculation soon began about who was really responsible for the assassination. As with all good whodunits there were suspects aplenty. In view of the recent bad blood between the king and Alexander and his mother Olympias it is no surprise to find Olympias and Alexander included among them, and in fact it was not long before the finger of suspicion was firmly pointed in their direction (Plutarch, *Alexander* 10.6). There was also Philip's nephew, Amyntas son of Perdiccas. Amyntas had recently been married to Cynanne, Philip's daughter by his second wife Audata, which suggests that the king was grooming him as his successor should the direct line of succession fail. As a contemporary of Alexander, he would certainly have been an attractive choice as the next king of Macedon had the Macedonians rejected Alexander, or if the prince had been killed in battle.

Also waiting in the wings were the sons of Aëropus. He was the man who had enjoyed a brief rule as king of Macedon back in the 390s BC after supplanting his young nephew Orestes, son of Archelaus. Finally there was the Great King of Persia. Unencumbered by the niceties of modern diplomacy, which frowns upon one head of state 'taking out' another, he had both the motive and the means for launching a pre-emptive strike against the commander-in-chief of the impending invasion force of Macedonians and Greeks.

After lining up the suspects and reviewing their possible motives, it is customary to find Olympias and Alexander not guilty of the assassination on the persuasive grounds that, though both of them had a strong enough reason to want Philip dead, neither had any need to take the tremendous risks associated with such a public act of regicide. Had she wanted to kill her husband, Olympias had ready access to more private and therefore less dangerous means of achieving her ends. Nevertheless there are those who continue to argue her guilt,[3] despite a growing tendency to view Olympias as more sinned against than sinning.

Alexander is an even less likely candidate as the murderer. He too could easily have arranged Philip's demise behind closed doors. Even more conveniently an 'accident' in battle on the forthcoming expedition would have left him in total control of the army and therefore the Macedonian state. As it was, the timing of Philip's death, just before the intended departure date of the main expeditionary force, almost proved a calamity for Alexander.

The case against Philip's nephew Amyntas and the sons of Aëropus is even weaker. The former had nothing to gain by causing the postponement of a hazardous military undertaking which might see both father and son killed and therefore open up the way for his own succession. The latter too had every incentive to wait. If Philip happened to be killed in battle, they could then raise a rebellion at home in the hope of securing Macedonia before the army returned from Asia Minor. In short, as far as we can see, none of the suspects from the Macedonian royal house had anything to gain from committing such a public act at such an inconvenient time.

That leaves the Persian king. Darius III had probably only just come to power himself,[4] in a way which despite the proverbial softness of the Persian race proves that here was a Persian who would have had absolutely no compunction about assassinating another monarch. The satrap of Armenia, Darius had been raised to the throne by Bagoas, the chief eunuch at the court of Artaxerxes III. Bagoas had already played the kingmaker once before when back in 338 BC he had disposed of his master by having him poisoned and had set up Artaxerxes' son Arses in his stead. When Arses in turn had refused to do what Bagoas wanted, the eunuch had him poisoned too and also wiped out his whole family for good measure. His new appointee was Darius. He too proved equally intractable but when Bagoas confidently went for the hat trick, Darius forestalled him. Taking from the eunuch the cup of poison which Bagoas had prepared for him, Darius forced him to drink the draught himself there and then and looked on as Bagoas died in agony. Darius therefore was not only ruthless but also well aware of the advantages of forward planning and it was certainly Darius and the Persians who stood to gain most from the timing of the murder of Philip. At best they would force the expedition's abandonment, at worst its postponement. In the event it was only postponed, but the delay (until early 335 BC) was long enough to enable Darius to put his own house in order.

It was also the Persians who stood to gain most from the public nature of the assassination. By the beginning of 336 BC some (if not many) of the Greek city-states, which had ratified the Common Peace at Corinth in early 337 BC and sworn to join Philip in the sacred war against Persia, had become less than enthusiastic about the merits of the forthcoming crusade. After calculating its likely costs to them in men and money, they had begun to wonder whether they were being asked to pay too steep a price to further Philip's personal glory. The Persian king for his part would have been well aware of this lack of enthusiasm, thanks to his extensive network of spies throughout Greece. He may therefore have anticipated that the Greek leaders assembled at Aegae would think even harder about the advisability of attacking a ruler who had the power to strike down their commander-in-chief in their very midst.

If there was a second hand on the Celtic dagger which killed Philip it is therefore more likely to have been that of Darius than any of the homegrown suspects. The Persians had long had links with the Macedonian court.[5] Pausanias' grievances were widely known and talked about in court circles and it would not have been difficult for Persian agents or sympathisers to prey upon the vengeful feelings of the young aristocrat and excite him into a state of homicidal paranoia. In Pausanias Darius may well have found a gun which was already loaded and aimed. All he would have needed to do was to pull the trigger. In fact Alexander himself was later to accuse Darius of boasting openly in his correspondence that it was he who had instigated the plot against Philip (Arrian 2.14.5). All the more strange therefore that in modern times so few have chosen to believe him.[6]

We shall probably never know for certain whether the assassination of Philip was the act of a lone madman or a carefully planned covert operation worthy of the CIA or the KGB. Either way the consequences were the same. Everything ground to a halt while the Macedonians got together to choose a new king, a process which would take them several months. Meanwhile, regardless of who was guilty or innocent, the plotting for the throne began in earnest.

By now it was traditional, if not obligatory, for every new Macedonian monarch to begin his reign with a purge of potential rivals and Alexander the Great on his accession was no exception to this rule. First to go after Philip's death were the sons of Aëropus. All three were arraigned for complicity in the murder of Philip. Two were found guilty and executed. The third, Alexander the Lyncestian, had been the first man to hail Alexander as his liege lord in the traditional manner, by donning his armour and taking his stand beside him ready to lay down his life for his chosen king. On that occasion the Lyncestian prince's quick wits had saved his life, for a few years at least. Acquitted thanks to Alexander's personal intercession, he remained in favour and even enjoyed high command until 334/3 BC when he was adjudged a traitor and put to death on a trumped-up charge of conspiring with the Persian king.

Amyntas was probably the next to go. Before the following summer he was condemned to death for allegedly instigating a plot against Alexander. However the greatest threat to Alexander at the time of his acclamation by the Assembly of Macedonians in the autumn of 336 BC came not from these immediate members of the royal family but from Attalus, the uncle of Cleopatra. It was not just his relationship with the murdered king as Cleopatra's uncle that made Attalus dangerous. He had also contrived to accumulate an inordinate amount of influence at court, for during the last months of his reign the king had come to rely upon him more and more as one of his closest confidants. Even more importantly, Attalus also had the backing of the Macedonian army.

Luckily for Alexander, at the time of the assassination Attalus was absent with the advance forces in Asia Minor. He was therefore able to bide his time before making any move. It was not long, however, before an opportunity presented itself in the form of a letter sent to Attalus by the Athenians suggesting a common revolt against the authority of Macedon. Attalus immediately turned the letter over to Alexander but that was not enough to save him. Having confronted the Athenians with the evidence and forced them to admit their complicity and eat humble pie, Alexander despatched one of the Royal Friends and a party of troops with orders to bring Attalus back alive or kill him if he resisted. Naturally enough Attalus resisted, although there can be little doubt that the result would have been exactly the same in the long run even if he had come as meekly as a lamb.

While Alexander was thus occupied with the menfolk, back in the women's quarters Olympias had begun to plot against Cleopatra and her child. When her own move was made is uncertain. Perhaps it was soon after Alexander's accession, perhaps somewhat later after Alexander had engineered the death of Attalus.[7] Now that the kingship was finally in her son's grasp, Olympias was determined to ensure that there should be no challenge ever again from that quarter. Whereas our sources lay responsibility for the disposal of Attalus and the other male members of Cleopatra's family squarely at Alexander's door, they are unanimous in identifying the elimination of Cleopatra and her infant daughter Europa as Olympias' personal contribution to this bloody spring-cleaning of the Argead house. Their only disagreement is about how Cleopatra and her child were put to death.

The most hair-raising version of their murder is that given by the Greek geographer Pausanias. In the course of a digression about the assassination of Philip which Pausanias has worked into his description of the region of Arcadia, he relates how after Philip's death Olympias had Cleopatra and her infant 'son' (sic) dragged onto a bronze dish, lit a fire underneath them and barbecued them to death (Pausanias 8.7.7). Like most barbecues just about all of this tall tale has to be taken with quite a large pinch of salt. As a travel writer describing the famous sites of classical Greece, Pausanias has proved extremely valuable as a source for modern archaeologists. But as a writer on history (and outdoor cookery) his work leaves a great deal to be desired, as his blatant error about the sex of Cleopatra's child Europa demonstrates. The sole excuse which can be offered on his behalf is that Pausanias was writing in the middle of the second century AD, almost 500 years after the event he purports to be describing.

The Latin author Justin, who wrote his abridgement of the universal history of the Augustan historian Pompeius Trogus a century after Pausanias had been travelling around Greece, does little better. His account is almost as silly, although slightly less blood-curdling. Justin (9.7.12) has Olympias forcing Cleopatra to hang herself, after killing the infant at her mother's breast – almost credible when taken in isolation, since hanging was a time-honoured form of suicide for women in the ancient Greek world, but ultimately unbelievable when we look back and read it in its context as just a small part of Justin's whole account of the murder of Philip. For Justin makes Olympias a fury incarnate, the open instigator of Philip's assassination. He represents her as personally providing the horses for the murderer's getaway and crowning the crucified assassin's corpse at dead of night with a crown of gold which no one but Alexander himself will dare to remove. She then cremates Pausanias' body over her own husband's remains before finally instituting annual rites at his tomb to celebrate his act of regicide!

In both these accounts Cleopatra has been stereotyped as the tragic victim just as Olympias has been typecast as the villain of the piece. Reality has so little part to play in either version that the only surprise is that neither of these ancient authors saw fit to reach right back into the mythological past in a search for inspiration and have Olympias wall up Cleopatra and her baby and starve them to death. After all, that is what had happened to Cleopatra's mythical counterpart.

All the characters involved in Philip's assassination and the accession of Alexander the Great are so much larger than life that perhaps we should not be unduly harsh on any ancient author for drawing upon tragic prototypes in his depiction of these events. Yet this myth-making tendency continues to the present day in modern accounts of what happened to Cleopatra after her murder. For in addition to worrying about how she was murdered, modern scholarship now finds itself faced with the further problem of Cleopatra's burial.

The venue for the fateful wedding of Philip's daughter to her uncle Alexander of Epirus had been the old royal capital of Macedon at Aegae and it was in the theatre at Aegae that Philip was stabbed to death. The administrative centre of the growing kingdom of Macedon had been moved to the more centrally located site of Pella at the end of the fifth century BC but Aegae had continued to be a place of importance. In the hot summer months it served as a royal retreat and it was developed as a place not only of ceremony for the living but also of repose for the dead. For it was here that all the Macedonian kings up to the time of Alexander the Great were buried.

Already in the last century travellers in the area had begun to suspect that the modern village of Vergina was the site of Aegae. An imposing monument above the village, which covered the remains of the hellenistic royal palace, was first described by a French archaeological mission in the 1860s but almost a century was to pass before work began in earnest on the site with the painstaking excavations of Manolis Andronikos. In the 1960s Andronikos worked on the Iron Age burial ground below the village, labouring away almost in the shadow of a great tumulus which dominated the village centre. At last in 1976 he finally got the necessary permission and financial backing to begin exploring the tumulus itself. The subsequent results more than justified his long wait for they have produced what is arguably the most important archaeological discoveries to be made in Greece in the last 50 years.

During the 1977 and 1978 seasons Andronikos uncovered three fourth-century tombs located under the tumulus. Two of them were unlooted and contained a wide range of extravagant grave goods. The amount of public interest aroused by these finds has been equalled only by the intensity of the controversy surrounding the claims which have been made about them. It is possible to present here only the briefest summary of Andronikos' finds, but such a summary is necessary in view of the claims that the bones of the double burial in the second tomb, which contained the richest of Andronikos' finds, are the remains of Philip II himself and his young widow Cleopatra.

Andronikos recovered four structures in all from beneath the great tumulus. On the southern edge of the mound were the foundations of a small building which was tentatively identified as a shrine for the hero cult of Philip. Close to it was a simple cist tomb, the marvellous frescoes painted on its inner walls still intact. This is Tomb 1. The tomb itself had been robbed in antiquity and was empty except for the scattered bones of a middle-aged man, a young woman, and an infant. Slightly further to the North, closer to the centre of the mound, is Tomb 2, a rectangular chamber tomb with antechamber and barrel-vaulted roof. The main chamber held a magnificent gold casket containing the cremated bones of a middle-aged man and a rich array of grave goods, including weapons and armour. In the antechamber was a second burial in a similar but less elaborate gold casket. Inside were the cremated bones of a young woman. The facade of this tomb bore an imposing painted frieze showing a Macedonian royal hunt. Further North again, near the centre of the tumulus, is Tomb 3. It is similar in form to Tomb 2, but less elaborate, and was also unlooted. In the main chamber was found a silver chest containing the bones of a teenaged male and an array of silver vessels and ivory relief carvings.

These tombs are clearly those of royalty. On that point at least there appears to be general agreement. Originally they must have formed but a small part of the Argead royal cemetery, the traditional burial place of the Macedonian kings. But whose tombs are they? This is the second part of our double mystery. There have been no inscriptional clues found associated with any of these structures. Consequently it is here that we begin a fascinating and highly complicated Macedonian version of the shell game. All the stylistic criteria and pottery evidence point to a date for the tombs sometime between the 330s BC (Tomb 1) and the 310s BC (Tomb 3). Since there is only a limited number of Macedonian royals who died in this period, the problem is to determine which one goes in which tomb.

The excavator himself argued from the very beginning that Tomb 2, the most magnificent of his finds, must be the tomb of Philip and that the remains found within the main chamber were therefore those of Philip while those in the antechamber must be the remains of one of his wives. It was not long, however, before that view was challenged, principally on the grounds that the architectural form of the tomb's barrel vault had been unknown in Europe until its introduction from Asia after Alexander's conquests, and that the silver gilded diadem discovered in the main chamber was also Asian in origin and consequently post-Philip in date.[8] Another royal pair was therefore put forward as candidates for Tomb 2: Alexander's successor, his mentally limited half-brother Philip III Arrhidaeus and his wife Eurydice. Arrhidaeus had been made king after the death of Alexander but in the course of a civil war in 317 BC he and his young queen Eurydice were captured and put to death on the command of Olympias. The following year, after defeating and murdering Olympias, the Macedonian general Cassander had the royal couple formally buried at Aegae with full royal honours in an attempt to win the support of their followers for his own grasp at the throne of Macedon.

It is easiest to begin any attempt to sort out who goes where with Tomb 3. If the identification of the bones from that tomb as those of a teenaged male is correct, the occupant is most likely to be Alexander IV. The posthumous offspring of Alexander the Great and the Bactrian princess Roxane, Alexander IV was the last of the Argead kings and his murder in 311 or 310 BC by Cassander saw the end of the dynasty. This leaves us with the identity of the double burials of Tombs 1 and 2.

Tomb 1's proximity to the supposed hero-shrine of Philip always meant that it too had to be in the running for consideration as the king's final resting place. Its case to be regarded as Philip's tomb was considerably strengthened by the belated revelation from 1980 onwards that the bones found there included those of an infant as well as a mature man and a young woman.[9] For a time at least therefore it began to look as if this complex problem could be solved very simply by taking the three tombs in their natural order. Tomb 1, the earliest and the nearest to the hero-shrine, would be that of Philip II, his last wife Cleopatra, and their child

Europa. Tomb 2 would belong to Philip III Arrhidaeus and his young wife Eurydice, and Tomb 3 belonged to Alexander IV.[10]

Unfortunately it seems that this neat solution must now be abandoned. A further examination of the bones from Tomb 1 has confirmed that they are those of a male in the prime of life, a young woman aged about 25, and an infant, but it has also revealed that the baby was only a day or two old at death, if that.[11] What is more, the remains of all three were inhumed and not cremated as we would expect a great king like Philip to have been.

Although they seem to imply a step backwards rather than forwards, these findings in fact represent a major contribution. They mean that, unless we are willing to believe that Cleopatra bore Philip another child some time after his assassination,[12] and that it was this child and not Europa who was murdered along with her mother, the infant remains in Tomb 1 cannot be those of Europa. Born while Philip was still alive and given her name by him, the little girl must have been several months old by the time that she and her mother were murdered by Olympias. Consequently the young woman buried in Tomb 1 is unlikely to have been Cleopatra, or the man Philip. The most natural inference to draw from the age at death of the baby is that this is another example of something which was all too common in the ancient world, as it is in today's Third World. The woman had most probably died in childbirth and the baby soon afterwards. But who she and her husband were, we simply do not know, except to say that they were not Cleopatra and Philip.

That leaves both royal couples still vying for occupancy of Tomb 2. Andronikos' original arguments for the identification of the main burial in Tomb 2 as that of Philip rested primarily upon the architectural details of the tomb's construction and the age at death of the occupants as determined by the initial examination of the bones. Unfortunately it has so far proved impossible to choose between Philip and Cleopatra and Arrhidaeus and Eurydice on the basis of either set of evidence.

The age at death of the man in Tomb 2 was between 35 and 55.[13] This would certainly fit Philip, who was about 45 or 46 years old when he was killed. But it could also fit Arrhidaeus, who must have been about 40 when Olympias ordered his death. The remains of the female in the antechamber were much more scanty, but they were sufficient to determine her age at death as being about 25, and not younger than 20 or older than 30. Again it is difficult to eliminate either Cleopatra or Eurydice in view of what little we know about their ages. Cleopatra is said by Plutarch (*Alexander* 9.6) to have been very much younger than her husband at the time of their marriage. Eighteen might be a likely age for a princess in that part of the world to have been married off but in Athens 14 was considered the ideal age for a girl to be married. So an earlier age cannot be excluded. Nor can a later one. There is slightly more information, albeit indirect, about Eurydice, which suggests that she too may have been as young as 20 or as old as 25 at the time of her murder.[14] Consequently she too fits the rather inadequate identikit picture which is all that the relatively new science of palaeopathology can give us at present.

The inferences which are drawn from the details of the tomb's construction can likewise be made to point to either couple. Tomb 2 consists of a main chamber, an almost equally large antechamber, a dividing wall with doors, a vaulted roof and a Doric-style facade. Andronikos discovered that the tomb had been built in two distinct stages. The first stage involved construction of the back wall, all of both side walls, the dividing wall and the barrel vaulting over the main chamber. The chamber's interior was roughly finished in undecorated plaster, suggesting a degree of haste in the construction work. This single-chambered tomb was then sealed after the burial of the male had been completed. Later, in the second stage, the antechamber was finished off more carefully, using finer decorated plaster. Then it too was roofed over with a barrel vault which is slightly lower than the roof of the main chamber. Finally the facade was added, with its magnificent full-width painted frieze of a Macedonian royal hunt.

What had started off as a hastily constructed chamber tomb with an antechamber for the deposit of grave goods was therefore converted within the space of a few months (perhaps even weeks) into a double-chambered tomb, unique among Macedonian tombs in containing burials in both chambers. It is this gap in time between the construction of the two parts of Tomb 2 which, Andronikos argued, points to the identity of its occupants as Philip and Cleopatra. Alexander had needed to respond quickly to events after his father's assassination and on the eve of the departure of the expedition to Asia there had been no time to waste on extensive preparations for the burial. So the murdered king's tomb was quickly constructed after the usual pattern of a 'Macedonian' tomb – a single burial chamber fronted by an antechamber for the grave goods – and as soon as Philip's cremated remains were decently interred, Alexander set off with the army.

The political situation which he left behind him was still very uncertain. Attalus may have been absent with the army but he and his family and supporters remained a power to be reckoned with at court. Blind to this fact, either because of her own hatred for Cleopatra or because she had misread the domestic political situation, Olympias jumped the gun in her eagerness to get rid of Cleopatra and her child. Alexander, we are told by Plutarch (*Alexander* 10.8), was furious with his mother when he found out what she had done. In an attempt to head off any angry backlash from Cleopatra's uncle and guardian Attalus and the rest of her family, he therefore decided to have Cleopatra buried with full royal honours. Philip's tomb was extended and the remains of the young queen were carefully laid to rest in the antechamber, which now became a second burial chamber. Alexander thereby succeeded in averting the possible anger of Attalus and his clan and could bide his time before making his own move against the still powerful general and his kin.

This scenario certainly fits what we may imagine was the situation in Macedon at the time of Philip's murder. Yet apart from the bare facts that Alexander left for Asia with the army soon after his accession, and that he is said to have been angry with Olympias for her savage butchery of Cleopatra and her child, there is very little evidence to support any part of this hypothesis. In fact we do not even know whether Cleopatra's murder took place before or after Alexander managed to dispose of Attalus. Had it taken place afterwards, then there would have been no reason to give Cleopatra anything more than a perfunctory burial. Indeed a royal burial for her at that stage would actually have been counterproductive, drawing sympathetic attention towards a figure who was now no longer of any significance.

Twenty years later at the time when Olympias had Arrhidaeus killed and forced Eurydice to kill herself, the political situation in Macedonia was equally unstable. The general Cassander, whom Eurydice had appointed as her champion just before her death, was already trying to sideline the young Alexander IV and set himself up as the country's first non-Argead ruler. This meant that he was under even more pressure to act rapidly than Alexander had been. The haste which apparently attended the burials in Tomb

2 will therefore fit the situation of early 316 BC just as well as that of 336 BC.

Furthermore to bury king and queen together would have been a much more politically significant act for Cassander to have undertaken than for Alexander to have interred Cleopatra with Philip II. Cleopatra was merely the last wife of a king who, like Henry VIII, had been married many times before. Her one role in life (which through no fault of her own she had been unable to fulfil) had been to bear Philip a son. Eurydice on the other hand was the sole wife of a king whose mental powers were always limited. Consequently she had as much, if not more of a role to play in the running of Macedon as Arrhidaeus had. It was she who had appointed Cassander as regent. It was she who in his absence led out the army in the ill-fated attempt to oppose the invasion by Olympias and her faction. And, unlike Cleopatra, Eurydice herself was of royal blood. She was the daughter of Philip's nephew Amyntas and Cynanne, offspring of the Illyrian princess Audata who had been Philip's second wife.

Eurydice was therefore much more politically prominent than Cleopatra had ever been. Furthermore her warlike nature, inherited from her mother's side, could help to provide an explanation for the martial character of the grave goods present in the antechamber of Tomb 2. Eurydice must accordingly remain in contention as an occupant of the antechamber just as Arrhidaeus must remain a possibility for the main burial. The splendour of Tomb 2 and its grave goods could be ascribed just as well to Cassander's desire to present himself as the legitimate successor of the royal allies he was interring as to a prudent act of piety by a young Alexander the Great. It would have been nice to have ended this chapter on a high note by agreeing with Andronikos that the young woman found in Tomb 2 was definitely Cleopatra and that, after her brutal murder, Philip's tragic young widow was finally accorded the honours which she deserved. But as matters currently stand, our evidence unfortunately no longer permits such an upbeat conclusion.

5

ALEXANDER'S SISTER

It is not often that a new bride can have woken up on the morning after her marriage to the shocking news that her father, who had given her away the previous day, had just been assassinated. That is what happened to Cleopatra, Philip II's other child by Olympias, in the disastrous aftermath to her splendid wedding to Alexander king of Epirus.

The murder of Philip in the theatre at Aegae had taken place before the astounded gaze of the entire Greek world. It is therefore only to be expected that such a blatant act of regicide should have drawn attention almost entirely away from the marriage itself and its contemporary significance. Yet the chief value of a Macedonian royal female always lay in her importance in binding the loyalty of another chieftain to her original family and Cleopatra's exalted status gave this particular marriage an added lustre. Not only was she the daughter of Philip II, the greatest king and conqueror of his age. She was also the full sister of Alexander, the male heir whom all the Macedonian court (except, no doubt, general Attalus and his coterie) fully expected to hail as their next ruler in the fullness of time. Hence the extravagant nature of her nuptials which, as we have seen, were merely the opening act of a great international media fest designed to serve as a showcase for Philip's power, wealth, and prestige.

Philip had intended his daughter's marriage to re-establish the ties between Macedon and Epirus which had been stretched very nearly to breaking point as a result of his own recent marriage to the other Cleopatra, the niece of Attalus, and the threat which this match had seemed to pose to the kingly ambitions of Alexander and his mother Olympias. As has been recounted, matters had come to a head at the famous drinking party where Philip's refusal

57

to do anything about Attalus' offensive remarks concerning Alexander had led to a drunken quarrel between the touchy young prince and his equally prickly father.

Alexander and his mother had subsequently withdrawn from court, thereby serving notice on the king that he could ignore them only at his peril. The places they chose for their self-imposed exile – Olympias returning to Epirus where her younger brother Alexander now ruled as king of the Molossians, Alexander taking temporary refuge among the Macedonians' ancient enemies, the Illyrians – left Philip in no doubt that what they saw as their legitimate claims could not be brushed aside in such a cavalier fashion. Had he continued to ignore them, he might have found his erstwhile ally manoeuvred into making common cause against him with his most dangerous enemy. A combination of these two powers against Macedon would have stretched his resources to the limit as Philip himself knew only too well. At the very least the expedition to liberate Asia would have had to be postponed and, given the then lukewarm attitude of many of the Greek states, a postponement at that stage might have meant the end of it altogether.

Consequently the intention of the Aegae extravaganza was not so much to honour Cleopatra or even her husband-to-be as to placate Olympias and Alexander. High born as she was, at this stage Cleopatra herself was little more than a pawn on the board of Macedonian power politics. If anyone was to be flattered by the wedding's splendour it was the bride's mother (and bridegroom's sister) Olympias, not the bride herself. Yet Cleopatra's fate was by no means as dreadful as it might at first appear. Although he was her mother's brother, Alexander of Epirus was not so very much older than his bride. He had been little more than 20 years old when he had succeeded to the Molossian throne in 342 BC. At the time of the marriage therefore Alexander was about 27 and Cleopatra about 18 so that the couple were well matched in age at least. Whether the marriage proved a happy one we cannot say. Perhaps it was, for Cleopatra had two children, Cadmeia and Neoptolemus, in quick succession. If it was not, at least she did not have to put up with her new husband for very long. It was not long before Alexander left on a military expedition to Italy (c. 334 BC) and it was there that he would meet his death in battle in the winter of 331/0 BC.

It is after her husband's departure for Italy that we find

Cleopatra first coming to political prominence in her own right in a way which seems to be hitherto unattested for Macedonian royal women. Her position probably owed a great deal to the unique fact that she was the sister of Alexander the Great as well as to the unusual role traditionally accorded to women in Epirus. Unlike the situation in mainland Greece where a woman always remained the 'property' of one man or another, an Epirote widow with sons was permitted to act as head of the family until her children came of age. So it seems very likely that it was thanks to her status as Alexander's sister that Cleopatra had been the natural choice as regent of Epirus at the time her husband left for Italy and that because of her son's youth she then simply continued in that position after her husband's death.

The first indication which we have that Cleopatra held an official position in the government of Molossia is a reference by the Athenian orator Aeschines (*Against Ctesiphon* 242) to the dispatch of an embassy from Athens sent to deliver condolences to the queen after the death of Alexander of Epirus. We also find her prominently involved as both a recipient and sender of official shipments of grain.[1] For example, at a time of widespread shortage in the late 330s BC her name appears on an inscription (SEG IX 2) from Cyrene in North Africa as the recipient of 50,000 *medimni* of grain and it was she also, it seems, who was responsible for shipping the surplus on to Corinth in about 330 BC (Lycurgus, *Against Leocrates* 26).

Of even more interest is the presence of Cleopatra in another inscription (SEG XXIII 189) which comes from Epirus itself. In it she seems to be acting as the religious head of state for the people of Molossia. The stone contains a list of *theorodoci*, 'welcomers of sacred ambassadors', for the recently established Epirote alliance which had been forged under Macedonian influence shortly after the death of Alexander of Epirus. Cleopatra's name appears in line 10 as *theorodocus* for Epirus and significantly she is the only female in the list. As we would expect from what we know of this office, all her colleagues from the other states were men. The job was a doubly important one in so far as Epirus was the site of one of the major sanctuaries of the ancient Greek world, the oracle of Zeus at Dodona. Cleopatra's position as 'official welcomer' would have enabled her to keep a finger on the pulse of whatever was happening anywhere in Greece as one group of civic envoys after another filed through the shrine on what was now a recognised sacred circuit.[2]

It has been suggested above that Cleopatra may originally have owed her political prominence in Epirus as much to her status as the sister of Alexander the Great as to the fact that she was the wife of the king. Unfortunately evidence for her relationship with her brother during this period is not as plentiful as we should like. Nevertheless there is enough to show that the two of them must have remained in close contact while Alexander was away on his campaigns in the East. Plutarch records that after the siege of Gaza in the autumn of 332 BC Alexander sent great quantities of booty home 'to Olympias and Cleopatra and his friends' (*Alexander* 25.6). We also hear of her interceding with her brother during the last years of his reign on behalf of a certain Dionysius who was the ruler of Heracleia. It therefore seems reasonable to assume that Alexander was closer to Cleopatra, his full sister, than to his other sisters. Indeed apart from his steadfast refusal to let Cynanne marry we know of no contact between Alexander and his half-sisters.

Cleopatra's relations with her mother Olympias during this same period are more complex. On the basis of Plutarch's statement that during Alexander's absence 'Olympias and Cleopatra even engaged in factionalism against Antipater (Alexander's regent in Macedon) and divided his realm between them, Olympias taking over Epirus and Cleopatra Macedonia' (*Alexander* 68.4) it used to be believed that Olympias herself had returned to Epirus soon after the death of her brother/son-in-law Alexander of Epirus and had asserted her own claim to control of the country. Either she had set herself up as queen or she had effectively ruled through her dominance over her daughter.[3]

This is somewhat difficult to believe given the evidence now of Cleopatra's role as *theorodocus* for the people of Epirus. It also seems very unlikely that if she had been left as regent on her husband's departure (as is generally believed), Cleopatra would simply have resigned her position and yielded pride of place to her mother without so much as a whimper, however forceful Olympias' personality may have been. In addition there is now some evidence to suggest that during the late 330s BC Olympias may have held the same sort of official positions in Macedon as her daughter concurrently occupied in Epirus, and this would seem to preclude her return to Epirus on any permanent basis.

Thus we find her sending a dedication to the goddess Hygieia (Health) in Athens in 333 BC in gratitude for Alexander's recovery from an illness and dedicating her son's spoils of war at Delphi in 331 BC. Both these actions suggest a similar religious role to Cleopatra's. And Olympias too is recorded as a recipient of grain shipments from Cyrene so that she may well have been Macedon's official representative in this sphere of interstate relations, just as Cleopatra was that of the Molossians.

Consequently it is much more probable that mother and daughter were acting in concert during Alexander's absence on campaign rather than in opposition to one another. While Olympias may have had some share in the rule of Epirus after her brother's death, she certainly did not attempt to oust Cleopatra from her position as regent. Instead Plutarch's tale of Cleopatra going back to Macedon while her mother took charge of Epirus is better explained by Hammond's theory that by c. 324 BC relations between Alexander's regent Antipater and his mother Olympias had reached such a low level that Alexander himself determined that it would be in the best interests of all concerned if Olympias removed herself to Epirus and let his sister Cleopatra take over her role in Macedon.[4]

It may be a cliché but there is a great deal of truth in the saying that behind every great man there stands a great woman. The details elude us but it looks as though in the case of Alexander the Great these words may have been true twice over. Behind him there stood two great women, his mother and his sister, working together to keep matters on an even keel at home while Alexander's ambitions of empire took him ever further away from the Macedonian court at Pella with its seething intrigues and incessant struggles for power. In fact it is not too fanciful to speak of Alexander, Olympias, and Cleopatra as a family team and this closeness to his own blood kin may have been a powerful factor in Alexander's own unwillingness to marry until quite late in his lifetime.

When Alexander died in 323 BC the situation of his mother and sister underwent a radical change, but it was hardly one for the better. During his lifetime both Cleopatra and Olympias had grown accustomed to the easy exercise of direct power, as we have seen. As long as the king was alive they had naturally been immune from any physical threat to their personal safety. Despite the intense enmity which had built up between Olympias and Antipater (and probably others too) none of their enemies would have had the audacity to move against someone as close to Alexander the Great as his mother or his sister. But now the game had become much more dangerous, and the stakes much higher, as Alexander's would-be successors rolled up their sleeves and got down to the serious business of playing for control of the largest block of real estate ever to come up for grabs in the ancient Greek world.

In such a potentially unstable situation the immediate problem for both women was how to ensure the continuity of the royal house of the Argeads for it was only by so doing that they could ensure their own personal survival. If they could not offer the Macedonians an heir to take the place of Alexander then they would quickly become expendable. When Alexander died, he had left a widow Roxane and an infant son, who would later become Alexander IV. But at this time they were not under Olympias' control, but in the firm grasp of her sworn enemy Antipater. So too were most of the other family members who might be capable of continuing the line of Philip and Alexander, either by ruling in their own right or by producing an Argead heir. Cleopatra therefore suddenly assumed a new importance. She was still of childbearing age. Any child of hers would carry Philip's bloodline and thus have at least as good a claim to the kingdom and the empire as any of the other contenders.

As a result it is no surprise to find that, not long after Alexander's death, Cleopatra is said to have written either on her own volition or at her mother's prompting to an old family friend Leonnatus, satrap of Phrygia, inviting him to return to Macedon and marry her. Leonnatus had been a trusted friend of her brother's and when they were children he had been brought up in the palace along with Alexander and Cleopatra. What is more, he may also have had a distant royal connection via his kinship with Philip's mother Eurydice. In his good looks he is said to have resembled Alexander the Great and after the latter's death he reportedly tried to play up that resemblance by deliberately imitating certain of Alexander's characteristics, such as his manner of wearing his hair long.[5] This looks a significant ploy at a time when image was becoming as important as reality in the projection of the royal persona. But Leonnatus was playing politics rather than fashion and we should not think of this personal likeness as having more than a marginal role, if that, in Cleopatra's decision to make him the object of her first approach.

Leonnatus jumped at Cleopatra's offer. His plan was to bring his army back to Europe on the pretext of assisting Antipater against the rival Successors but once he arrived home he would lay claim to Macedon itself (Plutarch, *Eumenes* 3.9). Tragically it all came to nothing. In early 322 BC Leonnatus was killed fighting in the first battle against the army of the Greeks in Thessaly (Plutarch, *Phocion* 25.5). This left Cleopatra in just as perilous a spot as before. As Elizabeth Carney has so perceptively observed,[6] the days of being a dowager queen with political clout of one's own were now long past. What Cleopatra really needed, and as soon as possible if she wanted to survive, was a Macedonian husband complete with a Macedonian army.

With that in mind Cleopatra next turned her attention to Perdiccas, the commander-in-chief of the Macedonian army in Asia. He was perhaps the most powerful of the Successors at this time and his qualifications appeared impeccable in other respects too. As chief confidant of Alexander during the king's last years it was Perdiccas who had been the recipient of Alexander's signet ring, a symbolic gift which was the nearest Alexander ever got to designating a successor. It was he too who was now serving as regent for the two Argead family members whom the Macedonians had acknowledged as co-rulers of Alexander's domains shortly after the king's death, his mentally deficient half-brother Philip Arrhidaeus and his infant son Alexander IV.

In 322/1 BC therefore Cleopatra travelled to Perdiccas' headquarters at Sardis in Asia Minor with the intention of making a dynastic marriage with him. According to the historian Arrian it was Olympias who first suggested she should go but, wherever the idea originated, it came too late. The same thought had already occurred to someone else. Cleopatra arrived at Sardis to find Perdiccas already betrothed, seemingly at his own request, to Nicaea, the daughter of their foe Antipater.

Perdiccas now really found himself on the horns of a dilemma. Whichever of the two women he chose, he would inevitably insult the other and make implacable enemies of her faction. In the short term an alliance with Antipater's daughter looked the better prospect for it was Antipater who controlled the armies. But Perdiccas realised that, if he was to have any hope of ruling all of Alexander's empire, he would be better served in the long term by a marriage with Cleopatra. Hence the farce which now ensued, with Perdiccas wavering this way and that as first his brother

Alcetas urged him to accept Nicaea and then his confidant
Eumenes (previously the go-between in Cleopatra's abortive
attempt to marry Leonnatus) sang Cleopatra's praises to him. In
fact at one stage Perdiccas is said to have sent Eumenes to
Cleopatra with a secret promise to repudiate the arrangement with
Nicaea as soon as he could, and there is doubt that the marriage
intended between them ever took place at all.

From then on matters began to go rapidly downhill for the
unlucky Perdiccas. Largely as a result of Cleopatra's arrival on
the scene, his previously amicable relations with Antipater started
to turn sour as Antipater's suspicions about his trustworthiness
began to grow ever stronger in the face of his shillyshallying. And,
to make matters worse, further domestic complications were
soon to follow with the arrival at Sardis of another forceful and
determined Macedonian princess intent on a dynastic agenda of
her own.

The newcomer was Cynanne, Philip's daughter by his Illyrian
wife Audata and therefore Cleopatra's elder half-sister. Her father
had married her to Amyntas, Alexander the Great's cousin and
Philip's alternative heir. But Amyntas was long gone, having been
executed by Alexander on a charge of treason soon after his
accession to the throne. Now that Alexander too had gone the
way of all flesh Cynanne, like Olympias, was determined to push
the claims of her own daughter Adea. As the granddaughter of
Philip and the daughter of Amyntas, Adea could claim to have
just as much Argead blood in her veins as any other contender, if
not more, and Cynanne's mission was to demand that she be
married to king Philip Arrhidaeus.

Perdiccas at once realised how great a threat such a match would
pose to his own ambitions to control the remnants of the royal
house and he got his brother Alcetas to arrange for Cynanne's
removal. This proved a serious error of judgement on his part.
The Macedonian rank and file still held their royal family in high
regard and Perdiccas' troops rioted at what they rightly saw as an
unprovoked and unjustifiable murder. Faced with a mutiny,
Perdiccas was forced to back down. Adea was married to Philip
Arrhidaeus, changing her name to Eurydice on her marriage, and
as we saw earlier it may be her royal remains which survive in the
antechamber of Tomb 2 at Vergina.

As if he did not have troubles enough with the living, Perdiccas
next had trouble with the dead too. He lost control of Alexander

the Great's corpse. The body of Alexander was an immensely prestigious relic for whoever wanted to lay claim to the succession. As we can see from some of the inheritance cases argued by the fourth-century Athenian orator Isaeus, since the duty of burial traditionally devolved upon the immediate male next of kin who was also most properly the deceased's heir, the performance of the burial itself could often be argued to determine succession even in the absence of any close ties of kinship. So whoever carried out the last rites for the dead king would be putting himself in pole position in the race to inherit Alexander's empire.

In early 321 BC the body still lay in Babylon while preparations were being made to convey it to what was to be Alexander's chosen resting place in the Egyptian oasis of Siwah, site of the shrine of Zeus-Ammon whose oracle had first hailed him as a god. In early summer the cortège set out from the city under armed escort. It had only got as far as Syria when it was met by Ptolemy, Alexander's satrap of Egypt, with a larger armed force. Perdiccas' men were outnumbered and had no option but to withdraw, and Alexander's body was effectively hijacked. Ptolemy took it temporarily to the old royal capital at Memphis, which was still the country's religious capital. There it would be embalmed in the manner of an ancient pharaoh before its eventual removal to a specially prepared mausoleum in Alexandria.

Perdiccas had to respond to Ptolemy's outrageous act of body snatching or else he would lose all credibility as a contender for the succession. In the spring of the following year (320 BC) he invaded Egypt to try to win back Alexander's corpse. All went well with the expedition as it advanced into Egypt until, at the end of a night march on Memphis, Perdiccas attempted to get his weary and confused troops across to an island in the middle of the Nile. In the course of their crossing the river level rose unexpectedly and over 2,000 men were washed away. Some drowned immediately, the rest were taken by crocodiles. Ever since the murder of Cynanne, Perdiccas' officers had been growing increasingly disenchanted with their commander's stiff-necked and authoritarian attitude and this disaster was the last straw. A plot was hatched by a group of cavalry leaders and Perdiccas was assassinated in an army *coup*.[7]

So much for Cleopatra's second attempt to get herself a Macedonian husband backed by a Macedonian army. After Perdiccas' death she stayed on in Sardis, no doubt because she felt she was more secure there than she would have been back home in either Macedon or Epirus. By remaining there she also stayed close to the men with the armies. Her very presence held out to any ambitious general who might be victorious in the struggle for Asia the heady promise of a dynastic connection with the Argead house, and therefore a claim to rule Macedon itself. Indeed, if we are to believe Diodorus (20.37.3–6), so distinguished was her lineage as the sister of Alexander that she was courted by practically all the Successors in turn – Cassander, Lysimachus, Antigonus, and Ptolemy.

In addition Eumenes, who had served as go-between for both Leonnatus and Perdiccas, now threw his own hat into the ring. Outlawed after the death of Perdiccas, he had turned up at Sardis eager to give battle to Antipater on the plain of Sardis in the hope of impressing her with the superiority of his cavalry (Plutarch, *Eumenes* 8.6). Afraid that he might overreach himself and thereby compromise her own situation, Cleopatra persuaded him to withdraw before battle could be joined. Her move probably saved his life for him,[8] but as she had feared even his presence spelt danger for her. Shortly after Eumenes' departure her old enemy Antipater arrived and publicly attacked her for her friendships with Perdiccas and Eumenes.

Confident in the strength of her own position Cleopatra rounded on him and gave as good as she got. Not only did she defend herself but she also defiantly counterattacked with charges of her own, 'in a way more like a man than a woman' (Arrian, *Succ.* fr. 1.40). She was well aware that Antipater knew of the uproar which the murder of Cynanne had provoked among Perdiccas' soldiers and she could take a gamble on his unwillingness to run a similar risk if he attempted to dispose of her. By this stage (*c.* 320 BC) the gamble was probably already a dangerous one, but it paid off. Antipater backed down and in time the pair were grudgingly reconciled. He may even have thought of taking her on himself, or giving her to one of his sons, so valuable was she as the key to the kingdom.

Cleopatra would remain at Sardis under the protection of Antigonus for over a decade more, a glittering prize on offer to all but ultimately available to none. The only asset she now had left was her marriageability and, as Cleopatra realised, she could never afford to cash that asset in. To give herself in marriage to any of the rival Successors would have had the effect of setting all the others against her and her chosen husband. As for Antigonus, despite his thoughts of marriage he too was aware that to marry Cleopatra himself would have acted as a catalyst to combine all his enemies against him. Far better therefore to keep her under his eye in what was virtual house arrest.

That was Cleopatra's lot up until 308 BC and during that time she succeeded in outlasting just about all of them, friend and foe alike. She would see the threefold division of her brother's empire, which took place at Triparadeisos in northern Syria after the death of Perdiccas, and the eventual emergence of the three major hellenistic monarchies, with Ptolemy controlling Egypt, Antigonus the king of a new dynasty in Macedonia, and the establishment of the Seleucid house in Syria. Next year came the death of Antipater followed by the defeat and execution of Eumenes by Antigonus (winter 317/6 BC). On the home front there was the brief but bitter civil war between her own mother Olympias and her half-brother Philip Arrhidaeus backed by his ambitious queen Eurydice (317 BC) which ended with the murder of the royal couple, followed swiftly by Cassander's revenge and the murder of Olympias in her turn.

The removal of Olympias opened the way for the marriage (at last) of Alexander's only other surviving half-sister Thessalonice, as Cassander in turn made an unsuccessful attempt to marry his way to the throne. It was Cassander too who, in his desperate quest for the kingship for himself, would murder Philip Arrhidaeus' co-ruler, the boy-king Alexander IV, and his mother Roxane (310 or 309 BC). The dispatch of Alexander's young son finally left Cleopatra and her half-sister as the last of the Argead line. Yet it was not the final murder in a house which had seen so much bloodshed since the time long past when the first Cleopatra had borne the first true Macedonian king to Perdiccas I, the young exile from Argos.

Alexander's empire may have been carved up at Triparadeisos but that had not meant an end to a falling out among thieves. Far from it. In 311 BC the dynasts had made an uneasy peace. By that time it was generally recognised that the surviving Successors were no longer satraps of a larger entity, and even if they did not yet dare to call themselves royal they were nevertheless already acting as kings, founding capitals for themselves and coveting each other's possessions. In 309 BC Ptolemy in Egypt had designs upon Greece, which was then in the domain of Cassander. The two generalissimos were already joined by a dynastic alliance for Cassander had given Ptolemy his sister to wife. But their relationship had hardly been improved by Ptolemy's blatant neglect of her in favour of his concubine Berenice, who after a cosy winter in Cos bore him a son, the future Ptolemy II, early in 308 BC.

It was against this background that in order to further his claim to Greece, and by implication Macedonia too, Ptolemy now proposed to marry Cleopatra – the only woman still living who had a better dynastic claim to Macedon than Cassander's own wife Thessalonice. For whatever reason Cleopatra accepted him. Maybe she had fallen out with her protector Antigonus, as Diodorus (20.37.3) suggests. Maybe the fact that the murder of Alexander the Great's own son the previous year had excited so little outrage compared to Cynanne's assassination twelve years earlier had alerted her to the harsh reality that the royal name had now lost almost all of its earlier magic. Maybe she felt that Ptolemy represented a better bet than Antigonus at that stage. Maybe she was just tired of being penned up in Sardis for so long and longed for a change of scenery.[9] At any rate Cleopatra set out to take ship for Egypt.

She did not get far before she was stopped by the governor of the city, who had his orders from Antigonus to detain her. She returned to her palace in Sardis and it was probably there that she was subsequently found murdered 'through the agency of certain women' who were acting under instructions from the governor. According to Diodorus (20.37.5) he was again following the orders of her 'protector' Antigonus. Later Antigonus would make a characteristic use of this 'cut-out'. To distance himself from the murder, he had the assassins executed and honoured his victim with a splendid royal funeral.

More than anything else, Antigonus' circumspection with regard to Cleopatra's murder emphasises for us the immense prestige which she must have enjoyed even at this late stage in her life. Although she must have been well past child-bearing age by the time of her death, as Alexander's sister and Philip's daughter she still represented a potent symbol of continuity in a changed world. That she was never able to fulfil her promise to link past and present together in the foundation of a new dynasty was regrettable but perhaps inevitable. And we should not lose sight of what was her greatest achievement. She did not merely survive through a period of unprecedented turbulence in the history of the Greek world. She survived with power and honour. Alexander's sister Cleopatra demonstrates more clearly than any earlier figure the sort of authority and influence a royal woman could now command, given the qualities of skill and determination with which, like her mother and brother, she was so abundantly endowed.

6

FROM AEGAE TO
ALEXANDRIA

The murder of Alexander the Great's young son, Alexander IV, by Cassander in 310/9 BC represented the fall of the curtain on the final act of the Argead royal house. A single dynasty had ruled Macedon since the mid-seventh century BC. So powerful and so well known had the family become that the kings had never even needed an official title. For a Macedonian king simply to say that he was the son of an Argead had been title enough.[1] Now that dynasty was over. All that survived of a distinguished, proud, and ruthless line were two middle-aged princesses, Alexander's sister Cleopatra, the widow since 331 BC of Alexander of Epirus, and her half-sister Thessalonice, who had been married since 316 BC to her nephew's assassin Cassander.

As we have seen, in 309 BC Cleopatra was still resident in Sardis in Asia Minor under the control of Antigonus. She was already under virtual house arrest when news reached her of the killing first of her nephew, who was just about to come of age, and then, shortly afterwards, of his slightly elder half-brother Heracles, Alexander the Great's bastard son by the Persian noblewoman Barsine. She must have realised at once what the murders meant for her. As long as she remained in the power of Antigonus, he had been unwilling to marry her himself out of a well-founded fear that his rivals might react by making common cause against him. At the same time he was even more loath to let her fall into another's clutches. So far her marriageability had protected her well, but it was no longer the asset it had once been.

Alarmed by the lack of public reaction to this latest round of royal deaths, Cleopatra most likely lost confidence in the power of the royal name to protect her any longer. If men could murder Alexander the Great's son and heir and get away with it, what hope was there for his sister? Nevertheless she determined on one last throw of the dice. Her final bet was to be on Ptolemy, on the reasoning perhaps that the man who had Alexander's body as backing for his claim to control of Egypt could have no interest in killing her off and a great deal to gain by keeping her alive. But when she tried to make a run for it, Antigonus had her murdered. Luckily Cleopatra's two children were far away and old enough by this time to survive. Nothing is known of her daughter Cadmeia but her son Neoptolemus had become king of Epirus in his own right after his grandmother Olympias had departed in 317 BC. He would rule there until his death in 296/5 BC. At the time of his assassination by Pyrrhus, Neoptolemus was therefore the last of the direct line of Philip II of Macedon.

The other survivor of the Argead line in 310/9 BC was Thessalonice, Philip's daughter by his fifth wife Nicesipolis. Cassander had married her shortly after he had eliminated Olympias in 316 BC. Although Alexander IV was still alive, he was already beginning to strive openly for the kingship for himself and his union with Thessalonice was merely one of a series of quasi-royal acts which he undertook at this stage in the hope of bolstering his claim to the Macedonian throne. Marrying her gave Cassander a direct link to the house of Philip, but more importantly it also made him the uncle of Alexander IV and thereby gave him a legitimate claim to be sole guardian of the boy-king and manager of all his affairs.

No doubt Cassander would have preferred to have married Cleopatra, given the greater prestige of her closer relationship to Alexander the Great. Indeed he is said to have been one of her suitors (Diodorus 20.37.4) but, had he ever succeeded, the fact that he had recently delivered up her mother Olympias to the vengeance of her victims' relatives might have caused a few awkward silences over the royal breakfast table. So he settled for Thessalonice instead. Not only was she on the spot, unlike Cleopatra. After the removal of Olympias from the scene she was totally at his mercy and would have had little choice in the matter.

Among his other acts as a man who would be king, Cassander marked the occasion of his marriage to Thessalonice by the foundation of cities named for himself and his new queen. Cassandreia, which he founded on the peninsula of Chalcidice, was an important city in ancient times but it has long since reverted to its earlier and better-known name Potidaea as Nea Potidea. Thessaloniki on the other hand, the first city to be named for a royal woman in what would become an increasingly common practice later in the hellenistic age, has endured to become the second largest and most important city of modern Greece. Although there would be few who would be conscious of the origins of the city's name, it is ironic to think that the name, if not the memory, of the most shadowy of Alexander the Great's female relatives has lived on while his much more forceful sister and mother remain trapped in the pages of the history books.

Thessalonice bore Cassander three sons. Philip, the eldest, succeeded his father as Philip IV after Cassander's death in May 297 BC but his unexpected death from a wasting disease after only a few months on the throne left the kingdom highly vulnerable. That weakness was compounded when Thessalonice, who is said to have favoured her third son Alexander, insisted that he be allowed to rule jointly with his older brother Antipater, with herself acting as their regent. Late in her life therefore Thessalonice seems to have started to exhibit the same fiery determination characteristic of all Philip II's offspring, but it did her little good. A couple of years later Antipater, then still in his mid-teens, rebelled against her domination and murdered her. His action led to the downfall within a few years of the dynasty which his father had tried unsuccessfully to establish on the ruins of the Argead house.

By that time Macedon was no longer the centre of the world as it had been under Philip II and Alexander the Great. Nevertheless it would be a grave misrepresentation to suggest that it reverted to being a peaceful backwater. Despite being considerably weakened by civil strife and incursions by marauding bands of Celtic tribesmen, the kingdom eventually recovered after a new king Antigonus II Gonatas won the country by force of arms in 276 BC. The house of the Antigonids which he established would last for just over a century. It would come to control much of mainland Greece as well as Macedonia and challenge for power in the Aegean until broken by the might of the Romans. Their attention had been drawn to Macedon when king Philip V, in an appalling and almost unbelievable error of judgement, made the mistake of openly siding with Carthage after Hannibal's annihilation of the Roman army at Cannae (216 BC).[2]

We lose sight of the name Cleopatra for a while during the years of the third century BC. The memory of Alexander the Great and all those who had been close to him had considerable talismanic power long after the Argead line had disappeared so no doubt there were still Macedonian princesses who bore the name in this period. But we know nothing of them. To pick up Cleopatra as a royal name once more, and find out how it gained its special place as a dynastic name among the Ptolemaic kings of Egypt, it is necessary to turn away from Macedonia and to focus instead upon what was happening politically in the area of the eastern Mediterranean at around the time that in the West the Romans had finally put paid to Hannibal (202 BC).

It was not until several years after all of Alexander's surviving family except Thessalonice had been assassinated that his Successors at last dropped the pretence of being only Alexander's governors and began openly to use the name of king. First to do so was Antigonus – not long in fact after his murder of Cleopatra. By 306 BC he was virtual monarch of much of the eastern part of Alexander's empire, including Asia Minor, and to take the title was almost a formality. If one could be king, so could they all. Within a year he had been followed by Ptolemy in Egypt and Seleucus in Syria. Yet the fact that these warlords had finally decided to creep out from under the fallen colossus of Alexander the Great and stand tall as rulers in their own right did not mean that any of them was about to stop coveting the possessions of his fellow kings. As a result there would never be a shortage of wars in the years which followed.

While there was never any dearth of matters about which to pick a quarrel if a war was ever wanted, one cause of war seems to stand out beyond any other in this period. It would not be too much of an over-simplification to say that as far as the Ptolemaic and the Seleucid kings were concerned the main bone of contention throughout the third century BC was always the question of who was going to exercise control over the region known as Coele (Hollow) Syria, where Ptolemy's Egypt marched on Seleucid Syria. The name had originally been coined by the ancient Greeks because geologically the place is quite literally a hollow. Coele Syria is the long depression running north to south between the Lebanon and Anti-Lebanon ranges where the Orontes river rises to flow northwards to the Mediterranean and, at the other side of the watershed, the Jordan begins its southward journey towards the Dead Sea.[3] In this period, however, depending on who was employing it and for what, the term Coele Syria was used much more vaguely to denote the whole of the Phoenician hinterland between Gaza in the South and Cilicia in the North. The region was important not only because it lay across the trade routes from the East to the Mediterranean, but also because it formed part of a strategic ring of possessions, including Cyprus, the Aegean islands and parts of coastal Asia Minor, which Ptolemy intended should act as a cordon to protect the heartland of Egypt from the rival Seleucid empire.

In 301 BC the opponents of general Antigonus joined together to challenge their ancient rival to a final test of strength on the battlefield. It was at Ipsus in Phrygia that the redoubtable Antigonus, now over 80 years old, was finally defeated and killed in battle. On the day of the engagement Seleucus' corps of battle elephants bore the brunt of the fighting while, crafty as ever, his supposed ally Ptolemy was conspicuous only by his absence. His sole contribution to the allied war effort was to invade Coele Syria. This he claimed was a diversionary tactic but everyone, including Ptolemy himself, recognised it for what it really was – a blatant Egyptian grab for territory.

It was the establishment of this early link between Coele Syria and Egypt under Ptolemy I (as he now was) which led to the immigration of large numbers of Jews to Alexandria throughout the third century BC. The result was the establishment there of a Jewish community second only to Jerusalem in its size and importance. The annexation also opened the way for the gradual exposure of the Jewish people to Greek ideas and institutions in their own homeland, thanks to the Ptolemaic foundation of new cities in Judaea and Phoenicia organised along Greek lines or the reorganisation of existing ones as Greek city-states. Within Egypt itself the process of hellenisation would lead in the next century to a drive to translate the Hebrew bible into Greek for the benefit of a Jewish congregation which was beginning to lose touch with its native language after living so long in the predominantly Greek-speaking milieu of Alexandria – hence the genesis of the ancient Greek version of the Old Testament known to us as the Septuagint.

These could be said to be some of the advantages which eventually accrued from Ptolemy I's occupation of Coele Syria. On the minus side his unashamed land grab gave rise to almost incessant friction between the two royal houses. Over the course of the next century and a half there would be six Syrian wars in all. They began with an unsuccessful attempt by Seleucus' son and successor

Antiochus I to win back the lands which he felt were rightfully his from Ptolemy I's heir Ptolemy II Philadelphus. Details of this First Syrian War (274–271 BC) are unclear except that Ptolemy II seems to have retained control of the areas he already held. He celebrated his success with a magnificent procession and banquet of which we have an almost contemporary account written by a Rhodian historian Callixeinus who was resident in Alexandria.[4] The splendour of the occasion and the sheer costliness of the show which Ptolemy II put on for his cheering subjects give an excellent idea of the immense wealth of the Ptolemaic monarchy at this stage in its history – and its essential vulgarity. For example, one of the floats in the procession was a wagon the length of a modern semi-trailer but nearly twice as wide, pulled by 600 men. On it reposed a 30,000-gallon wineskin sewn up entirely out of the skins of leopards. As the float was drawn along it spurted forth wine for the 'satyrs' who accompanied it (Athenaeus 5.199a–b). Then at the end of the day Ptolemy II awarded himself as well as his deified parents gold portrait statues which were mounted in gold chariots set on the tops of gold columns.

A decade later the Alexandrians had rather less cause for celebration when Ptolemy II made an unsuccessful attempt to take advantage of the death of Antiochus I and the accession of Antiochus II to push for further gains at Seleucid expense. The only result of the Second Syrian War (260–253(?) BC) seems to have been that the Egyptians lost territory formerly held in Asia Minor. Fighting also took place in Syria but the border between the two kingdoms apparently remained fixed at the Eleutherus river to the north of Tripolis. The exact terms of the settlement are unknown, except that it was sealed with a dynastic marriage. In what was a thinly disguised bribe, the new Syrian king received a huge dowry to put aside his wife Laodice and marry Ptolemy II's daughter Berenice.

The union established peace between Ptolemy II and Antiochus II for the rest of their lives, but after their deaths it was to be the cause of further trouble. Both kings died in the same year (246 BC), the latter in mysterious circumstances in the palace of his former wife Laodice. After she had been set aside, Laodice had set up a rival court in the city of Ephesus which had recently reasserted its independence, and she now claimed that with his dying words Antiochus II had designated their son Seleucus (later to rule as Seleucus II) as his chosen heir and successor. But Berenice too had borne a son to Antiochus II and she would have none of this. Proclaiming her own child king, she appealed for help to her brother Ptolemy III Euergetes, who had just become king of Egypt. So began the Third Syrian War (246–241 BC), known also for obvious reasons as the Laodicean War.

Delighted to represent himself as the champion of his sister Berenice and her son, Ptolemy III lost no time in invading Syria. As the supporter of a legitimate claimant to the Seleucid throne, his reception was more than friendly and his triumphal advance through the Levant went unimpeded until news of a native Egyptian revolt back home stopped him short and compelled a speedy return to Egypt (245 BC). Meanwhile in the northern and eastern parts of his vast realm Seleucus had been hailed as the rightful king and, after his supporters had successfully done away with Berenice and her son, Ptolemy III was eventually obliged to come to terms and recognise him as king. With no claimant to the throne to champion, he could appear only as a would-be conqueror, not a liberator. Accordingly although Ptolemy III may possibly have advanced into Seleucid territory as far as Bactria later in the war and may have made some slight gains in Asia Minor and Thrace, his successes there were short-lived.

Next it was the turn of a Seleucid to challenge the accession of a Ptolemy. Antiochus III, who would be known from his later conquests as Antiochus the Great, was Seleucus II's younger son. He had succeeded his brother Seleucus III on the latter's assassination in 223 BC. The death of Ptolemy III the following year and the accession of Ptolemy IV Philopator offered a golden opportunity which Antiochus III immediately grasped with both hands. Despite his own youth and inexperience (he was not yet 20 at the time) and the very great dangers still facing him from disaffected elements at home, in 221 BC he took personal command in the Fourth Syrian War (221–217 BC) and began the push southwards towards Egypt. His initial progress was slowed by stiff local resistance but by winter 218/7 BC he had control of most of Coele Syria, thanks in large part to the treachery of the local Ptolemaic governor, and had got as far south as Ptolemais on the coast of Phoenicia.

In the spring of 217 BC both sides prepared for a showdown. By skilful use of delaying tactics Ptolemy IV's diplomats had managed to buy themselves a breathing space the previous year and the Egyptians had used the time well. All available troops had been pulled back to defend the homeland, additional mercenaries had been signed on, and at the Egyptian end of the Gaza Strip the garrison town of Pelusium had been made ready to withstand a siege. In addition, in an unprecedented move which underlines how serious the situation was, 20,000 native Egyptian troops had been recruited and were being trained up by experienced Greek commanders in secret camps near Alexandria.

As spring turned to summer the Ptolemaic army, numbering about 75,000 men, advanced slowly northwards and met Antiochus III's forces near Raphia in Gaza, the southernmost settlement in Coele Syria. Compared to the Egyptian army the Seleucid troops were battle-hardened and vastly more experienced but they were also battle-weary and, just as significantly, they were now far outnumbered by the Ptolemaic forces. After a stand-off lasting several days battle was finally joined on 22 June 217 BC. The result was an overwhelming victory for the Egyptians. His army broken and utterly demoralised, Antiochus III at once withdrew to his capital Antioch. In the space of a single day Ptolemy IV had won back all of Coele Syria.

Although he could not know it at the time, his victory was to herald the final phase of Ptolemaic control of Coele Syria. When Ptolemy IV died in 204 BC his successor, his only son by his sister–wife Arsinoe III, was a mere child. Ptolemy V Epiphanes was no more than 6 years old when he became king under the regency of his ministers. As if that was not temptation enough for the Seleucid king to try his hand again, the country was in a mess. Egypt had been considerably weakened in the last years of Ptolemy IV's reign as a result of his growing indolence and self-indulgence and in 207 BC the upper part of the country had seceded to become an independent state ruled by a dynasty of local Nubian kings. It would not be brought back under Ptolemaic control until 187 BC. With one eye on this and the other on the growing unrest in the capital as the Alexandrians rioted in outrage at the unscrupulous conduct of the boy-king's self-appointed ministers, Antiochus III determined to make another attempt to win back Egypt's possessions in Syria and Palestine. In a secret pact made with king Philip V of Macedon, he arranged to invade Coele Syria while the Macedonians picked off the remaining Ptolemaic garrisons in and around the Aegean.

In the initial stages of the Fifth Syrian War (202–200(?) BC) Antiochus III succeeded in getting as far as Gaza but he did not have everything his own way. The Egyptians seem to have mounted a counterattack, probably in winter 201/0 BC, since we hear of them in the hill country of Judaea, well to the North of Gaza.[5] This allowed them to recover some lost ground at least temporarily but in 200 BC Antiochus III finally defeated them once and for all at Panium, a location near the source of the Jordan river named after the grotto of a local god whom the Greeks equated with Pan. The outcome was that Coele Syria was at last back in Seleucid hands. There it would remain. Never again would the Ptolemies gain a permanent foothold in the area, despite attempts to do so by Ptolemy V's son Ptolemy VI in the 160s BC and by the last Ptolemaic ruler, Cleopatra VII, in the first century BC.

Just over a century had passed since Ptolemy I had first annexed Coele Syria. But the political world of the eastern Mediterranean was quite different in 200 BC from what it had been 100 years before. There was a new player in the game in the form of the Romans, fresh from their victory over Carthage and clearly already prepared to take whatever action was adjudged necessary to protect their perceived interests in the East. That meant an interest in Ptolemaic Egypt and its grain supply, as well as what might be happening with Philip V in Greece and Macedonia or Antiochus III in Asia Minor.

Diplomatic contact between Rome and Egypt had begun as early as the 270s BC.[6] Initiated by Ptolemy II, it had elicited an embassy in return from the Romans, under the leadership of a distinguished ex-consul. This was the start of a cordial and initially undemanding friendship between the two countries. The early course of the relationship is impossible to trace but there had been an embassy to the Ptolemaic court only a few years earlier (210 BC), sent to procure Egyptian grain to help combat a shortage at Rome. In an interesting slip of the pen Livy (27.4.10) speaks of the ambassadors coming to 'Ptolemy and Cleopatra', substituting the much more familiar name for that of Ptolemy IV's queen Arsinoe III. Unlike Philip V of Macedon, Ptolemy IV had been careful to preserve a strict neutrality in the war between Hannibal and Rome, but it is likely that he acceded to the Romans' request on this occasion. In the following years he also offered his services several times as an intermediary in the conflict which had sprung up between the Romans and Philip V. Consequently it is hardly surprising to find that, faced with the threat from Antiochus III in 202 BC, one of the first diplomatic moves undertaken by the ministers of Ptolemy V had been to send an envoy to Rome.

Whether the envoy ever reached Italy is a moot point. He may have spent all his time *en route* visiting friends and relatives in Greece,[7] and a Roman embassy, which came on from Greece to Alexandria in 200 BC (Polybius 16.27.5), would attempt only to mediate, not to aid. A later tradition, preserved in the unreliable Justin (30.2.8), that before his death Ptolemy IV had entrusted the care of his infant son and heir to the Romans, who then delegated the task specifically to Marcus Aemilius Lepidus, one of the ambassadors of 200 BC, seems to be a piece of self-promoting propaganda stitched together by the family of the Lepidi later in the Roman Republic.[8] In short, however many embassies the Egyptians sent or received, it seems very likely that they got no help at all from Rome against Antiochus III.

This did not mean, however, that the Romans were taking no interest in what was happening between Egypt and the Seleucids. They were happy to stockpile Ptolemaic complaints about continued Seleucid annexation of Egyptian territories and use them later as ammunition in their diplomatic exchanges with Antiochus III. And they were equally happy to let Antiochus III weaken Egypt as long as he himself did not grow too strong in the process. Accordingly it soon became apparent to Ptolemy V's ministers that they could expect nothing from Rome. Their best course, they realised, lay in coming to a permanent arrangement of some kind with their enemy. As for Antiochus III, by 196 BC his interests no longer lay in the area of Coele Syria or Egypt. He had turned his attention westward towards western Asia Minor and Greece. In 195 BC he would begin his self-proclaimed 'liberation' of Thrace. But before doing so, he had to make sure his back was protected. At long last the rival dynasties would be joined together once more by marriage when Antiochus III sent one of his three daughters to become the wife of the young king of Egypt, Ptolemy V. That daughter was Cleopatra and in 194/3 BC she would come to Alexandria as queen Cleopatra I.

7

THE SELEUCID
CONNECTION (1)
Cleopatra I

Antiochus III had three daughters – Cleopatra, Antiochis, and a third whose name is not preserved. According to Appian it was because he was aware that his planned invasion of Thrace would put him on a collision course with the Romans that he decided to make use of his girls to establish dynastic alliances with three neighbouring kings before he set off to the West with his troops. Cleopatra was betrothed to the young Ptolemy V, his second daughter Antiochis was packed off to marry Ariarathes, king of Cappadocia, and the third was to be sent to Pergamum to become the bride of king Eumenes II. But to the great surprise of his brothers Eumenes refused her on the grounds that, if it came to a war between Antiochus III and Rome, he expected the Romans to emerge victorious in the long run. 'If the Romans win', he said, 'I shall be secure as king of my own kingdom. But if Antiochus wins, I can expect either that as my neighbour he will take everything away from me or, if I am suffered to continue ruling, that he will rule over me' (Appian 11.5).

Ptolemy V's advisers had no such qualms. In the autumn of 196 BC Antiochus III was able to announce the engagement of Cleopatra and the king of Egypt at a meeting held with the Romans at Lysimacheia in Thrace. The Roman delegates were thrown into consternation. They had come to Thrace to seek a reconciliation between Antiochus III and Ptolemy V and the peaceful evacuation of the Ptolemaic possessions in Asia Minor recently seized by the Syrians. The king's announcement that he was about to become Ptolemy V's father-in-law, coupled with his patronising assurance that he would ensure his new son-in-law thanked the Romans properly for the solicitude they had shown on his behalf (Appian 11.3), was a major diplomatic triumph for the Syrians. It completely cut the ground away from beneath the envoys' feet for it deprived the Romans at one blow of one of their main pretexts for what Antiochus III saw as their unwarranted interference in his affairs. He did not meddle in Italian affairs, he told them. Nor should they in the affairs of Asia.

At this time Ptolemy V was no more than 14 years old. Born on 9 October 210 BC, he had celebrated his coming of age only the previous year but, as the decree on the famous Rosetta Stone,[1] which is dated to March 196 BC, shows us, he was already regarded by the native Egyptians as full king in every respect. In the inscription he is identified as the living image of Amun and the beloved of Ptah, the patron god of the ancient capital of Memphis, and is accorded the full royal titulature appropriate to a divine king of Egypt and incarnation of the falcon-headed sky god Horus. Nevertheless, although a god was expected to have a consort, his marriage to Cleopatra did not take place immediately.

It was not until 194/3 BC that the wedding was celebrated at Raphia on the northern edge of the Gaza Strip. This may seem a strange choice for Raphia had been the site of Ptolemy IV's great victory over the young Antiochus III back in 217 BC. Yet it would be a mistake to regard the choice of venue as a symbolic way of rubbing Seleucid salt into Ptolemaic wounds. Antiochus III should not be compared to Adolf Hitler forcing the defeated French to sign the 1940 armistice in the same railway carriage in which the German high command had been compelled to accept the Treaty of Versailles just over 20 years before. Instead Raphia looks more like a compromise chosen to preserve face for both sides.

Whatever the occasion, in the ancient world the usual procedure for a royal visit was for the lower-ranking party to come to the court of the higher. The legendary Queen of Sheba had visited the court of King Solomon, Alexander of Epirus had come to Aegae to marry Philip II's daughter Cleopatra, the last Ptolemaic ruler Cleopatra VII would journey to Tarsus for her meeting with Mark Antony, the Magi would come to Jesus. In the case of Ptolemy V's marriage to Cleopatra I, it would have meant an unacceptable loss of prestige for either Antiochus III or Ptolemy V to have gone to the capital of the other king. The obvious answer therefore was for each of them to travel to what was currently the boundary of his own territory and to forge their alliance there at a town which was probably the nearest equivalent they could find to neutral ground. Both kings could then represent to their subjects back home that the other monarch had come to him. All that was needed was a slight stretching of the truth.

A more difficult problem to sort out is the question of the arrangements which were made for Cleopatra I's dowry. A generation later at the time of the Sixth Syrian War (170–168 BC) the Alexandrians would allege that Coele Syria, the original cause of all the conflict between the two royal houses, had been given back to them by Antiochus III as part of his daughter's dowry when she married Ptolemy V (Polybius 28.20.9, Appian 11.5). Another tradition, recorded by Josephus (*Jewish Ant.* 12.154), speaks of the cession of Samaria, Judaea, and Phoenicia on the understanding that their taxes be shared between the two monarchs, that is, between Cleopatra I and her new husband. This has usually been explained by arguing that although Antiochus III agreed to sign over the revenues from these areas to his daughter, he nevertheless retained political control over them himself.[2]

The modern view is that both these claims are arguably false.[3] They are seen as arising from the political propaganda of a later time when the Ptolemies were again attempting to win back Coele Syria. Certainly it is difficult to believe that at this stage in his career Antiochus III would have seen any need to make such a concession or that he would have voluntarily returned to the Egyptians a region which the Seleucid kings had always felt was theirs to rule. Indeed, to have acted in this way at a moment when he was attempting to reclaim the cities of Thrace and the Chersonese, the other part of what he felt was his legitimate heritage, would have been totally inconsistent, almost to the point of schizophrenia.

We therefore cannot be sure what material benefits Cleopatra brought to the marriage, although as the daughter of such a powerful king she would obviously not have come empty-handed. That would have entailed an unbearable loss of face for Antiochus III. What we can see though is what a welcome infusion of new blood she brought to a dynasty which already seems to have been running out of steam after a century of wealth and easy living. After all, her father Antiochus III was without any doubt the greatest monarch of his time and the one man who, had the Romans not been there to stop him, would have come closest to putting Alexander the Great's empire back together again. She also enjoyed a tough and distinguished lineage on her mother's side. Antiochus III's wife Laodice, whom he had married just before he set off on his first attempt on the Egyptians in 221 BC, was the daughter of king Mithradates II of Pontus and therefore the direct descendant of a Persian satrap who had carved out a kingdom for himself in Cappadocia during the time of the wars of the Successors after Alexander the Great's death. So Cleopatra I's heritage was as much Persian as it was Greek. More so if we also add in the contribution from the paternal side, for Antiochus III's great-great-grandmother on his father's side had been the Persian princess Apama.

We can also get some idea, however imperfectly, of what this particular Cleopatra looked like. From their coin portraits Peter Green has described her mother's forebears, the early kings of Pontus, as 'resembling a family of escaped convicts'.[4] The description is unkind but accurate. Fortunately their ill-favoured looks and boxers' noses seem to have passed Cleopatra I by. So too do the sharp features of her father Antiochus III, to re-emerge in the next generation in her son Ptolemy VI Philometor. Although there had been earlier efforts to identify several portraits as representations of her,[5] a unique gold octodrachm from Alexandria, which only came on to the antiquities market in the late 1970s and which was purchased by the British Museum, gives us for the first time a certain portrait of Egypt's new queen.[6]

The coin shows her in her maturity, when she was regent for her son Ptolemy VI. We see a serene and attractive woman with a long straight nose, full lips, and prettily rounded chin. Unfortunately it can tell us little about her eyes for they are treated in the round-eyed fashion characteristic of many Ptolemaic coin portraits and also of the mummy masks of this period. She is shown wearing a diadem and the type of head covering known as a *stephane* and she carries a sceptre, probably to symbolise her authority as regent for her young son, who appears on the coin's other face.

The portrait may be small but, unless it is more highly idealised than we would normally expect, it gives us enough detail to distinguish it from all the other portraits which have been tentatively associated with Cleopatra I. Their common feature is that they show a lot more heaviness around and under the line of the jaw than the representation on the octodrachm. Despite the great uncertainty which still surrounds the identity of these other portraits,[7] it may therefore be possible to discard Cleopatra I as a likely subject and narrow down the choice to her daughter Cleopatra II or her granddaughters Cleopatra III or Cleopatra Thea on the grounds that this heavy chin, which is present already in portraits of the first two Ptolemies, is a feature which they are likely to have inherited from the Ptolemaic side of the family.

Although all the evidence suggests that Antiochus III's primary motive in giving Cleopatra I to Ptolemy V was to strengthen his hand against the Romans and ensure that in the event of war with Rome the Egyptians did not try to attack him from behind, the view from Judaea seems to have been somewhat different. As the writer of the Book of Daniel saw it, his purpose in arranging the match was to bring about the destruction of Egypt itself:

> He shall give him the daughter of women to destroy Egypt but she shall not stand neither be for him.
>
> (Daniel 11.17)

This looks like wishful thinking, coloured perhaps by later events, for there is no reason to think that it was ever Antiochus III's intention to attempt to destroy Egypt. If it was he would have been disappointed. The Alexandrians, who had a penchant for nicknames, affectionately named their young queen 'the Syrian', presumably from her origins rather than the colour of her skin, and from the start there seems to have been a strong mutual liking between Cleopatra I and her new subjects. Even the steadily worsening relations between her father and the Romans do not seem to have affected their devotion to her, although many of Ptolemy V's courtiers no doubt had grave misgivings that they had ever agreed to the match when in the autumn of 192 BC they heard that Antiochus III had crossed over to Greece with his army and declared himself the champion of Greek freedom against Roman domination.

Antiochus III's action meant that war with Rome would be inevitable sooner or later and the Ptolemaic court hustled to distance itself from him. The Romans now looked decidedly the better bet and in 191 BC an embassy was sent from Alexandria to Rome bearing a large sum in cash and an offer to send troops to Greece to assist the Roman cause. The Senate declined both gestures (Livy 36.4.1–4), and happily the queen's loyalties were spared the test of a choice between the family of her birth and the family of her marriage.

Although we know nothing of Cleopatra I's involvement, if any, in these worrisome affairs of state, we can get a glimpse of her high standing in Egypt through the permutations of the royal titulature, in both Greek and demotic, which took place during her reign. From 199/8 BC Ptolemy V had already been designated as a living god and granted the title Theos Epiphanes (God made manifest). After her marriage to him Cleopatra too was granted this title. She also sometimes shares his other divine epithet Eucharistos (the beneficent [god]), so that after 194/3 BC the full form of the royal titulature was properly 'King Ptolemy and Queen Cleopatra, the manifest and beneficent gods'.

The English translation of these royal epithets can catch only a small part of what they must have meant originally to the native Egyptians who formed the bulk of Ptolemy V's and Cleopatra I's subjects. In fact 'manifest' and 'beneficent' are only translations of translations for both terms were ancient Egyptian in origin rather than Greek. Epiphanes has been equated with an Egyptian royal title which in its hieroglyphic form means 'he who comes forth' and signifies a complex of interconnected ideas – the notion of divine power manifested through the royal being, the incarnation of a new divinity in the king's body, or the epiphany of an existing deity in the person of the monarch.[8] The hieroglyphic equivalents of Eucharistos can be rendered equally variously to mean 'one of goodness', 'lord of beauties', or 'one whose favour is beautiful'. Both epithets emphasise the growing alignment which was taking place at this period between the Ptolemaic ruler cult and the native religious tradition. In this *rapprochement* the notion of the queen as well as the king as a living manifestation of a deity, usually the great goddess Isis, would come to play an increasingly important role.

A more unusual part of Cleopatra I's titulature, but one which is not unexpected given that the tradition of brother-sister marriage was already well established in the Ptolemaic house, is her description as the 'sister' of Ptolemy V as well as his wife. It seems likely that she inherited this title from her mother-in-law Arsinoe III, who was indeed Ptolemy IV's full sister as well as his wife and the first Ptolemaic queen to bear a child by her brother.[9] The fullest form of this titulature is found in a demotic text of 191/0 BC in which Ptolemy V and Cleopatra I appear as 'Pharaoh Ptolemy, son of Ptolemy and Arsinoe, the father loving gods, with his sister, his wife Queen Cleopatra, the manifest gods'.[10]

At about the same time, after the Roman defeat of Antiochus III, Livy (37.3.9) records that an embassy was sent to Rome 'by Ptolemy and Cleopatra, monarchs of Egypt' to congratulate the Romans on their success in expelling the Seleucid king from

Greece. Whatever feelings Cleopatra I may have had about what had happened to her father and his dreams of empire, the inclusion of her name with her husband's on this occasion is sufficient to demonstrate that her association with Ptolemy V in the royal titulature was something more than a diplomatic nicety intended only for home consumption. There may have been no official joint rule as such but the queen's role clearly extended beyond matters of royal cult and her authority would become greater still after her husband's death in 180 BC when she became regent for her young son Ptolemy VI.

Cleopatra I bore three children to Ptolemy V. Her daughter, who was named after her and who would become Cleopatra II, was perhaps the eldest. Then came two sons, both named Ptolemy. The elder, born c. 186 BC, would later take the title Philometor (Mother loving) in his mother's honour. He appears first in a dedication which the royal family made at the temple of Philae in Upper Egypt, probably in 185/4 BC soon after the final defeat of the Egyptian rebels under the native pharaoh Anchmachis and the reassertion of Ptolemaic control over Upper Egypt (186 BC). In the inscription (OGIS 98) he is simply called 'Ptolemy the son' and it is only after his father's death that we first find Philometor as part of his titulature, underlining his dependence upon his mother's regency.

At the time of Ptolemy V's premature death in September/ October 180 BC this elder son was no more than 5 or 6 years old and Cleopatra I took over the reins of government and governed as regent for him, with the aid of ministers. The royal titulature now changed to become 'the Pharaohs Cleopatra the mother, the manifest goddess, and Ptolemy son of Ptolemy, the manifest god'.[11] The demotic form clearly shows that this was now a recognised joint rule and Cleopatra I's name appears first to indicate that she was the senior partner in the co-regency.

Unlike the demotic, the Greek forms of the titulature, which usually put Ptolemy VI first, do not make this obvious but there are also two Greek texts to confirm that the Greeks too acknowledged Cleopatra I's pre-eminence as regent. First, in a papyrus of 177 BC (P.Coll.Youtie 12) a prisoner complains that he has been wrongfully confined for over three years and claims that he had already been acquitted 'by queen Cleopatra and king Ptolemy' (lines 14–15). The royal pardon on which he was basing his case must therefore have come to him with the names of the monarchs in that order. Second, part of an inscription (SEG XVI 788) from a broken statue base found on Cyprus records a dedication made to thank a dignitary whose name is lost for the services he has rendered 'to queen Cleopatra, manifest goddess, and king Ptolemy, and her other children, and to themselves'. The last named are most likely to have been the senior officers of the Ptolemaic garrison on the island who had set the statue up in honour of the island's governor.[12] In an official act of this kind they are hardly likely to have made a mistake in the order of their sovereigns' names.

It is implied by Diodorus (29.29) that shortly before his death Ptolemy V's thoughts had started to turn towards the possibility of recovering Coele Syria. Indeed he may well have been tempted to take advantage of what were difficult times for the Seleucids and resume hostilities against them. Antiochus III had met his death in 187 BC plundering the temple of Baal in Susa and it was Cleopatra I's brother Seleucus IV who now sat upon his throne. It is therefore only to be expected that for as long as she was regent, we should hear nothing more of these plans to attack Syria. Indeed her four years of co-rule with Ptolemy VI are marked by a general lack of Ptolemaic involvement in foreign affairs. This is not particularly surprising for conditions within Egypt itself were still very unsettled at the time of Ptolemy V's death and much needed to be done at home. The last native uprising in the Delta of Lower Egypt had not been put down until 184/3 BC and there is evidence of continuing problems of economic dislocation in these years.[13] So the lack of an aggressive foreign policy should not be held to Cleopatra I's discredit. Rather it is more the pity that she did not live longer, to allow her son to reach maturity and to give her adopted country a longer interval of peace before it was plunged into yet another senseless and destructive war with the Seleucids over the possession of Coele Syria.

Cleopatra I herself died probably some time between April and July 176 BC.[14] After her death she would be honoured by the establishment in Upper Egypt of an eponymous priesthood 'of Ptolemy and Cleopatra his mother' and from 165/4 BC we find this replaced by a special priestess 'of Cleopatra the mother, the manifest goddess'.[15] Like her predecessors Arsinoe II (sister–wife of Ptolemy II), Berenice II (the wife of Ptolemy III), and her own mother-in-law Arsinoe III, who all had their own cults and priestesses in Alexandria, Cleopatra I was therefore rewarded with the posthumous honour of an individual cult, albeit in the Thebaid and not in the capital itself. This was a fitting tribute for a royal woman who seems to have inherited her father Antiochus III's vigour and strength of character, traits which, as we shall see, she passed on in full measure to her daughter Cleopatra II. Not only was she addressed on equal terms with her husband both inside and outside Egypt, but she was also the first Ptolemaic queen to serve as regent and co-ruler with her son. With such qualities and achievements it is hardly surprising that henceforth Cleopatra should become the dynastic name *par excellence* of the Ptolemaic royal house.

8

CLEOPATRA II AND
PTOLEMY VI

Ptolemy VI was about 10 or 11 years old when his mother Cleopatra I died in 176 BC. His sister Cleopatra II was perhaps slightly older.[1] His younger brother, also called Ptolemy, was only 5 or 6. Despite the new king's youth there does not seem to have been any immediate problem about his succession and the demotic form of his royal titulature, 'Pharaoh Ptolemy, the god who loves his mother, son of Ptolemy and Cleopatra the manifest gods',[2] shows that he was recognised straightaway as sole king. Yet obviously he was too young to rule unaided. A further period of regency would be necessary, at least until his coming of age.

From this regency and from the strife between the three royal children which ensued as a result of the dynastic arrangements made by the regents there arose a disastrous period of warfare and civil unrest. The country was invaded and one brother set against the other. It was this strife more than anything else which led to the decline of the Ptolemaic house during the second half of the second century BC. During this time it was the females of the line, Cleopatra II and her daughter Cleopatra III, who succeeded in increasing their power at the expense of the males who were ostensibly their senior partners, so winning for themselves a significant place in the history of their dynasty.

The men who now found themselves elevated to the position of regents for the young king seem to have been totally unsuited to the task in every way imaginable. One was a eunuch called Eulaeus, whose name suggests a Macedonian origin, the other an ex-slave from Coele Syria called Lenaeus. Faced with this pair, our aristocratic sources typically throw up their hands in horror. According to Diodorus (30.15), Eulaeus had only recently put aside his comb and his pots of make-up, and what the historian coyly calls 'the works of Aphrodite', in order to enrol in the service of the war god Ares. Lenaeus, who may have been finance minister under the old king, had done the same with his abacus. Both of them lacked any knowledge or experience of military matters and, what is worse, they were without competent advisers to whom they could turn for help.

How Eulaeus and Lenaeus came to be regents is anyone's guess. The more kindly view is that of Bevan,[3] who suggests that Cleopatra I may have died suddenly before she could provide for the guardianship of her children. As a result Eulaeus and Lenaeus were able to use their position at court to seize power for themselves. A less charitable hypothesis is that it was the queen herself who had originally made them her ministers because she found eunuchs and slaves easier to manage and more willing to take a woman's orders than men of her own rank and class. This view seems offensively sexist from a modern point of view. Yet it is difficult to brush it aside as a typically anti-feminist comment when its author is Grace Macurdy writing on the development of female power in the hellenistic period.[4]

Whatever the origins of their power, Eulaeus and Lenaeus soon proved a recipe for disaster. The next few years show that the anti-Seleucid element at court had not disappeared with Ptolemy V's death in 180 BC. Those who had encouraged him in his hopes of regaining Coele Syria had merely been keeping a low profile while Cleopatra I was in effective charge. Once she was no longer present to ensure the continuation of peaceful relations between Egypt and Syria it did not take them long to show themselves once more. No sooner, it seemed, had the embers of the age-old animosity between the two superpowers begun to die down, than they were fanned into life yet again. The culmination was the Sixth Syrian War (170–168 BC).[5]

Despite their lack of military experience the new regents lost no time in setting their country on a collision course with king Antiochus IV, who now occupied the Seleucid throne after marrying his brother Seleucus IV's widow Laodice and adopting her young son, also called Antiochus. In order to put Egypt on a strong defensive footing one of their first acts was to consolidate their control over the royal family by marrying Ptolemy VI to his sister. Marriage between full siblings had been a frequent, although not an essential feature of the Egyptian monarchy in pharaonic times and for reasons which still elude us the practice had been revived in Ptolemaic Egypt by Ptolemy II's second marriage late in his life to his elder sister Arsinoe II. Then in 217 BC, at a time of national crisis when Antiochus III had seemed poised to invade Egypt itself, Ptolemy IV had married his sister Arsinoe III, probably in an attempt to cash in on the popularity of his grandfather, and thereafter the practice had achieved the status of a tradition.

It is easy to see the advantages to Eulaeus and Lenaeus of once more reviving the practice of sibling marriage. The union of Ptolemy VI and Cleopatra II in April 176 BC not only served to increase their authority over the royal family, but also ensured that Cleopatra II, who was now at or about the age of puberty, would no longer be available for any dynastic alliance outside Egypt. To marry her to her brother, even though he had not yet come of age, put her beyond the reach of any outsider who might hope to use a union with her to press a claim to the throne of Egypt. Brother–sister marriage within a royal house tends always to consolidate a dynasty and to emphasise the unique and godlike nature of the royal family, not only compared to ordinary people but also in relation to other royal families.[6] The arrangement was therefore as much an act of national unity as the regents' later much more explicit action in 170 BC when they named all three royal children as joint rulers of Egypt.

It did not take long for word to reach Antiochus IV of what was happening in Alexandria. The younger son of Antiochus III, he had recently come to power when his older brother Seleucus IV had been assassinated in an unsuccessful *coup d'état*. He was not the sort of man to quake in his boots at the prospect of being savaged by a pair of children and there has to be some suspicion that he would have been equally happy to take advantage of Ptolemaic weakness to launch an attack upon Egypt. In fact whereas our Greek sources generally agree in blaming Eulaeus and Lenaeus for starting the war, Jewish writers (along with Appian and Livy) charge that Antiochus IV wanted to be king of both kingdoms (I Maccabees 1.16) and that he was planning to seize Egypt, 'despising the youthfulness of its king and the inexperience of his tutors' (Livy 42.29.5). There may well be some truth in this view.[7] But Antiochus IV's hands were tied for the time being by the fact that he was co-ruler with his brother's son so that his own position was not yet as secure as he might have liked.

There were also the Romans to be considered. Since their defeat of Antiochus III and the subsequent Peace of Apamea (188 BC), they had left the Syrians alone, apparently content as long as the Seleucid king renounced all plans of westward expansion. In an optimistic mood Antiochus IV might have hoped that they would turn a blind eye towards any overt interference in Egypt but he probably had few illusions about them. After all he had been a 'guest' of Rome for 10 years, serving as hostage under the terms of the Peace of Apamea for his country's good behaviour. He would also have been well aware of the nature of Roman diplomatic ties with Alexandria.

Accordingly the last years of the 170s BC were taken up with a flurry of diplomatic activity. If and when it came to war, both Egypt and Syria wanted to be sure that they could rely on the Romans to side with them. And of course each wanted to find out what the other side was up to. In 174 BC Antiochus IV undertook a goodwill tour of Coele Syria to show the flag and assure himself of the continuing loyalty of his subjects there. At about the same time he sent a representative to Egypt to attend the celebrations marking the first anniversary of Ptolemy VI's accession. The reports which came back about the strength of anti-Seleucid feeling in Alexandria were hardly encouraging. Antiochus IV took the precautions of stationing an army in Phoenicia and sending off another embassy to Rome. Its brief was to renew the pact of friendship between the Seleucids and the Romans.

A copious dollop of flattery – how much their king had enjoyed his ten years as a hostage in Rome! – combined with the payment in full of the Seleucids' long-overdue tribute plus an additional 500 pounds' weight of gold vases helped to win a gracious reply from the Roman senate and a renewal of the treaty (Livy 42.6). But the Romans also sent off an embassy of their own, with instructions to proceed eventually to Alexandria and there renew Rome's friendship with the Ptolemies. Clearly the Romans intended a policy of even-handed neutrality and when the ambassadors returned the following year they had visited not only Ptolemy VI at Alexandria but also Antiochus IV in Syria. At this stage they were not to be seduced, however much they might be flattered or bribed.

The last year of this period of phoney war would see more embassies from both sides make their way to Rome with extravagant promises of assistance in the Romans' impending war against Macedon. According to Livy (42.29.6–7) this was all just so much window dressing. Both sides, he implies, intended to take advantage of Rome's preoccupation with king Perseus to attack each other openly at last. The synchronism has been doubted,[8] but it is difficult to say that an expectation of Roman involvement elsewhere can have had no influence on the conduct of one side or the other. Certainly the phoney war had given way to all-out hostilities by the end of 170 BC or early 169 BC at the latest.

It is in this context that we should probably locate the origins of the Ptolemaic claim that Antiochus III had ceded Coele Syria to Egypt in 194/3 BC as part of his daughter Cleopatra I's dowry. Since their own marriage both Ptolemy VI and his sister had been known as 'the mother loving gods' (Philometores), thereby emphasising their close link to Cleopatra I and their determination to win back for Egypt all that had been hers. The royal title and the propaganda about their mother's dowry fit together too neatly to be totally unconnected.

Also connected with the preparations which Eulaeus and Lenaeus were making for open war was the association of all three children – Ptolemy VI, Cleopatra II, and their younger brother Ptolemy VIII – in the joint rule of Egypt and the celebration shortly afterwards of Ptolemy VI's coming of age. The naming of Ptolemy VIII along with Cleopatra II as equal associates in the kingship is best explained as a further move by the regents to strengthen and legitimise the regime and their own place within it. Rather like the formation of a coalition of national unity in a modern state, it was designed to bring all parties together to face a common danger. It also lessened the possibility that any rival faction opposed to the regents' anti-Seleucid stance might be able to promote Ptolemy VIII as an alternative king. Less likely is Fraser's suggestion that the tripartite division of power was an initiative of Ptolemy VI himself.[9] Since he was now reaching the age of majority when he might reasonably expect to rule as king in his own right, Ptolemy VI could have had little incentive to dissipate his authority by splitting it three ways.

The joint rule is first alluded to in a demotic text of September 170 BC,[10] and Ptolemy VI's coming of age was probably celebrated that same winter. Exactly how the two events were related is unclear. The easiest explanation is to read the latter as yet another gesture of national solidarity, but there are also other possibilities. One suggestion is that it was a belated attempt by Ptolemy VI himself to assert his predominance over his brother and sister. Another view is that it constitutes evidence of a rival group opposed to the regents who were trying to force their hand by having the king's majority declared. Meanwhile, on the other side of the lines Antiochus IV had been busy with a little dynastic rearrangement of his own. In August 170 BC he had executed his young nephew who had been his co-ruler since Seleucus IV's assassination in 175 BC. Both sides were now ready for action.

When it finally began the Sixth Syrian War was a swift and sorry affair from the Egyptian point of view. In late 170 or early 169 BC Eulaeus and Lenaeus, full of misplaced confidence, led their forces out northwards towards Gaza. Antiochus IV was waiting for them. He had already covered himself with the Romans by informing them of Ptolemaic preparations for war (autumn 170 BC). Having thus secured the moral high ground, he had only to wait for the Egyptians to strike first. He could then launch his counterattack with greater justification. The Ptolemaic army had not even reached the southern boundaries of Coele Syria when he met them at Mount Casius and inflicted a crushing defeat.

Advancing towards the Nile Delta, Antiochus IV succeeded in taking the border town of Pelusium, apparently by treachery. Its fall opened up the way to an invasion of Egypt itself, something which had never happened since Alexander the Great had taken the country from the Persians over 150 years before. On the advice of Eulaeus, Ptolemy VI attempted to flee to the sacred island of Samothrace but he was intercepted and brought to the Seleucid camp. From there Antiochus IV had him conveyed to the ancient royal capital of Memphis where he set him up as puppet king under his protection. Although there is a tradition that the Seleucid king had himself crowned as pharaoh at Memphis,[11] it seems more likely that his aim in establishing Ptolemy VI there was to win the support of the powerful Egyptian priesthoods and through them the backing of the native population. Antiochus IV had already magnanimously spared the lives of the Ptolemaic troops whom he had defeated and had tried to win over the Greek population of Naucratis in the western Delta by distributing a gold stater to each citizen. So an attempt to win over the native Egyptians by setting up Ptolemy VI as pharaoh at Memphis is explicable as part of a two-pronged policy aimed at conciliating both Egyptians and Greeks.

The Alexandrians would not be won over so easily. Within the city the disgraced regents had been replaced soon after the disaster and they are never heard of again. The new regents were two upper-class Greek military men with considerable experience, Comanus and Cineas.[12] It was they who had initiated the negotiations with Antiochus IV which had led to Ptolemy VI's removal, voluntary or otherwise, to Memphis but the populace now reacted against the arrangements which they had made. They overthrew the new regents and set up Ptolemy VIII and Cleopatra II as joint rulers in Alexandria. Antiochus reacted by playing the role of kindly uncle, concerned to assert his elder nephew's right to be sole king (Livy 44.19.6–8). He marched on Alexandria but his attack on the city failed and by late summer he had abandoned his attempt to take it by siege. He accordingly had to leave Egypt with one king in Alexandria and another controlling the countryside from Memphis and, just for good measure, he kept his own foot in the door by stationing a garrison in Pelusium on the Egyptian side of the Sinai.

'Egypt had divorced itself from Alexandria', as a contemporary native oracle monger put it.[13] Such an unstable situation could hardly last. During the winter, negotiations were opened up between the two brothers and a reconciliation worked out, thanks in large part we are told (Livy 45.11.6) to the sane counsel and earnest entreaties of their sister Cleopatra II. Already therefore she had the opportunity to exert considerable influence in mediating between the two Ptolemies and that influence would increase as time went on. The result of her prayers was that Ptolemy VI agreed to return to Alexandria and the joint reign of Ptolemy VI, Cleopatra II, and Ptolemy VIII was revived. Antiochus IV was far from pleased. The new settlement not only reinstated the government of national unity set up by the original regents, but also undid all his own considerable efforts of the previous year. Any influence Antiochus IV might have expected to have on the government of Egypt through his 'alliance' with his client Ptolemy VI had been taken away from him.

Antiochus IV now dropped his kindly avuncular manner. In spring 168 BC he again invaded Egypt while his fleet took possession of Cyprus. In desperation the Alexandrians despatched envoys to meet him at Egypt's border. Antiochus IV relented enough to grant an armistice but the conditions he demanded to make peace – the cession of both Cyprus and Pelusium – were unacceptable. Without Pelusium to protect them the Egyptians would always have the Seleucids on their doorstep. The armistice expired, the envoys returned to the city, and the Syrians marched on to Memphis.

After accepting the surrender of Upper Egypt, Antiochus IV began to move down towards Alexandria by easy stages. His hope was that, given enough time, the joint rule would crack under the pressure which he was slowly but surely applying. But time had run out. On 22 June 168 BC the Roman general Lucius Aemilius Paullus finally defeated Perseus of Macedon at the battle of Pydna. At last the Romans had time to look up and take notice of what had been happening in the East. At last they had time to heed the Alexandrians' cries for help.

What follows is one of the most famous episodes in Roman history. As soon as news reached them of the victory, the Roman ambassador Gaius Popillius Laenas and his colleagues set out from Delos. Pausing only to snarl briefly at the people of Rhodes for their unhelpful behaviour during the Macedonian War, they arrived in time to confront Antiochus IV in his camp at Eleusis just outside Alexandria. Popillius handed him an ultimatum from the Roman senate, ordering him to desist at once from all acts of war against the Ptolemies and their territories. When Antiochus IV asked for time to consult his advisers, the senator took his stick and, drawing a circle in the sand around the king, demanded an answer before he stepped out of it. Taken aback by Popillius' unbelievable effrontery, Antiochus IV hesitated only briefly before caving in. Now that the Romans were free to deal with him, he knew he had no choice but to bow to their wishes. The Romans let him keep the booty his troops had seized but that was all. On 30 July 168 BC he embarked his army and set sail for home.

For the Greek intellectual Polybius, writing his history of Rome's drive to power, it was the Romans who had saved Egypt. In his eyes 'the day of Eleusis' marked the final establishment of Roman supremacy over the Mediterranean world just as surely as the battle of Pydna did. For the native Egyptians on the other hand it was the gods who had saved their country. Indeed the gods had actually foretold the date of Antiochus IV's discomfiture some three weeks before the event in a dream which they sent to Hor, an Egyptian prophet attached to the ibis temple at Saqqara:

> I was told a dream: Isis, the great goddess of Egypt and the land of Syria, walks upon the face of the waters of the Syrian

sea. Thoth stands before her and takes her hand. She has reached the harbour at Alexandria. She says, 'Alexandria is safe against the enemy. Pharaoh records within it with his brethren [i.e. Ptolemy VIII and Cleopatra II]. His eldest son wears the diadem. After him his son wears the diadem. This son's son wears the diadem after him. The son of the son of the son of this son wears the diadem after him, for a great length of days. The proof of this is that the queen bears a male child.'

(Ray, 1976: 11–12 (Text 1.11–18))[14]

What is most interesting for us is that the goddess Isis also chose to reveal Cleopatra II's pregnancy in the dream which she sent to Hor. Isis of course would have had a twofold interest in the pregnancy of the queen. Not only was she a goddess of childbirth and motherhood, but in one of her cult titles she was also 'the mother of the god' for in Egyptian mythology it was she who had borne the divine child Horus to her brother and lover Osiris. After avenging his father's murder by his uncle Seth, Horus had become the first ruler of Egypt by divine decree of the gods in council. Since each subsequent god-king of Egypt was regarded as a new Horus, Isis therefore had a particular concern with the royal heir. At the same time it was also customary for the Ptolemaic queens of this period to have themselves represented as Isis, a tendency which would culminate with Cleopatra II's daughter Cleopatra III taking a number of titles specifically identifying herself as Isis and Aphrodite.

The appearance of the queen's pregnancy as an item in Hor's dream can also throw some light on the perception which their native Egyptian subjects had of these Ptolemaic queens. Like a modern royal, Cleopatra II was an incredibly remote figure. The more so since for the Egyptians she was herself a divinity. At the same time she was intensely close to them for the whole of the country's prosperity and the well-being of all its people was inextricably linked to her ability to produce the new Horus, who in his turn would take over the task of ensuring the annual return of the Nile flood, the fertility of the land, and the order and good governance of Egypt.

In this area at least Cleopatra II and her brother certainly did the best they could. They had four children in all, Ptolemy Eupator, Cleopatra Thea, Ptolemy VII Neos Philopator, and Cleopatra III.

Although their birth dates are not known exactly, at least two of them must have been born before September 164 BC since a Greek papyrus of that date (UPZ I 110) speaks of 'children' in the plural. The child of Hor's prophetic dream is therefore likely to have been Ptolemy Eupator, and his birth may be referred to in another document from the archive of Hor, probably datable to December 166 BC, which mentions 'the confirmation of the fortune' and 'the salvation of the supreme inheritance'.[15] Nevertheless the assurance of the goddess that the direct line of Ptolemy VI and Cleopatra II would endure, with son succeeding son unto the nth generation, failed to come to pass. Although both their sons would share briefly in the kingship with Ptolemy VI, neither would live long enough to rule in his own right. The line would continue but only indirectly. It would be Ptolemy VI's and Cleopatra II's last child Cleopatra III who would ensure its continuation through the sons she would bear to her uncle, their younger brother Ptolemy VIII.

After Antiochus IV's departure it might be expected that affairs in Egypt would have begun to return to normal. But that did not happen. The tripartite rule continued but once the pressure of an external threat had been removed cracks soon began to appear in the facade of brotherly unity. The main problem was that Ptolemy VI and Ptolemy VIII were as different from one another as chalk and cheese. The elder was kind and gentle, more so we are told than any other Ptolemaic king (Polybius 39.7). Despite that he responded well to times of crisis and adversity brought out the best in him. On the other hand good fortune and success saw him relax his concentration and fall into a typically Egyptian state of indolence and enervation. Consequently things often went awry for him at these times. Even so he was a paragon of virtue compared to his younger brother.

Intelligent, cultivated, and determined, Ptolemy VIII was also cruel, petty, and vindictive. A ruler of great energy, he nevertheless managed to squander most of it and his main talent lay in an enormous capacity for self-indulgence. His decadent manner of life, combined with his gross obesity, would earn him two telling nicknames from the Alexandrians. He was Tryphon (The Magnificent), which can also mean 'The Decadent', and Physcon (Pot Belly). Given the differences between them, it is no wonder that the latent hostility, which seems always to have existed between the brothers, soon began to surface.

The first sign of unrest was an uprising fomented by an

ambitious courtier of Egyptian background called Dionysius alias
Petosarapis, who attempted to take advantage of the Alexandrians'
continued partiality for their younger king by putting about a
rumour that Ptolemy VI was planning to dispose of his brother
(Diodorus 31.15a). Their passions aroused, the Alexandrians
rushed to the stadium, ready to defend their favourite and murder
the other king, and the two Ptolemies had to make a joint public
appearance before the mob would calm down. Dionysius then
tried to raise an armed revolt · at Eleusis just outside the city.
Defeated by Ptolemy VI, he got away to Upper Egypt to continue
his resistance from there. Nothing is known of its outcome, but
we hear indirectly of rebels in the Fayum in Middle Egypt forcing
landowners to burn their title deeds in public (P.Amh. II 30)
and sacking a temple which had only just been restored after its
destruction by the invading Syrians (P.Tebt. III 781). There was
also more trouble further south as, encouraged by Dionysius'
example, other local resistance groups emerged among the native
population.

Ptolemy VI eventually succeeded in pacifying the South but
these uprisings only deepened the rift between the two kings.
While his brother was away campaigning in Upper Egypt, Ptolemy
VIII seized his chance to organise his own supporters and in late
164 BC he succeeded in ousting Ptolemy VI from Alexandria. The
joint reign was at an end, to be replaced by the rule of Ptolemy
VIII and Cleopatra II. Ptolemy VI made his way to Rome, there
to work towards his restoration, and for a short time younger
brother and elder sister ruled together, without as yet any
additional ties of marriage between them.

It was not long before Ptolemy VIII began to show his true
colours. The Alexandrians soon discovered their former favourite's
aptitude for indiscriminate persecution and arbitrary acts of cruelty
and they began to regret the choice they had made. Meanwhile in
Rome Ptolemy VI had enlisted the aid of his cousin Demetrius of
Syria, then a royal hostage there for Seleucid good behaviour, to
mount an elaborate charade designed to embarrass the senate into
supporting his restoration. Arriving at Ostia with a wretched entourage of a single eunuch and only three slaves, he ostentatiously
waved away the horse and royal regalia with which his cousin had
met him and proceeded to walk to the capital where he took
lodgings with an artist friend in one of Rome's seedier dwelling
houses. In an attempt to make amends the senators hastened to

apologise and bring him every regal honour, but in the end this complex scheme proved hardly necessary. At the Alexandrians' own request Ptolemy VI was back in Egypt by May 163 BC. They had risen up against Ptolemy VIII, overpowered his bodyguards, and set him aside. The day of the Alexandrian mob as kingmaker had arrived.

Throughout that summer a compromise was hammered out between the two kings, under the watchful eyes of a Roman embassy sent to urge a reconciliation. The outcome was that the remnants of the Ptolemaic domains were now partitioned. Ptolemy VI got the lion's share in the form of Cyprus as well as Egypt itself. His brother, who ought to have thought himself lucky to get anything at all, was given Cyrenaica. A decree of amnesty issued in September pardoned all crimes committed before 17 August 163 BC so that was therefore most probably the date of Ptolemy VI's resumption of power under the new arrangements.[16] By then Ptolemy VIII had gone off to his new 'kingdom', from where he in turn lost no time in trying to win Roman support for his restoration.

At this point the royal titulature changed yet again, to designate 'the Pharaohs Ptolemy and Cleopatra, the manifest gods' as the rulers of Egypt.[17] Although the period down to Ptolemy VI's death in 145 BC is often described as a sole rule, it is noteworthy that Cleopatra II's name is always found included alongside the king's in the official date formula. In fact from this time onwards the queen and consort would regularly be associated with the ruling Ptolemy in this fashion. Just how far the titulature truly reflects Cleopatra II's own political authority at the time is very difficult to say. Grace Macurdy speaks of her achieving a political equality with her husband,[18] but that may be an overstatement. On the other hand it would be wrong to dismiss the style of the official date formula as nothing more than a cynical attempt to accommodate native Egyptian expectations of a divine queen as well as a god-king.

It may not be a great deal but we do have some evidence for what looks like Cleopatra II's personal involvement in at least one important item of foreign affairs towards the end of the 160s BC. At that time Ptolemy VI was trying to regain a foothold for Egypt in Coele Syria by supporting the conservative Jewish faction in Jerusalem against the pro-Greek group favoured by the Seleucids. In the aftermath of the Maccabaean Revolt against Antiochus IV's vain attempt to suppress all Jewish rites and customs, Menelaus, the extremist leader of the 'hellenising' Jews who had been his protégé as High Priest, had been quietly removed to Syria and executed (162 BC). Antiochus IV's son and successor Antiochus V Eupator realised that 'by persuading his father to compel the Jews to abandon their ancestral religion' (Josephus, *Jewish Ant.* 12.384) Menelaus had been one of the main causes of the Revolt and he replaced him as High Priest by a man called Alcimus, or Yakim in Hebrew, who was another leader of the 'hellenisers'.

Even though Alcimus was supported by some of the most strictly orthodox,[19] Judas Maccabaeus and his followers, who were still under arms, were totally opposed to his appointment and as soon as the Seleucid army which had installed him had left for home they began open hostilities against Alcimus and his faction. It is not surprising that Ptolemy VI saw in this an irresistible opportunity to make further trouble for the Syrians and stir the pot on his own account by extending his assistance to one who thought he should have had the High Priesthood by hereditary right.

Onias IV was the son of Onias III who had been High Priest when Antiochus IV had first become king. 'A zealot for the laws' (2 Maccabees 4.2), Onias III had been deposed by Antiochus IV in favour of his brother Jason (174 BC) and was later murdered when Jason in turn was supplanted by Menelaus (170 BC). The first we hear of his son is when Onias IV turns up in Egypt to request asylum after Alcimus' appointment as High Priest (Josephus, *Jewish Ant.* 12.387). Although the details are unsure,[20] it seems most likely that he had remained in Judaea throughout the Revolt and the subsequent restoration of the Temple in 164 BC, hoping that he would eventually be appointed High Priest. When that did not happen and he saw Antiochus V remove one 'helleniser' only to replace him with another, he finally gave up the struggle and emigrated to Egypt. He was given a kindly reception by Ptolemy VI and Cleopatra II and later successfully petitioned them for the right to build a temple similar to the one in Jerusalem at Leontopolis near Memphis.

In his account of the temple's foundation (*Jewish Ant.* 13.62–73), Josephus includes an exchange of letters which purportedly took place between Ptolemy VI and Cleopatra II and Onias IV about the advisability of siting the new temple at a ruined sanctuary of the Egyptian cat goddess Bastet. The royal couple are made to query whether such a contaminated place so full of sacred animals would be pleasing to the Lord before they give their assent 'if this is in accordance with the Law so that we may not seem to have committed any sin against God' (*Jewish Ant.* 13.71). As scholars have seen, these letters are obviously not authentic. Nevertheless they do reflect the friendly attitude which Ptolemy VI and Cleopatra II are felt to have had towards the Jewish people.

While it would be pleasing to believe that the Ptolemaic king and queen still felt a duty of care towards the inhabitants of their mother Cleopatra I's former homeland, their pro-Jewish stance is much more likely to have been motivated by a strong element of self-interest. The unusual location of 'the territory of Onias' and the site's obvious unsuitability for a temple to Yahweh quickly alerted modern writers to the fact that, despite what Josephus says, although Onias IV might have come from a family of High Priests, Leontopolis was never meant to be a second Jerusalem for all the Jews of Egypt. The temple was merely a local foundation to serve the needs of a large group of Jewish military colonists settled in the area and its location in the eastern Delta suggests that they had been put there primarily to guard the route from Pelusium to Memphis.[21]

When they were younger Ptolemy VI and Cleopatra II had twice had the unpleasant experience of seeing a Seleucid army march along that road into the heart of Egypt. To settle Jewish refugees, particularly ones combining military skills with a strong hatred for the Seleucids, in such a location therefore made a great deal of sense. Indeed the next time we hear of Onias' family it is in a military context. After Ptolemy VI's death in 145 BC, when Alexandria split into two armed camps, Onias IV would come to Cleopatra II's support with a small contingent of Jewish troops (Josephus, *Against Apion.* 2.50). Later his sons Chelkias and Ananias would serve as generals for her daughter Cleopatra III in her civil war against Ptolemy IX (Josephus, *Jewish Ant.* 13.285–7, 348–55) and the only region which would remain steadfastly loyal to the queen would be 'the territory of Onias'. The continuing loyalty of these Jewish settlers and their descendants towards both royal women strongly suggests that the original act of royal kindness towards Onias IV may have been due as much to queen Cleopatra II as to her husband. It was an act which would pay handsome dividends for both her and her daughter in years to come.

PLATES

1 Cleopatra I's father, the Seleucid king Antiochus III the Great.

2 Cleopatra I's husband Ptolemy V Epiphanes, to whom she was married in 194/3 BC.

3 The only certain portrait of Cleopatra I, probably as regent for her elder son Ptolemy VI Philometor, who appears on the other side of this gold octodrachm. There are no certain representations of her daughter Cleopatra II or her granddaughter Cleopatra III.

4 Ptolemy VI Philometor, brother and first husband of Cleopatra II. His sharp features seem to be inherited from his maternal grandfather Antiochus III.

5 This copper coin from Cyprus may represent Cleopatra II or III. The legend reads 'Basilisses Kleopatras' (of queen Cleopatra). The elephant skull head-dress recalls a very early coin type of Ptolemy I, which showed Alexander the Great similarly clad.

6 Cleopatra Thea and her first husband Alexander Balas, the pretender to the Seleucid throne, to whom she was married in 150 BC.

7 Cleopatra Thea's second husband, Demetrius II Nicator, shown as a young man during his first period of kingship (146–40 BC).

8 Demetrius II Nicator during his second period of kingship (129–125 BC) after his return from captivity, shown wearing the beard and long hair characteristic of his captor, the Parthian king Mithradates I.

9 Cleopatra Thea's third husband, her brother-in-law Antiochus VII Euergetes nicknamed Sidetes, whom she married in 138 BC shortly after the defeat and capture of Demetrius II by the Parthians.

10 Cleopatra Thea shown as sole ruler (126/5 BC) on a silver tetradrachm from Sykaminos. She was the only Seleucid queen ever to issue coins in her own name.

11 The reverse gives Cleopatra Thea's title as 'queen Cleopatra Thea Eueteria (Goddess of plenty)' and shows a double cornucopia.

12 Cleopatra Thea as co-ruler with her son Antiochus VIII Grypus.
The origin of his nickname Grypus (Hook-nosed) is clear from this
coin portrait. Grypus was the first husband of Ptolemy VIII's and
Cleopatra III's eldest daughter Tryphaena and second husband of their
youngest daughter Cleopatra Selene.

13 Antiochus IX Cyzicenus, second husband of Ptolemy VIII's and
Cleopatra III's middle daughter Cleopatra IV (who was his second
wife) and third husband of her younger sister Cleopatra Selene (who
was his third wife).

14 Cleopatra Selene's stepson and fourth husband Antiochus X Eusebes, whom she married in 95 BC.

15 Cleopatra VII's father Ptolemy XII Auletes. The coin portraits of him are rare and of poor quality.

16 Cleopatra VII on a tetradrachm of Antioch, *c.* 34 BC.

17 The other side of the tetradrachm shows Mark Antony.

18 Cleopatra VII and the baby Caesarion, her child by Julius Caesar, shown on a bronze coin from Cyprus, *c.* 47/6 BC.

19 Juba II of Mauretania, husband of Cleopatra VII's daughter Cleopatra Selene, to whom she was married *c*. 20 BC.

20 Cleopatra Selene, daughter of Cleopatra VII and Mark Antony, as queen of Mauretania.

21 Ptolemy of Mauretania, son of Juba II and Cleopatra Selene, as a young man.

9

CLEOPATRA II AND
PTOLEMY VIII

The Jewish colony at Leontopolis where Ptolemy VI and Cleopatra II allowed the High Priest's son Onias IV to found a temple when he came down into Egypt with his followers was probably only one of a number of similar settlements established at this time.[1] They were designed partly to police the local population, partly to serve as a bulwark against further incursions from Syria. As matters turned out this inner defensive ring would prove unnecessary. The last decade and a half of Ptolemy VI's kingship would see a remarkable turnaround in the fortunes of Egypt. In his final years he not only managed to play his troublesome younger brother Ptolemy VIII to a standstill, but also succeeded in regaining for a brief time much of the territory in Coele Syria which Egypt had lost 50 years before, and at the time of his death he was virtual ruler of Antioch itself.

In 154 BC a combination of diplomatic skill and decisive military action enabled him to frustrate the last of Ptolemy VIII's manoeuvres to regain Cyprus. After the collapse of an earlier attempt to win back the island (162 BC) and further vain appeals to the Roman senate, Ptolemy VIII had mounted a second invasion. He found himself pinned down in the harbour town of Lapethus, just west of modern Kyrenia, and was forced to make an unconditional surrender. Ptolemy VI had him totally at his mercy, but instead of having him summarily executed (as perhaps anyone else would have done) he preferred to show his brother clemency yet again. He allowed Ptolemy VIII to return to Cyrene, granted him a fixed amount of grain each year from Egypt (thus allowing him a share of the country's wealth but not its territory), and to seal the bargain offered him one of his own daughters as wife.

It is not known whether this was Cleopatra Thea, who was probably Ptolemy VI's and Cleopatra II's elder daughter, or Cleopatra III, whom Ptolemy VIII would eventually take as his second wife after his brother's death. Nor does it matter greatly since in the event Ptolemy VIII declined the alliance. In so doing he fell right into Ptolemy VI's hands. Up until then he still had a number of powerful backers at Rome. His brother shrewdly guessed that a public reconciliation strengthened by the offer of a marriage alliance would have the effect of cutting the ground from under their feet as well as neutralising any residue of support which Ptolemy VIII might still command in Cyprus or Alexandria. His guess was correct. After 154 BC Roman support for Ptolemy VIII rapidly ebbed away and he found himself effectively sidelined.[2]

That left Ptolemy VI free to pursue his other plans. His inclusion of his son Ptolemy Eupator in the kingship, probably in early 152 BC,[3] together with the prince's appointment as governor of Cyprus show his intentions in regard to Egypt's internal affairs. His son, not his brother, would be his successor. Further afield he turned his considerable energies to fulfilling a long-standing ambition to win back Coele Syria. Apart from siding with the Seleucids' Jewish enemies, he had already had one attempt at meddling in Seleucid affairs but it had backfired on him. In 162 BC a Ptolemaic envoy had been one of those assisting Ptolemy VI's Seleucid cousin Demetrius to escape secretly from Rome where he had been serving as royal hostage under the terms of the Peace of Apamea. Once back in Antioch, Demetrius had quickly eliminated the young king Antiochus V and his regent Lysias and set himself up as king, but Ptolemy VI's hopes that this would lead to a favourable shift in Seleucid foreign policy were disappointed. A few years later (155/4 BC) Demetrius I repaid him by trying to get control of Cyprus through bribing the island's governor.[4]

Accordingly when the opportunity presented itself Ptolemy VI was only too happy to join in a coalition with several other kings to get rid of Demetrius I and replace him with someone more amenable. The man they chose was a supposed son of Antiochus IV called Alexander Balas. Demetrius I was finally defeated and killed in battle after an extended campaign and Balas was set up as king in his place. As the major contributor to the coalition on the military side Ptolemy VI at last had a direct say in whatever took place in Syria. Balas was effectively his vassal and he set about maximising his influence over him. He brought his elder daughter Cleopatra Thea to Ptolemais and married her off to the 23-year-old Balas. It was a mirror image of the dynastic relationship which Antiochus III had established almost half a century before when he had betrothed his eldest daughter Cleopatra 'the Syrian' to Ptolemy VI's father Ptolemy V. This time though it was the Ptolemaic king who would be the father-in-law and the dominant partner in the relationship. Balas, young, genial, and good looking, would be under his control, not vice versa.

Unfortunately for Ptolemy VI his new son-in-law turned out to be a broken reed. He was completely dominated by his mistresses and court favourites and before too long a challenger for the kingship emerged. Demetrius I's son Demetrius II, who had recently come of age, landed in Cilicia with a force of Cretan mercenaries intent on regaining the throne (147 BC). In this crisis Ptolemy VI saw his chance. He immediately set off from Egypt at the head of a large army. His ostensible purpose was to bring support to his son-in-law but as he advanced northwards he garrisoned the key towns of Coele Syria on the way. At Ptolemais, where the marriage of Balas and Cleopatra Thea had been celebrated only three years before, there was an attempt made to assassinate him. Or so Ptolemy VI said.[5] Claiming that Balas had instigated the plot, he at once switched sides, throwing his considerable weight behind Demetrius II. Annulling his daughter's marriage to Balas, he transferred her to his new protégé.

The teenager got both the crown and the princess but there was no fairy tale ending to the story. Ptolemy VI had already repossessed Coele Syria and through his hold over Demetrius II he was now in a position to control Seleucid Syria itself and all its other possessions. Indeed it is said that when he entered Antioch at the end of his march northwards the Antiochenes offered him a double crown as king of Asia as well as Egypt (Josephus, *Jewish Ant.* 13.113–15). But he wisely declined for fear of upsetting the Romans. In fact he had no need of the title since thanks to his tutelage of the naive and inexperienced Demetrius II he already had everything which the title implied.

At that moment Ptolemy VI stood on the brink of re-establishing Egypt as the major power in western Asia and completely redrawing the political map of the entire area. But a sudden mishap swept everything away. Returning from Cilicia, Alexander Balas offered battle. He was no match for the combined forces of Ptolemy VI and Demetrius II and was soundly defeated, but in the battle Ptolemy VI was thrown from his horse and surrounded. Barely alive by the time his own men reached him, he was carried from the field with severe wounds to his head. For four days he lay in a coma while the Egyptian surgeons, with centuries of trepanning experience to draw upon, desperately worked to close his wounds. On the fifth he recovered consciousness just long enough to have the pleasure of seeing Alexander Balas' head brought to him before he slipped away (June/July 145 BC).

Ptolemy VI's sudden and unexpected death left Cleopatra II as queen of Egypt and regent for her younger son. Their elder son Ptolemy Eupator had died young (152 BC) and Ptolemy VII had been associated with his father just before Ptolemy VI set out for Syria. But he would not live to see out his first year as king. As soon as the news of Ptolemy VI's death reached him, Ptolemy VIII was on his way back from Cyrene, pausing only long enough to secure Cyprus before he made for Egypt.[6]

It is difficult to gauge how much support he had in Alexandria or how much resistance he met. There may have been some fighting, but it cannot have lasted very long for the latest date by Ptolemy VI is in a demotic text of 15 July while the earliest document of Ptolemy VIII and Cleopatra II is dated to barely a month later (14 August 145 BC).[7] The literary sources suggest that Ptolemy VIII's forces may have been able to rely on some popular support among the Alexandrians to get them into the city. At the same time Cleopatra II was probably short of loyalist troops to oppose them as a result of the sudden reversal of fortune in Syria. Ptolemy VI's soldiers had been so shocked and demoralised by their leader's demise that they had simply abandoned everything at Antioch, including their battle elephants, and left Demetrius II and his advisers to resume unopposed control over all the territory their king had won so brilliantly and held so briefly. They were already streaming back to Egypt but by the time they reached Alexandria it was all over.

It is at this point that we hear of Onias IV again. Conscious of his people's debt to Cleopatra II, he brought a small force of Jewish troops, no doubt from Leontopolis, into Alexandria to support the queen in her hour of need. Josephus (*Against Apion* 2.53–6) tells a lurid tale of how, rather than face them, the cowardly Ptolemy VIII responded by rounding up all the Jews in the city – men, women, and children – and chaining them up naked to be trampled to death by his elephants. But they were saved by a miracle. Although Ptolemy VIII got the animals totally drunk for the occasion, the intoxicated elephants adamantly refused to tread on any of the Jews. Instead they turned on his own men and killed a large number of them. Unfortunately the miracle of the drunken elephants is later repeated by the writer of the Third Book of Maccabees, who attributes it to Ptolemy IV (3 Maccabees 5–6). It therefore looks like a late invention, made up perhaps to explain the origins of a local festival among the Jews of Alexandria.[8]

No less lurid is the story of Ptolemy VIII's wedding night. Having made himself master of Alexandria, probably without too much difficulty, Ptolemy VIII reached an agreement with his sister that she would become his wife and queen, thereby giving a semblance of legitimacy and continuity to his seizure of power. Cleopatra II's side of the bargain may have included a condition that her son Ptolemy VII would be allowed to live, perhaps even that he could continue as co-ruler under the guardianship of his uncle and new stepfather. If so, the agreement was not worth the papyrus it was written on, for Ptolemy VIII is said to have had the boy killed on the very day of his marriage to Cleopatra II. Justin (38.8.4) tells us that after the rites had been performed and the guests had taken their places at the marriage feast, Ptolemy VIII himself killed his young nephew as he clung to his mother's embrace. Then he made his way to his sister's bed with the blood of her son still fresh on his hands.

To round out this classic picture of horror, Justin (38.8.9–10) also invites us to imagine Ptolemy VIII dressed in a sort of see-through nightdress as he dragged his great weight, puffing and panting, towards his brother's widow. Cleopatra II's new husband, he says, was not only short, ill-featured, and grossly obese, but was also given to wearing thin translucent robes. These had the extraordinarily unpleasant effect of emphasising his grotesque pot belly rather than concealing it, as any self-respecting man with an ounce of decency would have tried to do!

All of this is part of the standard identikit portrait of the ancient tyrant and, while there may be an element of truth in it, as evidence it needs to be treated very circumspectly. On the one hand there can be little doubt about Ptolemy VIII's corpulence or enthusiastic vindictiveness. One does not get the nicknames Physcon (Pot Belly) or Kakergetes (Malefactor), instead of Euergetes (Benefactor), for nothing, and the rare coin portraits of Ptolemy VIII show a man with blown-out cheeks, a bull neck, and cruelly flaring nostrils who looks ready to bulldoze his way through any obstacle to satisfy his appetites. On the other hand the diaphanous robes seem different when it is an eye witness who is describing them. The Stoic philosopher Panaetius, who accompanied the younger Scipio on a Roman embassy to Alexandria a few years later,[9] describes the king thus:

> Thanks to his over-indulgence his body had been utterly ruined by fat. He had an immense belly. You could not have got your arms around it. Over it he wore a short tunic which covered his feet while the sleeves came down to his wrists.
> (Athenaeus 12.549e)

Panaetius confirms most of what Justin says about Ptolemy VIII. He was short, almost to the point of dwarfism.[10] He was immensely fat and he had a horrible distended stomach. Yet what is missing in this contemporary account is the exhibitionism implied by Justin and as a result the image in our mind's eye is no longer so repellent. Without the see-through robes of Justin's account Ptolemy VIII at once becomes a different figure. No longer is this a monster to be feared, a Ptolemaic elephant-man. Instead the king becomes a human being, to be pitied rather than despised. In fact we almost feel sorry for him as we see him hobbling around Alexandria, trying to keep up with the towering and supercilious Romans, and overhear Scipio's snide comment whispered behind his hand to Panaetius: 'The Alexandrians have already got one thing from our visit. Thanks to us they've finally seen their king walking' (Plutarch, *Moralia* 201A).

This is not to imply that Ptolemy VIII deserves historical rehabilitation. His dealings with his sister–wife and any who supported her, like the Jews, or offended him, like the Cyrenaeans who had returned to Alexandria in his entourage, amply demonstrate that Grace Macurdy was right to call him 'the most cruel of all the Ptolemies'.[11] Yet on a sliding scale of nastiness Ptolemy VIII would rank far behind the likes of Hitler, or Stalin, or even Idi Amin. A major part of the problem is the image of him which has come down to us because the difficulty of assessing his character accurately is compounded by the fact that among his victims he unwisely chose to include the intelligentsia attached to Alexandria's great institutions of learning, the Library and the Museum. The scholars and writers whom he purged would fan out across the Mediterranean so that even the smallest towns and islands of the Greek world benefited from the cultural fallout.[12] But these same scholars would exact a telling revenge on their persecutor by ensuring that the portrait they left of Ptolemy VIII was drawn in the very darkest of hues.

The Romans may have laughed at Ptolemy VIII as they looked down on him. Judged by modern standards he may be only an also-ran in the all-time tyranny stakes. Yet had the contest been on grounds of his own choosing – feasting or fornication – then despite his physical shortcomings (and perhaps other congenital defects of which we know nothing) the fat little king could have left most others struggling in his wake. Devoted as he was to the lower appetites, he managed to father seven children that we know of, a far better score than many of his more illustrious predecessors.

Ptolemy VIII's eldest child was Ptolemy Apion, most probably the offspring of his concubine Eirene. His relationship with her was a long-standing one and we get the impression that she gave him a lot less trouble than either of his domineering wives Cleopatra II and Cleopatra III. By this time Ptolemy Apion was perhaps 10 or 11 years old. Later he would become governor of Cyrenaica and eventually its king, when the Ptolemaic possessions were partitioned under the terms of his father's will. His own bequest of Cyrenaica to the Romans in 96 BC would be the first step in the final break-up of the Ptolemaic realm.

Ptolemy VIII's second child was his son by Cleopatra II, for this was no more a marriage in name only than her union with their elder brother Ptolemy VI had been. Born in the second part of 144 or, at the latest, 143 BC the boy was naturally called Ptolemy but he was also named Memphites since his birth took place at the time of Ptolemy VIII's coronation by Egyptian rites at Memphis. This was not a lucky coincidence. The Egyptian coronation was no doubt deliberately arranged to take place after the birth, thus allowing Ptolemy VIII (who had already alienated the Alexandrians once again) to gain the support of the native Egyptian priesthoods by presenting them with a complete version of the divine triad of father, son, and sister–wife/mother which was such an important feature of late Egyptian religious thought.[13]

The occasion was also marked by a change in royal titulature. Immediately after his seizure of power in 145 BC Ptolemy VIII and Cleopatra II had been known as 'the Pharaohs Ptolemy and Cleopatra, the offspring of Ptolemy and Cleopatra the manifest gods' and that form had been used until 144/3 BC.[14] Then from 143/2 BC both king and queen bear the demotic version of Ptolemy VIII's Greek title Euergetes (Benefactor). Demotic documents were henceforth dated by the year of 'Pharaoh Ptolemy the beneficent, son of Ptolemy and Cleopatra the manifest gods, with queen Cleopatra his sister, his wife, the beneficent goddess'. It seems therefore that at the time of the Egyptian coronation Ptolemy VIII extended his title Euergetes to Cleopatra II, who had formerly been Cleopatra Philometor through her marriage to Ptolemy VI Philometor. Disregarding the double incest, Mrs Cleopatra Philometor had become Mrs Cleopatra Euergetes, except that the acquisition of her new 'surname' was connected not with her second marriage but with the much more important occasion of her production of a male heir.

The birth of Ptolemy Memphites may have been important but it did little to improve relations between the king and his sister–wife. Cleopatra II is hardly likely to have already forgotten the murder of her last child Ptolemy VII and right from the start she seems to have had ambitions to rule in her own right. Moreover within the space of a year Ptolemy VIII had fathered another son.[15] But this child, who would eventually succeed as Ptolemy IX, was not Cleopatra II's. He was the offspring of her own younger daughter Cleopatra III, who would only become Ptolemy VIII's second wife some years later.

The story of Cleopatra III's 'rape' by her uncle will be discussed later but, whatever the origins of the relationship between uncle and niece, it is not too fanciful to guess that behind it lay an attempt by Ptolemy VIII to bypass his sister–wife by putting some other dynastic arrangement in place. Now that Cleopatra II had another child of royal blood in Ptolemy Memphites, there must have been a real danger that she might try to mobilise her widespread support among the Greek and Jewish elements of the population to throw out her brutal and unpopular brother. If she could drive him out, she would again be in a position to reign herself, as she had done briefly in 145 BC as regent for Ptolemy VII. She could re-establish the same arrangement with Ptolemy Memphites substituted for Ptolemy VII. She knew that the Alexandrians and the Jews would accept her rule and, after the successful presentation of the baby Memphites to the Egyptian priests assembled in synod at Memphis, she was confident of their backing too, or at least their acquiescence.

Ptolemy VIII for his part, if he was to head off a plan like this, would either need to mend his ways (which was hardly likely by this time) or he would have to find a new power base for himself and then work towards getting rid of his sister–wife and neutralising the support she enjoyed. This is exactly what we see him doing during these years. The Egyptian coronation and the presentation of Ptolemy Memphites to the priesthoods was an attempt to create a new basis of support among the native population of the countryside after his realisation that the Alexandrians were still totally opposed to him and would continue to favour Cleopatra II, or indeed any member of the royal family connected with the 'good king' Ptolemy VI. It is in this setting that we can probably locate the attempt by a former general of the previous king called Galaestes, now in exile overseas, to foment a mutiny against Ptolemy VIII by producing a supposed son of Ptolemy VI and Cleopatra II and crowning him (Diodorus 33.20). The attempt failed when Ptolemy VIII's loyal general Hierax undercut Galaestes by the expedient of paying out the discontented troops' arrears of pay from his own pocket.

Ptolemy VIII's sustained efforts to purge various elements of the population which he saw as hostile to him can be understood as part of a wide-ranging plan to undermine Cleopatra II's position within Alexandria. There were persecutions of the Jews, whose primary loyalties still lay with the queen. There was the expulsion of writers and scholars from the Alexandrian Library and Museum. There were reprisals against the Cyrenaeans who had accompanied the king on his return to Egypt. There was an attack on the upper-class elite among the Alexandrian citizenry when the king's troops surrounded a crowded gymnasium in the city and wiped out all the young men they found there. Except for the last atrocity, which is connected by Valerius Maximus with the later murder of Ptolemy Memphites,[16] our sources assign all these acts of savagery to the early part of Ptolemy VIII's reign. Indeed the murder of the Cyrenaeans is expressly associated with the birth celebrations for Ptolemy Memphites in 144/3 BC. They are said to have attracted the king's wrath by their comments about his concubine Eirene (Diodorus 33.13) but there was probably more to it than that[17] – speculation perhaps about Ptolemy Apion's place in the succession now that there was another child?

Finally there was the problem of how to dislodge Cleopatra II herself, for it was not enough merely to destroy her bases of support among the population. To conciliate the bulk of his Egyptian subjects and meet their expectations about the kingship, Ptolemy VIII had to be able to offer them another Isis figure who would be an acceptable substitute as queen and consort. That meant replacing Cleopatra II with someone whose blood was as royal, and therefore divine, as hers. The substitute would also need to be easier to control than Cleopatra II was proving herself to be. Furthermore it would be necessary to find a substitute for Ptolemy Memphites. After the Egyptian priests assembled at Memphis had acknowledged Memphites as the third essential element of the divine triad – the Horus child who would follow his divine father and uphold his acts – it would have been little use for Ptolemy VIII to go back to them with a replacement Isis if he could not also supply a replacement Horus.

Hence the king's liaison with his niece Cleopatra III and an explanation why he did not marry her until after she had given birth to their first son. Cleopatra III's bloodline was as good as her mother's if not better, for as the daughter of Ptolemy VI she offered a way of conciliating and winning back the allegiance of those still yearning to be ruled by the stock of the late lamented god-king. The credentials of any son of hers as the Horus child were likewise just as good. Last but by no means least, she was still only a girl when Ptolemy VIII took her to his bed so that he might confidently expect to be able to exercise a greater degree of control over her than over Cleopatra II.[18] It was not his fault that she would turn out to be even more intractable and domineering than her mother.

Without excusing Ptolemy VIII's atrocious record of persecution, let us suppose that he was not the tyrannical monster portrayed by our sources, a fiend whose acts were motivated only by lust and cruelty. Instead he was like his brother Ptolemy VI, a clever and calculating politician, and the only difference between them was that his heavy-handed methods brought him far less success than Ptolemy VI's lighter touch. The problem which confronted him on his return in 145 BC was how best to secure and legitimise his kingship against strong opposition from those who would have preferred to see the dead king's son Ptolemy VII confirmed as the next king of the dynasty, with his mother Cleopatra II as his regent. I suggest that, faced with such a situation, Ptolemy VIII's original plan may have involved the removal of both Ptolemy VII and his own sister Cleopatra II, followed by marriage to his niece Cleopatra III and her eventual promotion to the position of queen and consort. After all, Cleopatra III (or perhaps her elder sister) had been offered to him by Ptolemy VI back in 154 BC when the kingdom had been partitioned. In the event of any objection from the Alexandrians (or more seriously the Romans) he could therefore claim that he was only carrying out his dead brother's wishes now that the girl was approaching marriageable age. But the strength of the opposition which he encountered among the Alexandrians forced him to shelve this plan temporarily after achieving only the first part of it (the murder of Ptolemy VII).

The strategy which Ptolemy VIII chose for his fall-back position was one which he had already used once before in 164 BC. Faced with an outright revolt from a hostile population, he negotiated an arrangement with his sister under which he gained legitimacy by making her his queen, as he had done at the time of his successful expulsion of Ptolemy VI in 164 BC. But this time she would be his wife as well as his queen. When Cleopatra II gave birth to Ptolemy Memphites a year or so after the marriage that was a bonus for him in so far as it gave him a means of ingratiating himself with the native Egyptian population, as we have seen. Yet the child was also a potential trump card for Cleopatra II in that both the Greek and Egyptian elements of the population would have been just as glad to return to the arrangement which they had had immediately after Ptolemy VI's death and be ruled by a son of hers with herself as regent. The arrival of Ptolemy Memphites therefore paradoxically made Ptolemy VIII's position both more and also less secure since there was now the possibility that Cleopatra II might be able to use their child against him. To ensure that he stayed on top of the game, the king needed another higher card with which to overtrump his wife.

He had that card the following year when Cleopatra III bore his son. All along, it seems, he had been secretly pursuing his original plan to marry his niece and advance her as his queen. It is not too difficult to believe that he could have done this without his wife's knowledge. Relations between Cleopatra II and Ptolemy VIII were already so strained that it is hardly likely that they indulged in much pillow talk and Cleopatra III was probably already old enough and ambitious enough to conspire actively with her uncle to conceal their relationship from her mother. Once her child was born, and was found to be male and healthy, further concealment became unnecessary, indeed counterproductive from Ptolemy VIII's point of view. By publicly acknowledging the child as his, the king would put himself in a position where ancient Greek sensibilities would compel him to marry his niece, which is precisely what he had always intended to do. As a corollary he would be 'forced' by public opinion to set aside Cleopatra II. In any case that union would have been considered to be automatically annulled by the subsequent marriage, as had happened with the marriages made by the dynasty's founder Ptolemy I to the Persian princess Artakama (324 BC), then to Antipater's daughter Eurydice (321 BC), and finally to his mistress Berenice (316 BC).

We know that Ptolemy VIII did indeed marry his niece, most probably at some time between May 141 and January 140 BC.[19] By that time the child had survived the perils of earliest infancy and Ptolemy VIII could acknowledge his paternity, confident that the boy was likely to live long enough to be accepted as a potential successor. Now that he had Cleopatra III and her son he had no further need of Cleopatra II. In fact both Livy (59) and Justin (38.8.5) speak of him divorcing her after the birth of Ptolemy IX and the marriage to his niece. But that does not seem to have been what happened. As the royal titulature shows us, Cleopatra II had other ideas. Since 170 BC when the regents Eulaeus and Lenaeus had first established the tripartite rule of the three royal children, she had been the mainstay of the Ptolemaic house. She had later been queen at one time or another with both of her brothers, with each in turn, and with her younger son. Throughout the whole period he alone had managed to remain in Alexandria and, more importantly, to retain the affection and loyalty of the notoriously fickle Alexandrian mob, which now had the power to make or break kings (and knew it too). She was not about to fade quietly into the background and leave the field to her younger brother and her own younger daughter.

Ptolemy VIII may have created a new Isis and a new Horus child to replace Cleopatra II and her son Ptolemy Memphites. But, divorce or no divorce, Cleopatra II was not going to let herself be consigned to the scrapheap as last year's model. She would remain queen even if it meant a joint rule with her daughter. The texts of the time tell a confusing story but the confusion of the scribes who wrote them probably mirrors only too accurately the confusion of society as a whole. Unpalatable as it might be, Ptolemy VIII was still king. But who was his queen? Who was his wife? Cleopatra II? Cleopatra III? Or both?

The documents provide a kaleidoscopic array of answers. For example a demotic papyrus from Thebes, dated to 8 May 141 BC, speaks of Ptolemy VIII as pharaoh along with 'queen Cleopatra and Cleopatra the beneficent'. It also mentions the eponymous priestesses for the cult of each of the two Cleopatras. Their titles are 'the priestess of queen Cleopatra' and 'the priestess of Cleopatra the daughter of the king'.[20] It therefore looks as though Cleopatra III already had the title Euergetes from her uncle, that is, the same title which her mother had acquired at the time of the Egyptian coronation and Ptolemy Memphites' birth. But she was not yet hailed as queen, or wife, at least in Upper Egypt.

The next step in the process is illustrated by a Greek papyrus (P.Amh. II 45) of July 141 or 140 BC.[21] Here the same priestesses are called 'the priestesses of queen Cleopatra and of queen Cleopatra the daughter' so that, unless the latter is a courtesy title inserted by the scribe to cover his bets, there were now two queens. But still only one was recognised as wife for in another demotic text of September 140 BC we find Ptolemy VIII still reigning with 'the queen Cleopatra, his sister, his wife, the goddess, the beneficent one' and the priestesses are still 'the priestess of queen Cleopatra' and 'the priestess of Cleopatra, the king's daughter'.[22]

It was not until the end of 140 BC that the mist finally clears and the royal titulature settles down into a form which would last until 132 BC. A royal circular, written in Greek which was the official language of the country and sent out in early February 139 BC, begins with the words 'king Ptolemy and queen Cleopatra the sister and queen Cleopatra the wife'. Then a little later (138/7 BC) essentially the same format occurs in a fuller form in the demotic date formula as 'Pharaoh Ptolemy the beneficent god, son of Ptolemy and Cleopatra the manifest gods, with queen Cleopatra his sister and with queen Cleopatra his wife, the beneficent goddess'.[23]

It seems therefore that, after several years spent trying to undermine Cleopatra II by carrying out a series of pogroms aimed at her different groups of supporters, Ptolemy VIII then wasted a further two years attempting to replace her with Cleopatra III. But it all came to nothing, just as his earlier plans to win back Egypt from Ptolemy VI had come to nothing. Then he had been outmanoeuvred diplomatically and militarily by his elder brother.

Now he found himself outmanoeuvred dynastically by his elder sister. There was no way that he could get Cleopatra II to give up her hold on the kingship short of murdering her, and that he dared not do.

Not only had Cleopatra II survived his latest complicated attempt to replace her, but also, if anything, she had grown in strength and stature as a result. In the confused conditions of 145 BC Ptolemy VIII had been able to get away with his nephew's murder without any repercussions that we know of. Yet he had still needed his sister beside him as queen and consort to secure his place as king and win the support of the native priesthoods. Although he had subsequently tried to work towards a position where he could do without her, all his efforts to cut away the bases of her support and ultimately dispense with Cleopatra II herself had proved fruitless. She had been too powerful and too popular for him to dislodge. Now it was Ptolemy VIII who was the meat in the sandwich. With two wives and two potential heirs (not counting his mistress Eirene's son Ptolemy Apion), he found himself trapped between his seemingly unassailable sister and her equally forceful and ambitious daughter.

Such was the dynastic situation which the Roman ambassadors led by the younger Scipio found when they landed at Alexandria and took Ptolemy VIII on the unexpected and unwanted walking tour of his own city. At this stage the Romans had no interest in annexing Egypt, but they were nevertheless concerned that the country remained stable enough to ensure undisturbed continuity to the Egyptian grain supply. Consequently the uneasy peace which existed between the royal trio over the next few years may have owed as much to a diplomatic nudge and a wink from Rome as to any new-found depth of family feeling within the Ptolemaic household.[24] Yet given the basic instability of the arrangement, with mother and daughter both acknowledged as co-rulers alongside their joint husband, it is no surprise to find the tripartite rule eventually foundering and a resumption in 132 BC of hostilities between Ptolemy VIII and Cleopatra II.

A lack of information about internal affairs in Alexandria in the 130s BC makes it difficult to pinpoint the exact cause of the renewed strife. One suggestion is that by the mid-130s BC Ptolemy VIII had become infected with the same fatal desire to meddle in the dynastic affairs of Syria which had afflicted his brother a decade earlier, and Cleopatra II had seen in this an opportunity to move against her brother while his attention was distracted.[25] There could be some truth in this (although not enough is known even to start trying to reconstruct Ptolemy VIII's external policies), but there are other factors which are much more likely to have encouraged Cleopatra II to make a move at this stage. One is the fact that Cleopatra III had continued to bear children to Ptolemy VIII at quite an alarming rate. Although exact dates are not known, probably all five of her children had been born by 135 BC. There was a second son, who would eventually rule as Ptolemy X (107–88 BC), so she now had an heir and a spare. Then there were three daughters, Cleopatra IV, Cleopatra Selene, and Cleopatra Tryphaena, which meant that she also had sister–wives for both of them plus a spare. Cleopatra II on the other hand was past child-bearing age by this time. Unless she moved soon, she and her son Ptolemy Memphites would be locked out of the dynasty's future. Her daughter and her brother would have overwhelmed them by sheer weight of numbers.

Another factor influencing the timing of Cleopatra II's attempt to reassert her claims was the age that Ptolemy Memphites was at. Ptolemy Eupator, her elder son by Ptolemy VI, had been about 12 years old when his father had associated him in the kingship in 152 BC, and Ptolemy VI himself had been about the same age when Cleopatra II had been married to him by the regents Eulaeus and Lenaeus. In 132 BC Ptolemy Memphites was therefore coming up to the age when he would be acceptable to his native subjects (if not yet the Greeks) as king in his own right – with his mother there, of course, as regent to guide him. But the window of opportunity which was opening up for Cleopatra II and her son was a narrow one by any reckoning. Another year and Ptolemy IX, Cleopatra III's first-born son, would be old enough for Ptolemy VIII to take him on as co-ruler and heir designate. A year or so after that and her second son would be in the same position.

It was in 132/1 BC that the revolt against Ptolemy VIII co-ordinated by Cleopatra II came to a head. In Alexandria the mob attacked the palace and Ptolemy VIII was forced to flee the city. He went into exile in Cyprus, taking Cleopatra III and her children with him. Ptolemy Memphites had already been sent away by his mother to a safe refuge in Cyrene but somehow or other Ptolemy VIII managed to have him brought to Cyprus. An impasse had been reached and for a time matters degenerated no further than a war of words. For his part Ptolemy VIII endeavoured to present an image of happy family unity. A contemporary inscription from Delos reads:

> I, king Ptolemy son of king Ptolemy Euergetes [i.e. Ptolemy VIII] in honour of queen Cleopatra Euergetis [i.e. Cleopatra III], my father's wife, my cousin, on account of my gratitude towards her [have dedicated this] to Apollo, Artemis, and Leto.
>
> (OGIS I 144)

It looks therefore as if, in return for being associated in the kingship with his father, Ptolemy Memphites was persuaded to turn his back on his mother and recognise Cleopatra III as the only true queen of Egypt.

On her side Cleopatra II responded in the only way she could. In Upper Egypt, which was still in ferment after the recent collapse of a brief rebellion led by a native pharaoh called Harsiesis (132/1–131/0 BC), she proclaimed herself sole ruler with the title 'queen Cleopatra, the mother loving (Philometor) goddess, the saviour (Soteira)'. The resumption of her original title Philometor recalled her dead husband Ptolemy VI with the implication that he had been Egypt's last legitimate king while Soteira equated her with the dynasty's founder Ptolemy I Soter. The Theban scribes, who had seen it all before, quite sensibly took a wait-and-see attitude and adopted a system of double dates of the type 'Year 39 which is also Year 1', but her brother's reaction was rapid and predictable. He gave orders for Ptolemy Memphites to be murdered.

Although he was Ptolemy VIII's own son, the disposal of Ptolemy Memphites was a logical move for the king to make for it deprived his sister once and for all of any hope of ever setting up a dynasty of her own. Even if the native Egyptians rallied behind her as sole ruler, she would no longer be able to offer them the prospect of a successor, as he and Cleopatra III could. The murder story is credible not because of Ptolemy VIII's savage character but because we can see the logic behind it. Far less credible is its sequel. Hearing of the murder, the Alexandrians are said to have risen up against the king and pulled down all his statues. Believing that his sister was behind this act of lèse-majesté, the king had the dead boy's body cut up and sent it to Alexandria in a chest as a birthday present for Cleopatra II (Diodorus 34/5.14, Justin 38.12–13).

It is difficult to believe the details of this gruesome tale but what is certain is that the country quickly descended into a state of civil war, which the papyri of these years euphemistically call a time of *amixia*, 'a breakdown of civil intercourse'. Ptolemy VIII managed to return to Egypt in 130 BC, only to find that the Alexandrians had raised an army against him. He succeeded in defeating them in battle but it was not until 127 BC that he won back control of the countryside. Meanwhile Cleopatra II had taken refuge at Antioch with her Seleucid son-in-law Demetrius II. It was 124 BC before she finally returned. Under the terms of the official reconciliation she again became 'queen Cleopatra the sister' and the reign of brother, sister, and niece was resumed, with both sides tacitly admitting that despite so many years of strife the best that either could hope for was a drawn game.

Egypt itself remained in a state of turmoil for several more years and it is only in 118 BC that we find an amnesty decree (P.Tebt. I 5 = Sel.Pap. II 210) aimed at restoring law and order and drawing a veil over the excesses of the past. This important and comprehensive document opened the way to a long-overdue reconstruction of a country ravaged by almost ten years of intermittent civil war. It is usually interpreted as evidence of a final compromise hammered out between Ptolemy VIII and Cleopatra II under which she managed to extract considerable concessions from him for the benefit of their long-suffering subjects. Yet the unpleasant truth is that Cleopatra II was just as responsible as her brother for the desolation which now lay upon the land of Egypt. She had enjoyed great power, more so than any previous Ptolemaic queen, but although greatly provoked by her younger brother she had abused that power in her search for total authority. Her brief taste of absolute rule in 145 BC and her obsessive desire to have a child of her own on the throne had led her to embark on a destructive war which she could never hope to win.

All her sons were now dead of natural causes or murdered. Yet Cleopatra II had the final satisfaction of surviving long enough to see her brother predecease her. Ptolemy VIII died on 28 June 116 BC, leaving the kingdom to his niece Cleopatra III to rule over with whichever of her two sons she should choose. Her choice fell on the elder, Ptolemy IX Soter II, but Cleopatra II was still alive and demanded to be accommodated. The last reference we have to her is in a demotic text of 29 October 116 BC which refers to 'Year 2 of the queen Cleopatra and the queen Cleopatra and pharaoh Ptolemy her son, the mother loving, the saviour'.[26] After that she disappears and the assumption is that she died soon afterwards, probably of old age. She had had 57 years of almost unbroken rule as queen of Egypt, a record equalled by few monarchs before or since.

10

CLEOPATRA II, CLEOPATRA III, AND PTOLEMY VIII

When Ptolemy VIII and Cleopatra II died within a few months of each other in 116 BC it left Cleopatra II's daughter Cleopatra III virtually in charge of the country. The terms of Ptolemy VIII's will were that she had the right to choose whichever of their two sons Ptolemy IX (later Ptolemy IX Soter II) or Ptolemy X (later Ptolemy X Alexander I) she wished to have associated with her in the kingship. The other stipulation was that his first-born son Ptolemy Apion, the illegitimate child of his concubine Eirene, should have the five Greek cities of Cyrenaica to rule as a separate kingdom. Intentionally or not, by laying down these conditions Ptolemy VIII set his kingdom on a downhill course from which it would never recover. There were two outcomes assured by his will, as certainly as if they had been foretold by a god in a Greek tragedy.

First, the establishment of Cyrenaica as a separate kingdom paved the way for the final break-up in the first century BC of the remnants of what had once been a powerful and wealthy empire. Rather than allow it to revert to the control of Egypt and its then king, his obscenely gross and grossly obscene half-brother Ptolemy X, in 96 BC Ptolemy Apion instead chose to bequeath his mini-kingdom with its lucrative monopoly of the silphium trade to the Roman people. Meanwhile that other important Ptolemaic possession, the island of Cyprus, would also function henceforth as a virtually autonomous state as first one Ptolemaic pretender and then another took refuge there, declaring himself its king against the day of his hoped-for return to Alexandria. In 80 BC it too would be bequeathed to the Romans under a will allegedly made by Ptolemy XI Alexander II, the puppet-king briefly set up in Alexandria by the dictator Sulla.[1] The island would finally become a Roman province in 58 BC. Its last king, Ptolemy IX's younger son, chose to commit suicide rather than lose his royal title.

Second, the provision made by Ptolemy VIII that Cleopatra III might choose either of her two sons to reign alongside her guaranteed that Egypt would once again be racked with discord as she obstinately struggled to assert her own will against that of her children and against the Alexandrians, who in their preference first for one king and then the other remained as unpredictable as they had ever been back in the days of Ptolemy VI and Ptolemy VIII. Although she would never have the need to declare herself sole ruler of the country as her mother had done in 132/1 BC, Cleopatra III was without any doubt the dominant figure in the royal house throughout the final years of her life, until she finally pushed her second son too far and he murdered her (101 BC). Her importance in what we know of the events of these years is confirmed by her place in the royal titulature. There she always takes pride of place before whichever of her 'mother loving' sons had the dubious privilege of being associated with her at the time.

How had Cleopatra III managed to get herself into a position of such prestige? Part of the answer must be that she took over the mantle of authority which her mother had put together so carefully over so many years while she was following her own political agenda. Part of it must be that, although she was used by Ptolemy VIII as one of his main weapons in his propaganda war against Cleopatra II, she succeeded in dissociating herself in the public mind from her uncle's cruelties and excesses. She was thereby able to build up a basis of popular support in her own right. Part of it was her shrewd use of religious titulature as she associated herself ever more closely with the great goddess Isis until the two of them eventually became one.

In 116 BC Cleopatra III was in her early forties. She already had some 25 years' experience of palace intrigue and political infighting to draw upon. So she could be said to have been at the height of her powers when opportunity came her way. We should therefore not be surprised at the intensity of her desire for power when she found herself free at last from the strait-jacket of the triple rule with her mother and her uncle and stepped into the sunlight in her own right. Her 'passion for sovereignty and grandeur', as Grace Macurdy put it,[2] is not hard to understand. What is more difficult is to pinpoint its origins and track its growth. To do this it is necessary to return in time to Cleopatra III's girlhood and the enforced induction which her uncle had given her into dynastic affairs.

If we can believe Justin's (38.8) account of it, soon after Ptolemy VIII's return from Cyrene and seizure of power in 145 BC he forced himself upon her although she was still only a young girl and then took her as his wife, repudiating his marriage to her mother Cleopatra II. All this is heady stuff, particularly in the light of Justin's subsequent pen portrait of the king as an overweight and ugly manikin who had already murdered her younger brother Ptolemy VII only minutes before climbing into bed with her mother. Consequently the tendency in the past was to represent Cleopatra III, who at that time must have been somewhere between 12 and 17 years old, in a highly sympathetic light. She was seen as very much an unwilling and innocent participant in the ghastly *ménage à trois* which Ptolemy VIII subsequently set up.[3] She was a victim not only of her uncle's abominable lust but also of his cruel determination to find a way of wounding her mother as deeply as he could.

As we have already seen, the sequence of events was not quite as simple and straightforward as Justin implies. More recently, too, there has arisen a sneaking suspicion that Cleopatra III may not have played quite such a passive role in the initiation of the relationship.[4] If we put her birthdate nearer to 160 than 155 BC, then at the time of the 'rape' she was nearer to 17 than 12.[5] That is, in the context of a society in which girls were regularly married at an early age, she could certainly be regarded as already mature enough and probably ambitious enough to see the advantages in submitting to her uncle. Those advantages began to accrue in a very short time, culminating in her marriage to Ptolemy VIII probably in late 141 or early 140 BC after her success in bearing a boy child to the king.

In the light of the revised chronology outlined in the previous chapter, which puts the birth of their son Ptolemy IX before Cleopatra III's marriage to her uncle, we can see that many of the honours which she gained in this early period were connected with her production of a son and heir rather than with her marriage. The first advance in status which we see her achieving as a result of her fruitful liaison with the king is the acquisition of a religious cult of her own. This put her on an equal footing with her mother, who had been an object of devotion since her first marriage to

Ptolemy VI in 172/1 BC. Thus we find the existence of a 'priestess of Cleopatra daughter of the king' as well as a 'priestess of queen Cleopatra' in Thebes from 142/1 BC.[6] Although she was not yet termed queen, we also find that at about the same time Ptolemy VIII extended his title Euergetes to her, making her 'Cleopatra the beneficent one'.[7]

Whether she acquired this title before or after Ptolemy IX's birth, there is no doubt that Ptolemy VIII's acknowledgement of the child and the recognition by the native priesthoods that the baby was 'distinguished in his birth together with that of the living Apis' brought further prestige. The most natural interpretation of the native title accorded the infant Ptolemy IX is that the king's son (as he now was officially) had been born on the same day as the new Apis bull, that is, on 18 February 142 BC.[8] The religious significance of the Apis was that the animal was believed to be an embodiment of the ancient Egyptian creator god Ptah. Since Ptah was also the patron god of Memphis, the second city of the land after Alexandria and the royal capital and coronation site of pharaonic Egypt, there was always a close link between the cults of Ptah, the Apis bull, and the Ptolemaic royal family. Any ruler who needed to assure himself of the backing of the native population, as Ptolemy VIII now did, would take especial pains to emphasise his connections with the Apis cult.

Although there was only ever one Apis at a time, an Apis bull might be born anywhere in Egypt. Just as on the death of the Dalai Lama his Tibetan followers scour the land to discover his reincarnation in a child with certain physical characteristics, so the death of an Apis bull led to a systematic search throughout Egypt until his successor was found reincarnated in a specially marked black and white bull calf.[9] On this occasion, as we know from the hieroglyphic and demotic inscriptions associated with the burial vaults of the Apis bulls at Saqqara, Ptah chose to reincarnate himself in his Apis form within his own high temple at Memphis.[10] Not only was this extremely convenient, but it was also probably regarded as particularly auspicious. If that is the case, the reincarnation would have given added lustre to the royal birth which coincided with it and brought added honour to the child's mother.

Cleopatra III might not yet be Isis in her aspect as the royal consort. That would follow later when Ptolemy VIII married her. But there were already two ways in which the girl and the goddess could be equated. Since she had given birth to the king's child,

Cleopatra III was now Isis 'the mother of the god', that is, the Horus child who would succeed in time to the kingship. And since the child shared the same birthday as the Apis bull, she was also the goddess in her manifestation as the 'Isis cow', the mother-of-Apis whose cult stood alongside that of Apis at Saqqara.

What part Cleopatra III herself played in acquiring these different honours we do not know. But knowing what we do of her blatant self-promotion as Isis in later years, it is difficult to regard her as altogether an unwitting pawn in the struggle between her uncle and her mother for the throne of Egypt. On the other hand, it is equally difficult to imagine that she could already have been sophisticated enough to have thought up a strategic plan of her own to wrest control of the country from her mother. So to suggest that she was 'fighting her way to the throne through her uncle's bed'[11] is to make her too manipulative, a sinister and exploitative Lolita with Ptolemy VIII an undersized and overweight Humbert Humbert bumbling along behind her. On the other hand, to picture her as a complete innocent turned against her own mother by the lustful ways of her wicked uncle is probably also somewhat wide of the mark.

Cleopatra III's acquisition of honours in this early period culminated in her formal marriage to Ptolemy VIII and her official recognition as 'queen Cleopatra the wife'. This distinguished her from Cleopatra II who now became 'queen Cleopatra the sister' but both mother and daughter were now fully queens of Egypt. The marriage is probably to be dated to some time between May 141 and January 140 BC, a year or so after Ptolemy IX's birth.[12] Any estimate made of how far Cleopatra III herself might have foreseen or even planned such an outcome, and at what point before or during her affair with her uncle she might have decided the throne lay within her grasp, will inevitably affect our judgement of her relations with her mother during these years. While we can never know for sure what actually happened during this early period, we can nevertheless outline a possible scenario to help explain what little is known of events just prior to the outbreak of hostilities between Ptolemy VIII and Cleopatra II in 132/1 BC. It was at that time that Cleopatra III became the object of further cultic honour and was identified even more closely with Isis.

According to the traditional view of events at the Ptolemaic court in the 130s BC, the breakdown of law and order in Egypt and the eventual uprising of the population in support of Cleopatra

II was the result of the intense rivalry between mother and daughter which had been provoked by Ptolemy VIII's unprecedented act of marrying his niece and at the same time keeping Cleopatra II as his wife.[13] Ptolemy VIII's heavy-handed ways of governing are acknowledged as a contributory factor in the gradual shift in public sentiment from passive discontent to active rebellion, but it was the growing jealousy between Cleopatra II 'the sister' and Cleopatra III 'the wife' which is usually held to lie at the root of the problem. The struggle between them for control of the king's favour and, through him, of the land of Egypt is taken to be the key to explain everything.

My own view would be to put the emphasis elsewhere. I suggest that we should look for the cause of the civil strife in this period not in any sexually-based rivalry between the mother and her daughter as they vied with one another for ownership of the same husband. The primary rivalry and hence the root cause of the civil war was rather the deep seated antipathy which already existed between Cleopatra II and her younger brother Ptolemy VIII. That antagonism can be traced back over 30 years to the time when Ptolemy VIII had first driven out his elder brother, Cleopatra II's husband Ptolemy VI, and had then attempted to give his takeover legitimacy by obliging her to become associated in the kingship with him (164/3 BC).

Cleopatra II had again been forced by circumstances into a similar situation in 145 BC when Ptolemy VI's unexpected death in Syria had allowed Ptolemy VIII to return from Cyrene. But that time he had not merely obliged her to lend legitimacy to his position by agreeing to be associated with him in the royal titulature. He had also forced a marriage upon her and to clear the way for his own succession he had summarily disposed of her younger son Ptolemy VII, through whom Cleopatra II had confidently expected to rule Egypt in her own right. Had she not already realised it, that action must have made it abundantly clear to her that her brother had every intention of getting rid of her too as soon as he thought he could get away with it. All that stood between Cleopatra II and the assassin's knife was her personal popularity.

In the years immediately after her brother's return she therefore had to be constantly on her guard as he tried every means at his disposal to whittle away her bases of support to the point where he could dispose of her without fear of any repercussions. Thus the series of persecutions subsequently carried out by Ptolemy VIII were not the random acts of a brutal tyrant suspicious of all and incapable of discriminating between friend and foe, as our sources would have us believe. They were all part of a master plan aimed at isolating his sister by ridding himself of any whom he saw as sympathetic to her cause, be they the Jews, the elite among the Alexandrian Greeks, or the intelligentsia attached to the Library and the Museum. In short, the reason why civil war broke out in 132/1 BC was not because of any rivalry between Cleopatra II and Cleopatra III (although that is not to say that it did not exist). It was because Cleopatra II was mortally afraid of what her brother might do to her, given the chance. She also knew that, once their child Ptolemy Memphites came of an age to threaten his father's hold on the throne, then he might try to dispose of the boy just as he had done away with Ptolemy VII back in 145 BC. She had to act first to forestall him.

When she broke away from Ptolemy VIII and her daughter and set herself up as sole ruler late in 132 BC,[14] Cleopatra II took on a new cult title to mark the beginning of her autonomous reign. As well as initiating a new series of regnal years for herself, she began to call herself 'Cleopatra the mother loving goddess, the saviour' (Cleopatra Thea Philometor Soteira).[15] The new titulature not only stressed her divinity, but also proclaimed her solidarity with both her deceased brother Ptolemy VI Philometor and her mother Cleopatra I and with the founder of the dynasty, Ptolemy I Soter. We do not know whether this self-proclaimed titulature ever gained universal acceptance throughout Egypt for so far it has yet to be found in texts written in demotic. Nevertheless the claims which it made, that Cleopatra II stood as a goddess in her own right with special links to the dynasty's founder as well as to her immediate forebears, and that she and her son therefore represented the true line of succession, were serious enough that the opposition could not afford to overlook them.

Ptolemy VIII had already used Cleopatra III in several similar attempts to exploit the propaganda value which these cult titles obviously had for his subjects. As we have seen, before their marriage he had granted her a share in his own cult title Euergetes so that even before she was officially recognised as queen she was termed 'Cleopatra the beneficent one' in the demotic texts. Then at the time of the marriage she had been made one of the 'beneficent gods' (Theoi Euergetae), who now became a threesome instead of a pair as a result of Cleopatra II's reluctance to go gracefully. Finally, as well as her place in this collectivity, we find her promoted a few years later as 'Cleopatra the wife, the beneficent goddess' (Thea Euergetis)[16] in a formula which appears to emphasise the unique and individual nature of her divinity. Meanwhile Ptolemy VIII had given their second son (born c. 140 BC or later) the name Ptolemy Alexander in what seems to have been an effort to link himself and his younger wife not just with any old Ptolemy of earlier times but with the deified Alexander the Great himself. It was Alexander's name which took pride of place in the titulature of the Ptolemaic dynastic cult in Alexandria and the titles and names of the cult's officiants, who each served for a year, often appear in documentary texts alongside the regnal year of the king.[17]

Once Cleopatra II had established her independent rule under a new religious banner, it did not take Ptolemy VIII long to think up a new title for Cleopatra III which made even more extravagant claims for the junior queen's divinity. In 131 BC the royal couple and their five children were in temporary exile in Cyprus where they had been forced to take refuge after the Alexandrians had risen up and driven them from the city. It was probably while they were on the island that a remarkable new form of worship was first instituted for Cleopatra III within the context of the dynastic cult. Designed to promote her person as of far greater sanctity than that of her mother the saviour goddess, the new cult sought to identify the queen directly with the goddess Isis. In a transparent attempt to use cultic terminology for self-advertisement, it is at that time that we first come across a priest in Alexandria who is known as 'the holy colt (*hieros polos*) of Isis Great Mother of the Gods'.[18]

The institution of the 'holy colt', so named perhaps from the youthfulness of the priest who held the office, meant that Cleopatra III alone among the royal women had the exceptional honour of a cult administered by a priest rather than a priestess, just as Isis herself had been ministered to by priests and not priestesses. Hitherto all Ptolemaic queens who had been the object of cult, including Cleopatra III herself in her Upper Egyptian cult as 'Cleopatra the daughter of the king', had made do with a priestess. Even more striking though than the grant of a personal cult in Alexandria to parallel her cult in Thebes or the decision to appoint a male rather than a female ministrant of the office is the complete identification of Cleopatra III and Isis which now took place. Although Cleopatra III had already been identified with the goddess in a limited number of important aspects, she was now presented to her adoring subjects as one with Isis in all of her diverse manifestations.

The omission of Cleopatra III's name from the titulature of the 'holy colt' is particularly significant. Except for Alexander the Great himself, all previous rulers of the Ptolemaic line had been received into the dynastic cult under their own names and titles with the addition of 'god' or 'goddess' to emphasise their divine nature. What they were therefore was the manifestation of the deity in a particular royal individual. Now for the first time one of them appeared directly as a goddess herself, without the title 'goddess' and without the inclusion of her own name. Other Ptolemaic queens – Berenice I (the last wife of Ptolemy I), Arsinoe II (the sister and second wife of Ptolemy II), Berenice II (the wife of Ptolemy III), and possibly Arsinoe III and Cleopatra I – had been identified as Isis. But they had always been known as 'Isis Mother of the Gods So-and-so'. The new cultic formula, unique to Cleopatra III, meant that at a single bound her divinised image was elevated far beyond that of her mother the rebel queen, or indeed that of any previous member of the Ptolemaic house.

Queen and goddess had become one. No longer was Cleopatra III merely Isis the mother of the god in her ancient Egyptian aspect as the consort of Osiris and mother of Horus. She now spread her benign influence to assimilate aspects of many other deities, both Egyptian and Greek, as Isis herself had been doing throughout the hellenistic period. As well as Isis the king's consort and mother of the divine heir, she was now also Isis in her aspect as a goddess of love, equated by the Greeks with Aphrodite. She was also Isis in her guise as Demeter, the goddess of fertility and justice, for Demeter's priest in Messenia on the Greek mainland had also borne the title 'colt'.[19] She was also Isis as Cybele for the title 'Great Mother of the Gods' served to identify her with the great Phrygian mother goddess. In short, Cleopatra III had become the epiphany of Isis in all her myriad forms and so she would remain for the rest of her reign. Despite attempts to attribute the same cult to her mother,[20] there is no evidence to connect 'the holy colt of Isis Great Mother of the Gods' with any other Ptolemaic queen. The last recorded example of the office occurs in 105/4 BC,[21] just a few years before Cleopatra III's murder. After her death no more is heard of it.

We have no idea how convinced her subjects were by this latest blatant attempt to present Cleopatra III in such a catch-all guise designed to appeal to every section of the community, Greek or Egyptian. Probably not very much, if we can judge from the apparently scurrilous nickname Kokke, meaning 'the scarlet one' or perhaps even 'cunt',[22] which the populace gave her or the high level of support which they continued to give to Cleopatra II. Even though Ptolemy VIII was able to return to Alexandria in 130 BC it took him another three years to win back the rest of the country. During that period the rest of the royal family may have stayed out of harm's way in Cyprus so that despite her divine status it may have been several years before the living goddess herself actually dared to set foot in the land where she claimed to be the chief female deity.

As was recounted in the preceding chapter, Ptolemy VIII and his sister eventually agreed to bury their differences and the joint rule of Ptolemy VIII, Cleopatra II, and Cleopatra III was re-established in 124 BC. Unfortunately nothing is known of the doings of Cleopatra III between this date and her emergence as the major figure on the political scene in 116 BC after the deaths of her uncle and her mother. All that can be said is that her new status as Isis incarnate seems to have cut very little ice at the negotiating table when terms were hammered out for the renewal of the tripartite rule. Despite every effort which had been made against her, Cleopatra II was successful in defending her pole position in the royal titulature. As long as the king was alive 'queen Cleopatra the sister' took precedence over 'queen Cleopatra the wife' in the official dating formula, and even for the few months in 116 BC when Cleopatra II ruled jointly with her daughter and grandson the protocol was 'queen Cleopatra (II) and queen Cleopatra (III) and her son king Ptolemy, the mother loving one, the saviour', with the older woman coming first.

When Cleopatra II died in the autumn of 116 BC it was probably from old age. After all she was nearly 70 years old and there is no evidence to support the suspicion that her daughter might have done away with her. Ironically her death left Cleopatra III in a similar position to that in which Cleopatra II had found herself back in 145 BC. She was capable of ruling in her own right and eager to do so. Yet she was obliged not only by the terms of her husband's will but also by public pressure to rule with and through another. But there was an immense difference in as much as her son Ptolemy IX was no mere lad as Ptolemy VII had been when he had briefly become king under the tutelage of his mother. Ptolemy IX was 26 or 27 years old by this time. As the first-born he should have succeeded to the kingship in the normal way, and he would have done so had it not been for Ptolemy VIII's will and his mother's obtuseness.

11

CLEOPATRA III AND HER CHILDREN

In 116 BC the kingship should have come to Ptolemy IX regardless of the fact that his mother was still alive. Why Ptolemy VIII chose to override the customary rule of succession by primogeniture and permitted Cleopatra III not only to remain as queen but also to take as co-ruler whichever of their two sons she wished can only be surmised. The usual assumption is that his decision was a result of the enormous pressure which she brought to bear upon the king during his last years in her passionate desire to continue and extend her own authority. Her actions immediately after Ptolemy VIII's death certainly lend support to this view.

Before his father died Ptolemy IX had been sent off to Cyprus as governor, to give him some experience of the responsibilities of power. While Cleopatra III may not have engineered the appointment to get him out of the way, she seized upon his absence as an opportunity to pass him over in favour of her younger son Ptolemy X whom she preferred, perhaps because she felt he would be more malleable than his brother. It was therefore Ptolemy X Alexander I who was her first choice as co-ruler, but the Alexandrians would not have him. Within a short time they compelled her to set him aside (116/5 BC) and take his elder brother in his place. So Ptolemy IX returned from Cyprus to become king with his mother as Ptolemy IX Philometor Soter II while his brother in turn went off to the island where he set up a court of his own and proclaimed himself king in 114/3 BC.

It is probably to this period when, much against her will, Cleopatra III was forced by popular pressure to depose her younger son and take the elder as her co-ruler that we can assign the next efflorescence of cult titles found associated with her name. From 115 BC there appear for the first time three eponymous priestesses of different aspects of Cleopatra III's divinity.[1] There was a 'crown-bearer' (*stephanophoros*), a 'torch-bearer' (*phosphoros*), and a priestess (*hiereia*) of 'queen Cleopatra the mother loving goddess, the saviour, mistress of justice, bringer of victory' (Cleopatra Thea Philometor Soteira Dikaiosyne Nikephoros).[2]

The sudden appearance of not one but three new personal cults of the queen looks suspiciously like religious overkill. Any reasonable person might suppose that the dual aspects of justice and victory were present already in Cleopatra III's identification as Isis which had been made some fifteen years previously with the institution of the 'holy colt of Isis Great Mother of the Gods'. Why go to all this trouble to make her association with justice and victory yet more explicit? One explanation might be that, although they also occur in a demotic form, these new titles were aimed primarily at the Greek section of the population, particularly the Alexandrians who still obstinately refused to recognise what a paragon they had in their midst and persisted in trying to thwart her divine will. Another might be that the new offices just happened to give Cleopatra III precedence over all previous queens who were the object of individual cult, just as earlier the priesthood of the 'holy colt' had given her precedence over the cult of her mother Cleopatra II, who was served only by a priestess.

In addition to the royal priest for the cult of Alexander the Great and all past Ptolemaic rulers and Cleopatra III's own 'holy colt', there were at this time three eponymous priestesses in Alexandria. The 'basket-bearer' (*kanephoros*) of Arsinoe II Philadelphus, Ptolemy II's deified sister–wife, is attested from 267/6 BC, a few years after her death (270 BC). She was now outranked by Cleopatra III's 'torch-bearer'. In 211 BC Arsinoe's 'basket-bearer' had been joined by another annual priestess, the 'victory-bearer' (*athlophoros*) of Berenice II Euergetis, when in a belated act of filial piety Ptolemy IV had established a cult for his mother, whom he had poisoned some years before. The *athlophoros* now yielded place to the 'crown-bearer' of Cleopatra III. Finally, Cleopatra III's new priestess took precedence over the last of the pre-existing offices, the priestess of Arsinoe III Philopator, the deified wife of Ptolemy IV, whose cult had been established in 199 BC. The queen was therefore pre-eminent at last in all parts of the dynastic cult. In this aspect of religious life she dominated everything and everyone, as she expected to dominate everything and everyone in the political sphere.

It will be noted that these women were all priestesses of Cleopatra 'the mother loving saviour'. After her mother's death Cleopatra III ceased to call herself 'the beneficent one' (Euergetis), the title which she had had from Ptolemy VIII and which she had used throughout her marriage to him. Instead she assumed the titles which Cleopatra II had taken when she had made her bid for sole power in late 132 BC. Furthermore, her son Ptolemy IX also became 'the mother loving god' as well as 'the saviour' (Soter) on his association with her, and the pair of them together sometimes took the title of 'the mother loving saviour gods'. What we seem to have in this is an attempt by Cleopatra III to take over her mother's political constituency and distance herself completely from Ptolemy VIII and his excesses, while simultaneously presenting an image of unbroken dynastic continuity.

In the event the epithet Philometor (Mother loving) would turn out to have rather a hollow ring to it. Despite strenuous expressions to the contrary, there was as little family feeling between mother and son as there had been earlier between mother and grandmother. In fact when he mentions the statues of the Ptolemies which he had seen outside the Odeon in Athens on his visit to the city, the second-century antiquarian Pausanias says that Ptolemy IX was given the surname Philometor 'in a spirit of ironic mockery. For we know of no king hated to such an extent by his mother' (Pausanias 1.9.1).

While this may be an exaggeration, there was certainly no love lost between Cleopatra III and Ptolemy IX after he was foisted on her as king and she wasted no time in trying to bend him to her will. One of her first acts was to compel him to set aside his sister–wife Cleopatra IV and marry his younger sister Cleopatra Selene instead. Justin (39.3.2) may well be right to imply that this was a precondition of his acceptance into the joint rule, but we do not have to believe that the fact that Cleopatra IV was 'very dear to him' necessarily influenced Cleopatra III's decision to separate them. Her action was dictated by prudence, not by spite. As her later history shows, Cleopatra IV was just as spirited as her mother and grandmother. Had Cleopatra III left her alone, it is highly likely that sooner or later she would have egged her brother on to arrange their mother's expulsion, or even her death, so that she could be queen in her own right.

As it was, immediately after the divorce Cleopatra IV made for Cyprus where she raised an army with the initial intention, it seems, of returning in force to Egypt. Whether or not the exiled Ptolemy X, who was then governor of Cyprus, was privy to any of her plans is unknown. It used to be thought that she may have offered to marry him, for such an alliance could have paved the way for their eventual return together to Alexandria where they might have been able to depose Ptolemy IX and Cleopatra III and set themselves up as Egypt's rulers. Unfortunately there is no evidence to support such a hypothesis and in the event Cleopatra IV took another tack. Hoping either to engineer her return to Alexandria via Antioch or to avenge herself on her mother by thwarting Cleopatra III's dynastic schemes to get control of Syria, she now took her army off to Syria.

There she offered herself and her soldiers to the Seleucid king Antiochus IX Cyzicenus. Since c. 121 BC Cyzicenus had been locked in a struggle for control of the dynasty with his half-brother Antiochus VIII Grypus. Both of them were the children of Cleopatra III's sister Cleopatra Thea. Since Grypus' queen Tryphaena was also Cleopatra IV's sister, what had previously been a war between brothers now took on an extra dimension of nastiness as the two sisters locked horns over the pitiful scraps of the once mighty Seleucid empire. With the welcome assistance of his new wife, Cyzicenus succeeded in regaining the throne for a brief time in 114/3 BC. But Grypus got back the next year and Cleopatra IV, who had been left in charge in the palace while Cyzicenus went out on campaign, found herself trapped in Antioch.

When the city fell she managed to get away and take refuge at Apollo's sanctuary at Daphne. Grypus was all for sparing her but the more he pleaded with Tryphaena to allow her to live the more suspicious his wife became, fearful that he had some ulterior motive for wanting her kept alive. Finally Tryphaena took over and ordered the troops to drag her from the sanctuary. Cleopatra IV's hands were hacked off as she clung to the cult statue and she died cursing her sister. Only a year later her curses would be fulfilled when Tryphaena in turn was captured by Cyzicenus, who sacrificed her to the shade of his dead wife (Justin 39.3.5–12).

Cleopatra III's directive to Ptolemy IX to put his original sister–wife aside and take Cleopatra Selene in her stead had only served to aggravate the ill feeling which already lay between them. He wanted to rule on his own. So did she or, failing that, she wanted his more tractable brother Ptolemy X as her co-ruler. Not surprisingly therefore we like to think that we can catch the occasional glimpse of them trying to undermine each other during these years. Thus while it is certain that in 107 BC Cleopatra III was finally successful in ousting her elder son and reinstating Ptolemy X as king alongside her, it has also been argued that she may have managed to bring him back, albeit briefly, on at least two earlier occasions.[3] Given her determined character it is not hard to believe that there may have been several abortive attempts before she succeeded in getting rid of Ptolemy IX, but the evidence of the different dating formulas in contemporary documents is regrettably quite ambiguous. All the texts in question can be dated just as convincingly to the time of the known expulsion in 107 BC.[4] It is perhaps safer therefore to stick with the notion of a single successful act of expulsion, particularly as the literary sources (such as they are) are silent about any earlier attempt to expel Ptolemy IX.

When Cleopatra III did make her move, it was brilliantly planned and ruthlessly executed. What she did shows a woman who would stop at nothing to get her own way. In front of the Alexandrian mob she openly accused her son of plotting to kill her. To back up her tale she had deliberately wounded a number of her palace eunuchs beforehand and she paraded them before the crowd in their bloody and battered state, claiming that their wounds had been sustained in defending her against Ptolemy IX. The hysterical mob rushed at the king and he barely escaped with his life (Pausanias 1.9.2). Clearly Cleopatra III had hoped to see him torn to pieces but Ptolemy IX proved too quick for her. Meanwhile Ptolemy X, who had already left Cyprus, was waiting at Pelusium on Egypt's borders for the summons to Alexandria. As he set off for the city, his elder brother in his turn took ship for Cyprus.

Cleopatra III hoped that her association of her younger son with her as co-regent would lead to a reamalgamation of Egypt and Cyprus into a single kingdom and so henceforth all official documents were given a double date, beginning with her Year 11 and Ptolemy X's Year 8, since it was now the eighth year since he had proclaimed himself king of the island (114/3 BC). To celebrate the inauguration of their joint reign towards the end of October 107 BC and symbolise the recovery of the island which had been the birthplace of the goddess Aphrodite, Cleopatra III also took on yet another religious title. For the first time in 107/6 BC we find an Alexandrian priestess 'of queen Cleopatra, the goddess Aphrodite, who is also the mother loving one'.[5] At the same time, in what must be an attempt by the queen to play down any association with the disgraced fugitive Ptolemy IX Soter (Saviour) II, the 'saviour' element was tacitly dropped from the titulature of her three eponymous priestesses. In a return to her earlier sobriquet as 'the beneficent goddess' (Thea Euergetis) they now became the 'crown-bearer', the 'torch-bearer', and the priestess of 'queen Cleopatra the beneficent goddess who is also the mother loving one, mistress of justice, bringer of victory'.[6] Like the return of the mini-skirt, which the world of fashion revives every ten years or so, it had taken only a decade since the death of Ptolemy VIII Euergetes for the title 'beneficent' to become respectable once more.[7]

Unfortunately Cleopatra III's hopes for Cyprus proved misplaced. In her haste to get rid of Ptolemy IX she had taken no account of the possibility that he might escape with his life. Ptolemy IX seems to have been well liked during his governorship of Cyprus before he first became king and once he got back to the island he soon won the local garrison over to his cause. The queen despatched an army to winkle him out and bring him back alive, but he eluded his pursuers and continued his flight to Seleucia-in-Pieria on the mainland. Cleopatra III was furious and the general in charge of the Egyptian army is said to have been executed for his failure to capture the fugitive. Eventually Ptolemy IX would return to the island, recapturing it in 106/5 BC.[8] Cleopatra III had not seen the last of him by any means.

Early in 103 BC the feud between mother and elder son erupted once more and spilled over into Syria as Ptolemy IX, now king of Cyprus, attempted to get back to Egypt via Coele Syria. By that stage the Seleucid kingdom had entered on its final period of disintegration, being split between the two half-brothers and cousins Antiochus VIII Grypus and Antiochus IX Cyzicenus, who both claimed to be its rightful king. After a period of struggle (112–108 BC) Grypus had almost completely re-established himself and controlled Cilicia and most of Syria, but Cyzicenus still kept a tenuous hold upon the coastal region and parts of Coele Syria. Their division of the country had allowed most of the southern part of Coele Syria and Palestine, over which earlier Ptolemaic and Seleucid kings had spilt so much blood, to fall under the control of the newly emergent Hasmonaean kingdom of Judaea under the leadership successively of John Hyrcanus I, Aristoboulos I and Alexander Jannaeus (Jonathan). It was only with great difficulty that the free Greek cities on the coast were able to maintain their independence in the face of a confident and resurgent Jewish state eager to expand wherever the domestic squabbles of Grypus and Cyzicenus presented an opportunity.

Ptolemy IX was already on friendly terms with Cyzicenus. While he was still king of Egypt he had sent 6,000 Egyptian troops to aid Cyzicenus in his tussle with John Hyrcanus over possession of the city of Samaria (c. 108 BC). Cleopatra III, who had inherited the Jewish loyalties so assiduously cultivated by her mother, had objected most strenuously and 'just about threw him out of the kingdom when she heard about it' (Josephus, *Jewish Ant.* 13.278). Indeed it may have been her anger at Ptolemy IX's interference which hardened her resolve to move against him the next year. None the less Ptolemy IX's action stood him in good stead for it was no doubt thanks to the favour which Cyzicenus owed him as a result that he was able to take refuge at Seleucia-in-Pieria in 106 BC after he had been chased out of Cyprus.

In 104 BC, soon after becoming king, the Jewish leader Jannaeus took advantage of a resumption of hostilities between Grypus and Cyzicenus to attack another of the independent Greek cities, Ptolemais (modern Acre) on the Phoenician coast. With no prospect of help from either Seleucid king, its citizens appealed for aid to Ptolemy IX. Seeing an opportunity to win the support not only of Ptolemais but also of several of the neighbouring cities which were still independent, Ptolemy IX quickly crossed from Cyprus with a large army said to have numbered some 30,000 in all (Josephus, *Jewish Ant.* 13.333).

When he landed, however, he found that the people of Ptolemais had changed their minds. Even so Alexander Jannaeus was overawed enough to raise his siege of the city and withdraw his army. Preferring to try trickery instead, he opened friendly negotiations with Ptolemy IX but also sent a secret mission to Cleopatra III to propose a joint attack on him. When he discovered Jannaeus' treachery Ptolemy IX was outraged. Breaking off his agreement he attacked Ptolemais himself and, having left part of his army to carry on the siege, he set off southwards with the rest, determined to invade Judaea and punish Jannaeus for his deceit.

All this took place in the first months of 103 BC and a small group of papyri from Pathyris in Upper Egypt, together with three inscriptions written in demotic, Greek, and hieroglyphs respectively, give some tantalising glimpses of how Cleopatra III responded to what was both an alarming emergency and at the same time a marvellous opportunity. The earliest document shows Egyptian troops being mobilised in Upper Egypt in late June 103 BC,[9] but before she despatched a land and sea force to block Ptolemy IX's southward advance from Judaea (where he had already defeated Jannaeus in a pitched battle) Cleopatra III opened an offensive on the diplomatic front.

So far the Seleucid kings Grypus and Cyzicenus had cancelled each other out and neither had entered the fray. In the event neither would do so but Cleopatra III was not to know that. Given Ptolemy IX's initial success against Jannaeus and his previous record of friendship with Cyzicenus, the queen felt that if he combined with his former ally he might prove more than she could handle militarily. So she secured Grypus' support by offering him another dynastic alliance. Grypus, it will be remembered, had already been her son-in-law once before through his marriage to her eldest daughter Tryphaena. That alliance had ended tragically in 111 BC when Cyzicenus had executed her in revenge for her butchery of his wife (and her own sister) Cleopatra IV. Cleopatra III offered to provide a replacement. With the Alexandrian mob baying for his blood, Ptolemy IX had had to make such a hasty departure from the city in 107 BC that he had left his second sister–wife Cleopatra Selene and their two children behind. It was Cleopatra Selene who was now packed off to Syria to take Tryphaena's place as the spouse of Grypus and so ensure his support, or at least his neutrality, in the coming conflict.

At the same time Cleopatra III despatched much of her treasure, her last will and testament, and her grandsons (by both her sons) to the sanctuary of the healing god Asclepius on the island of Cos. These preparations show both the extent of the danger which the queen felt threatened her as Ptolemy IX moved inexorably southwards towards the frontier zone of Gaza and the depth of her resolve to win her way through. She was determined to meet the threat head on, rather than meekly waiting for Ptolemy IX to come to her.

The decks were now cleared for action. The Ptolemaic army, led by Cleopatra III's Jewish generals Chelkias and Ananias, sons of the Onias whom her mother had welcomed to Egypt so many years ago, began its advance across the Sinai. At the same time her co-ruler Ptolemy X set sail with a naval force for Phoenicia. Their intention was to meet up at Ptolemais and invest the city. The third of the papyrus letters found at Pathyris was sent from there on 27 September 103 BC, by which time the combined forces had apparently succeeded in their mission. The widespread and total destruction of the site which has been uncovered by modern archaeologists and ascribed to this period fleshes out Josephus' bare reference to their successful siege of the city.[10]

Cleopatra III's swift and decisive action at once turned the tide of battle firmly in her favour. Ptolemy IX tried to make a dash for Egypt, hoping to find it undefended, but it would be too little too late. His brother had time to double back and by the time that Ptolemy IX had passed through Sinai he found Ptolemy X and his army waiting to meet him at Pelusium. He was forced to fall back to Gaza where he spent the winter of 103/2 BC while Ptolemy X remained guarding the approaches to Egypt against any further offensive. But Ptolemy IX would not try again. The following year he returned to Cyprus while he still had the chance to do so. He realised that, had he lingered, his escape route would have been cut off now that Cleopatra III controlled the few harbours on the Phoenician coast and the island itself could have been raised in revolt against him. His campaign, which had started out so splendidly, had ended in less than a whimper. Ptolemy IX would not return to Egypt until after his brother's death (89/8 BC) and, as far as we know, he would make no further attempt in the intervening years to win back his throne.

There is a hint that, for just a moment after their success in taking Ptolemais, the Egyptians might have dreamt of trying to win back the whole of Coele Syria once more. Lines 18–24 of the demotic papyrus from Pathyris mentioned above read:

> I am sending you this letter on the high ground [?][11] of Ptolemais. The king has gone to Damascus. He left one company of army men [?] in the town.[12]

Despite the difficulties in the text, the king in question can only be Ptolemy X and it seems that by late September 103 BC when the letter was sent he had divided up his forces. One group stayed at Ptolemais, either to continue the siege or to garrison the newly captured town. The other group set off with Ptolemy X for Damascus, which lay about 100 km north and 100 km inland.

What was the reason for Ptolemy X's journey? Presumably it was something more than a desire to shake his new brother-in-law Grypus by the hand and see how his sister Cleopatra Selene had settled into her new home. Indeed we do not even know who was in possession of Damascus at this time. Ptolemy X may have been going there to Grypus' assistance, or his intention may have been to wrest control of the city from Cyzicenus and occupy it himself. Had he succeeded in doing so, then Cleopatra III and Ptolemy X would have been well on the way to a complete Ptolemaic reconquest of Coele Syria. They already held Ptolemais and the southern coastline. With Damascus in their power too, they would have been able to push southwards and encircle Ptolemy IX and his forces in a pincer movement, cutting off his line of retreat either along the coast or up the Jordan valley. They would also have been able to corner Alexander Jannaeus, who had already been weakened by his defeat by Ptolemy IX, and proceed to a leisurely conquest of Judaea. They now knew that neither Seleucid king would interfere. Grypus had been bought off with the marriage to Cleopatra Selene and Cyzicenus had sensibly kept well out of it as the opposing Ptolemaic armies rampaged through his former domains.

According to Josephus (*Jewish Ant.* 13.353–5) some of Cleopatra III's advisers actually suggested just such a course of action as this when, soon after Ptolemais had been taken, Jannaeus approached her seeking an alliance. But Ananias, one of her Jewish generals, counselled against it on the grounds that an attack on Jannaeus, who was already perceived as an ally, would turn the whole Jewish people against her and Cleopatra III heeded his wise advice. By that time too, of course, the moment had been lost. Ptolemy IX had begun his race for the Egyptian border, hoping to find the country undefended, and Ptolemy X had been obliged to turn around, probably even before he reached Damascus, and hasten back to defend the frontier at Pelusium.

Cleopatra III therefore granted Jannaeus' request for an alliance. After her armies eventually withdrew, he would go on a miniature rampage of his own, marching down the coast and storming one city after another as far as Gaza. Meanwhile, however, the Egyptians continued to occupy Ptolemais. They were still there in September 102 BC, long after Ptolemy IX's return to Cyprus.[13] Ptolemy X too seems to have remained at Pelusium well after his brother's abortive invasion attempt. He probably did not return to Alexandria until winter 102 BC and even after his departure a strong garrison was kept at the border town for several months. The last of the texts from Pathyris, which was sent from Syria or the Delta, shows Egyptian soldiers still waiting there in early January 101 BC for a ship to take them home to Upper Egypt.[14]

So for Cleopatra III too this Syrian venture finally came to nothing. What if anything had she achieved by it? Remarkably little, to judge by the dismissive comments of some historians. Bevan wrote of 'her futile operations in Palestine', Macurdy of her return to Egypt 'without having accomplished anything against Cyzicenus, her hated ex-son-in-law, or Ptolemy Soter, her hated son'.[15] Yet these judgements are surely far too harsh. She had succeeded in defending Egypt's territorial integrity and her own place as its ruler against what was clearly a determined and well-organised effort by Ptolemy IX to force his way back into the kingdom. That defence had not been without its costs. Egypt's border had been briefly pierced and her general Chelkias met his death while pursuing Ptolemy IX's forces through Coele Syria (Josephus, *Jewish Ant.* 13.351). Furthermore, Cleopatra III had managed to keep a stake in Seleucid affairs by renewing her dynastic alliance with Grypus, who looked the better bet at the time as monarch of Syria. Then by letting Jannaeus have his head after the capture of Ptolemais she had ensured that Grypus' rival Cyzicenus would have enough to worry about for several years to come without giving any further assistance to her elder son.

As for winning back Coele Syria, that was surely a pipe dream at this stage in the dynasty's history. The presence in Cyprus of the once and future king (for after his recall Ptolemy IX would rule again until his death in 80 BC) meant that whoever was in charge of Egypt could undertake any overseas venture only at their utmost peril. No sooner had their troops left Alexandria than the exile's supporters would be out among the crowd, fomenting trouble and working towards their master's recall. And there were also the Romans to think about. Rome had had an alliance with Judaea since 161 BC[16] and Cleopatra III was doubtless well aware of that fact. She would have weighed both these factors and many more besides before arriving at the only sensible decision, which was to get out while she was ahead. Ptolemy IX might not be dead yet but at least he was back in Cyprus. That was the most important outcome from her point of view.

Whether Ptolemy X felt the same way is a moot point. The evidence of contemporary papyri proves beyond doubt that within a few months of the end of the Syrian campaign Cleopatra III was dead. The latest text bearing regnal years of both Cleopatra III and Ptolemy X is dated 14 October 101 BC. Next comes a year date by Ptolemy X and his 'sister'–wife Berenice III (actually his niece, the daughter of his exiled brother) in a text dated 26 October.[17] From then on Ptolemy X continued to reign with Berenice, or Cleopatra Berenice as she was now called after assuming the name which had become as much a dynastic name for the princesses and consorts of the royal house as Ptolemy was for the kings of the line.

Both texts come from Upper Egypt. As it always took some days for news of any dynastic change to make its way up the Nile, we can probably confidently say that Cleopatra III just made it into her Year 17 in September 101 BC. But how she died remains a mystery. She was not especially old, being not far off 60, so death from natural causes is by no means a foregone conclusion. In fact three of our ancient sources concur in agreeing that it was her own son who killed her because she had conspired against him earlier.[18] But they then add that, as a result of his act of matricide, the Alexandrians rose up against Ptolemy X, drove him out and recalled Ptolemy IX from Cyprus. Yet the royal titulature shows us that this did not happen until 89/8 BC. Is the whole tale therefore to be rejected? After all, the Alexandrians are hardly likely to have sat around quietly for twelve years waiting for their passions to become inflamed. Or can we accept one part of the story and not the other? Perhaps we can if we can see it in its context.

Suppose that there had been a drastic breakdown in relations between Cleopatra III and Ptolemy X as a result of the events in Coele Syria in 103–102 BC. In 103 BC for probably the first time in his life Ptolemy X found himself in personal command of a military force. It was probably only with reluctance that Cleopatra III let him become involved at all for Josephus implies that he was summoned to Phoenicia with the Egyptian navy only after she herself had already departed for Syria (*Jewish Ant.* 13.348–50). Yet desperate times demanded desperate measures and he had got his command. Then, almost as soon as he landed, he had tasted success. The city of Ptolemais had already successfully resisted sieges by Alexander Jannaeus and then Ptolemy IX but it quickly fell before the combined naval and land forces of Cleopatra III and Ptolemy X. All at once the way lay open, or so it must have seemed, not only to get rid of Ptolemy IX but also to regain Coele Syria.

With the scent of victory still fresh in his nostrils, Ptolemy X had set off immediately for Damascus with an expedition of his very own. There was no mother and no canny Jewish general looking over his shoulder any longer and telling him what to do. If the Egyptians could take Damascus as well as the coast, they could split the Seleucid kingdom and isolate Coele Syria. All that would then be needed would be a gradual push southwards to corner Ptolemy IX and to mop up the Jews, who had already been softened up by their defeat by Ptolemy IX. But Ptolemy X had not even reached Damascus before his brother's dash for Egypt meant that he was abruptly recalled and packed off with the fleet back to Pelusium to defend the frontier against possible invasion. There he would have to languish throughout the autumn and winter, forced back onto the defensive just as suddenly as he had been put on the attack.

Under the circumstances of course the defence of Egypt was a matter of the utmost importance but Ptolemy X, who was no strategist, could probably not see that. To him it may have seemed an arbitrary and inexplicable relegation to the bench just when he had begun a brilliant drive for the line. Meanwhile in Coele Syria Cleopatra III was apparently doing nothing. Instead of pressing home their advantage by pushing on to Judaea, she had listened to Ananias and, mindful of her Jewish supporters back home, had let Jannaeus off the hook. Ptolemy IX too had been allowed to escape scot-free and the two Seleucid kings had managed to stay aloof from the conflict and keep their power intact. And all the time Ptolemy X, the great warrior, the sacker of Ptolemais, was forced to sit idle in the grubby border town of Pelusium, utterly frustrated and powerless to do anything.

Ptolemy X's exasperation at the injustice of it all was no doubt aggravated by his unhappy memories of what had happened at court just before the Syrian expedition had set out. According to Justin (39.4.3) even before the expedition Ptolemy X's relationship with Cleopatra III had deteriorated to the extent that he had fled from Egypt for a time out of fear of her enmity towards him. Although Justin alone is hardly a reliable source for anything, his statement now seems to be confirmed, partially at least, by a contemporary papyrus (P.Köln II 81). All that survives is the document's prescript but that alone is enough to suggest that by 105/4 BC Cleopatra III may have been starting to move against her younger son and co-ruler.

From 116/5 BC onwards it had been customary for the king himself to act as priest of the dynastic cult honouring Alexander the Great and the earlier Ptolemies.[19] Ptolemy IX had served as the eponymous priest of Alexander for as long as he was king (116–108 BC) and after his expulsion we find Ptolemy X in the office in 107–105 BC. But in 105/4 BC he was no longer the Alexander priest. According to the papyrus (line 3) it was the queen, Cleopatra III, who was acting as the priest of Alexander. So she had contrived to establish a whole series of priesthoods for herself (including a 'lifetime priest' from 107 BC), which allowed her to outrank all previous Ptolemaic queens. She had a male, 'the holy colt', as ministrant of one of her cults whereas all other consorts had to make do with priestesses. Not only this; she had also now taken over the most prestigious male office in the dynastic cult for herself and thereby blocked Ptolemy X's access to this powerful position. Furthermore, the same text later seems to show Cleopatra III removing her son's supporters from other important priesthoods (including her own) in order to replace them with her own adherents.[20]

It may be too far-fetched to see this as a *coup* in the making. Yet it could certainly be construed as evidence for the 'secret plots' mentioned by Justin (39.4.5), and the recollection of his replacement as the Alexander priest would surely have added to Ptolemy X's sense of bitterness as he watched in dismay while his mother frittered away what seemed to him to be the military opportunity of a lifetime. No doubt too many of the army officers with him at Pelusium would have felt equally betrayed as Cleopatra III pussyfooted around with Jannaeus in her anxiety not to lose the loyalty of the Jewish communities of Egypt.

Ptolemy X knew all about her Jewish supporters just as he knew all about her ability to manipulate the Alexandrian mob or to use the priesthoods of the dynastic cult against him. But, by a lucky chance of fate, her uncharacteristic inertia after the sack of Ptolemais had opened up to him an alternative source of support which she had hitherto been careful to keep well closed off. In the aftermath of the Syrian campaign, when the Egyptian troops were at last returning home not in defeat but not in triumph either, Ptolemy X may well have felt that he had enough backing from sympathisers within the army to make a move against his mother before she tried another move against him. He could pitch an appeal to the Alexandrians as the conqueror of Ptolemais for with Chelkias dead there would be no one to contradict him. He could also point to his successful role in defending the homeland while Cleopatra III had dallied in Coele Syria and achieved nothing. He could have regained their lost dominions for them but she would not let him for fear of alienating her Jewish friends. The Alexandrian Greeks would love that. There is no shortage of ingredients here for a political campaign against Cleopatra III. Whether they also add up to a recipe for matricide is best left an open question.

However she met her death, there were probably few who really mourned the passing of Cleopatra III in autumn 101 BC, apart from the functionaries of her personal cults who now found themselves out of a job. For after Cleopatra III's death her priesthoods disappear from the official documents as swiftly and as surely as all trace of her mother Cleopatra II had disappeared from the record after 116 BC. But not all traces of her reign were suppressed as quickly and as easily. As late as the fourth century there were several Egyptian villages, as well as a town in Nubia, still called Cleopatra. They had probably been named after Cleopatra III rather than her mother or grandmother since the first attestation of them coincides with her reign.[21] The important provincial city of Oxyrhynchus in Middle Egypt also had a Street of Cleopatra Aphrodite which must have been named after her identification as Aphrodite in 107 BC.[22] It was probably the site of a temple dedicated to her worship as Aphrodite for there is also evidence of the existence of temples of Cleopatra in several other localities.[23]

While it is difficult to be sure which of the first three Cleopatras was responsible for their foundation, probability must again favour Cleopatra III in view of her incessant self-promotion as a divinity either in her own right or under the guises of Isis, Cybele, or Aphrodite. She is also more likely to have been their inspiration in as much as she reigned longer and, thanks to Ptolemy VIII's unusual will, had far more scope for the exercise of power than either her mother or her grandmother had. This is not to belittle their achievements for both Cleopatra I and Cleopatra II were undoubtedly better rulers than she ever was. What is more, they are both far more sympathetic personalities than Cleopatra III whose imperious nature (if we are to believe our sources) at last became so unbearable that her younger son was willing to go to any lengths, even matricide, to free himself from the stranglehold she had upon him.

Whether or not we accept the tale of Ptolemy X's matricide, there can be no doubt that during this period it was Cleopatra III who held the real power in the state. The many titles which she was accorded or in later life awarded herself were no empty honours acquired out of feminine vanity or a fascination with the trappings of power rather than its actual substance. They are a true reflection of the real status and political influence which she continued to amass throughout her lifetime and they preserve a record of the genuine awe and devotion which she apparently inspired in her followers. Although it may have been Ptolemy VIII who initially promoted her recognition in order to strengthen his own hand against her mother Cleopatra II, it is inconceivable that Cleopatra III would have continued to appear in these ever more splendid transformations, culminating finally in her total identification with Isis, had she not had enough popular support to sustain her chosen image.[24]

No other queen before her had even approached the status which Cleopatra III finally held in the dynastic cult of the Ptolemaic house. Unfortunately for us her true position in the later years of her life is obscured by the tangled grandiloquence of her Greek titulature, and not revealed as it would have been to her contemporaries. For once the Egyptian hieroglyphic titulature can tell us more. Some 80 km south of Thebes is the Ptolemaic temple of El Kab whose construction the queen began at the start of her joint reign with Ptolemy IX in 116 BC. While here as elsewhere the reliefs most usually show her in company with her son as co-ruler, in one unique example at El Kab she is depicted alone in an attitude of ritual, almost as if she were the sole ruler of Egypt.[25] Her titles, as they are given at El Kab, appear as 'the female Horus, wife of both countries [i.e. the Two Lands of Upper and Lower Egypt], mighty bull'.[26] Here at least, it seems, her will to power has lifted Cleopatra III far beyond the earthbound ties of gender and mortality to become both king and queen, both god and goddess. She has finally succeeded in uniting the masculine potency and invincibility of the god-king Horus with the cherishing femininity of Isis, the great goddess whose combined roles as sister, wife, queen, and mother she herself had duplicated on earth over the course of her long career.

This is the image of absolutism which these titles expressed for the native priests and it was this image which must have obsessed Cleopatra III herself during the final years of her life. But she failed at the last. It would be left to another greater monarch, Cleopatra VII, to revive her dream. As we know, the famous

Cleopatra would also call herself 'the new Isis' (Plutarch, *Antony* 54.9). She too would represent herself as the goddess Aphrodite when she came to Mark Antony at Tarsus in 41 BC. She too would be known to her native subjects as 'the female Horus'.[27] It was Cleopatra III who had provided her with her inspiration.

12

THE SELEUCID
CONNECTION (2)
Cleopatra Thea and her Husbands

By the time that she died or was done away with by her son Ptolemy X in 101 BC Cleopatra III had survived far longer than any other child of Ptolemy VI and Cleopatra II. Her elder brother Ptolemy Eupator who had been made co-regent with his father in 152 BC had died prematurely, perhaps of some congenital defect. Her younger brother, Ptolemy VII, had been assassinated by his uncle Ptolemy VIII when the latter returned from Cyrene and seized the throne in 145 BC. Her elder sister Cleopatra Thea, whose career we now consider, would become embroiled in the bitter feuding over possession of the throne of Seleucid Syria.[1] Although she would fare better than her nieces Cleopatra IV and Tryphaena in the next generation, she too would fall victim to the convulsions which racked the Seleucid house in the later stages of its history. And, like her sister, she too finally made the fatal mistake of standing in the way of one of her own sons for far too long.

Cleopatra Thea was the wife of three Seleucid kings in succession, Alexander Balas, Demetrius II Nicator, and Antiochus VII Sidetes, of whom only one turned out to be a good bet. In 150 BC she was little more than a girl of 14 or 15 when her father Ptolemy VI first took her with him to Ptolemais on the coast of Lebanon to marry her off to Balas, the pretender whom he had been promoting for the Seleucid throne. In fact it was thanks largely to the Egyptian king's funding and military assistance that Balas found himself victorious and in undisputed possession of the kingship. Just as half a century earlier her grandmother Cleopatra I 'the Syrian' had been betrothed to the boy-king Ptolemy V in order to establish a Seleucid presence in Egypt, in the same way Cleopatra Thea's dynastic marriage to Balas, celebrated at Ptolemais 'with great pomp as the manner of kings is' (1 Maccabees

10.51), formed a cornerstone of Ptolemy VI's grand plan to establish Egyptian dominance over the Seleucids and eventually regain control of Coele Syria.

To begin with, the Syrians were delighted to see the last of their former king. Demetrius I had passed his boyhood at Rome as a royal hostage for the Seleucids under the terms of the Peace of Apamea. The company he had kept there during his formative years with men of affairs like Scipio Aemilianus and Greek intellectuals like the historian Polybius and the Stoic philosopher Panaetius had bred in him a contempt for his fellow countrymen which he found difficult to conceal when he returned to Syria. This aloofness, coupled with an increasingly morose and surly manner (the result of alcoholism), did as little to endear him to his subjects as the over-ambitious schemes for the conquest of Cappadocia with which he tried to saddle them. Consequently they were happy at first to welcome their new monarch, the alleged son of Demetrius I's predecessor Antiochus IV Epiphanes to whom the handsome young man is said to have borne a remarkable likeness.

Their jubilation was short-lived. Demetrius I may have been too severe and withdrawn but Balas quickly proved far too easygoing. Before too long he was totally under the thumb of his mistresses and hangers-on at court and had surrendered the government to the corrupt and murderous whims of his minister Ammonius (whose name suggests that he may have been a Ptolemaic appointee). By 148/7 BC the backers of Demetrius I's son, who was also called Demetrius, decided that the time was ripe to try to win back the throne. Putting together a small army of Cretan soldiers of fortune, they made a landing in Cilicia and raised their standard.

Balas hurried northwards to confront them and forestall a revolt in Antioch but, almost as soon as he left Ptolemais, his governor of Coele Syria threw in his lot with Demetrius. The disaffection quickly spread and the kingdom's rapid descent into civil war prompted Ptolemy VI to invade in force. His entry into the country was ostensibly motivated by a need to bring aid to his vassal and son-in-law and protect his daughter Cleopatra Thea, who was still in the royal palace in Ptolemais. But soon after reaching Ptolemais his shaky alliance with Balas broke down in a spectacular fashion when Ptolemy VI claimed to have discovered an attempt on his life by Balas' minister Ammonius.

Ammonius fled to Antioch and when Balas resisted Ptolemy

VI's demands for his surrender the Egyptian king immediately renounced their alliance and threw his weight behind Demetrius. Although his daughter had already borne a child to Balas, Cleopatra Thea's marriage was annulled and her father handed her over forthwith to Demetrius 'as if she were a piece of furniture'.[2] Balas, who found himself completely isolated in the midst of the hostile population of Antioch, had no option but to abandon the city and seek refuge in the mountains of Cilicia. Before he fled, he sent Antiochus, his young son by Cleopatra Thea, away to Abae to the safekeeping of a friendly Arab chieftain. Meanwhile Ammonius too tried to escape from Antioch, dressed as a woman, but the Antiochenes recognised him and he was cut down (Josephus, *Jewish Ant.* 13.108).

By 145 BC Balas had gathered enough support to attempt a return. He descended into the plain of Antioch and began to lay it waste. The upshot of the battle which ensued has already been related.[3] Balas' forces were completely routed by the combined armies of Demetrius and Ptolemy VI and he was once more forced to flee, but in the subsequent mêlée Ptolemy VI was thrown from his horse when it took fright at the trumpeting of a battle elephant and he was set upon by Balas' mountain men. He was barely alive by the time he was rescued and five days later he died, but not before he had had the satisfaction of gazing upon Balas' severed head.

So perished Cleopatra Thea's first husband, assassinated by his own officers in return for a promise of free pardon from Demetrius. She was still only 20 years old. Meanwhile her new husband, the 14-year-old Demetrius, had been crowned king of Syria as Demetrius II Theos Nicator Philadelphus (God, conqueror, and brother loving). But without Ptolemy VI there to help him his hold on the kingship was far from secure. The Antiochenes had not liked his father and they did not like him any better. In fact, rather than have him as their king, they had initially offered the crown to Ptolemy VI and called upon him to rule as monarch of both Egypt and Asia. Ptolemy VI had demurred but he prevailed upon them to accept Demetrius only by promising that he would not allow his new son-in-law to purge those who had opposed his father Demetrius I or supported Balas. That worked for a while but after Ptolemy VI's death there was nothing to prevent the boy's foreign mercenaries from looting and murdering exactly as they pleased.

Matters came to a head when Demetrius II tried to follow the advice of his Cretan commander Lasthenes, who was by then his chief minister, to dismiss and disarm his native Syrian troops. Such an action would have left the city's population totally at the mercy of the mercenaries and the Antiochenes arose as one in armed rebellion when the Cretans attempted to use force to carry out the order. As the situation rapidly deteriorated and fighting spilled out into the streets, Demetrius II appealed to the Jewish leader Jonathan, who responded by sending 3,000 crack troops to Antioch to support him. By that time the hostile mob had the king barricaded in his palace and it would have been all up with him had the Jewish troops not been there. Although heavily outnumbered, they managed to rally and turn the tables on their attackers by taking to the rooftops and setting the city ablaze. In the panic which followed the Jews fell upon the terrified citizens and put them to the sword. According to the writer of 1 Maccabees (11.45–7), when they returned home, laden down with plunder, the Jews boasted of killing 100,000 of the people of Antioch.[4]

The suppression of the revolt was followed by a reign of terror. Any who were suspected of implication in the resistance were proscribed and had their property confiscated. Refugees streamed out of the city in every direction. All that they had left was their hatred of the king (Diodorus 33.4.3–4) and it was not long before their burning desire for revenge provided an ideal opportunity for one of Balas' former generals, a native soldier called Diodotus from Apamea in the military heartland of Syria, to grasp at the throne for himself. Diodotus' first move was to get hold of his former master's son Antiochus, then little more than an infant of 2 or 3 years old, and proclaim him king under the splendid title of Antiochus VI Theos Epiphanes Dionysus (The manifest god Dionysus).

With the native soldiery firmly behind them, Diodotus and Antiochus advanced in triumph on Antioch and Demetrius II was forced to flee before them (summer 144 BC). He would continue to hold the outermost regions of the Seleucid empire while Diodotus and Antiochus proceeded to occupy the greater part of mediterranean Syria. The Jewish leader Jonathan, who had previously helped Demetrius II against the rebel Antiochenes, also threw in his lot with them when Demetrius II reneged on an undertaking he had made to withdraw the Seleucid garrisons from Judaea and he and his brother Simon were made generals of the new king (1 Maccabees 11.54–9). But their subsequent successes and Jonathan's open policy of Jewish expansionism soon alarmed Diodotus so much that he captured Jonathan by treachery and later had him put to death (143/2 BC).

At about the same time he also disposed of his young protégé and had himself proclaimed king as Diodotus Tryphon (The Magnificent). He announced that the boy had an internal disorder which required an operation. When it proved fatal, the general belief was that it was Diodotus who had bribed the surgeons to ensure that he died under the knife. But he lost more than he gained by this underhand action. He had already alienated the Jews by his treacherous capture of Jonathan and without the boy-king as a focal point for their loyalties they soon went back to the cause of Demetrius II. When Simon sent envoys to renew his allegiance, Demetrius II reciprocated by confirming him in his privileges and at last fulfilled his undertaking to withdraw the Seleucid garrison from the citadel of Jerusalem. It was 25 years since Antiochus IV had first occupied Judaea but the Jewish people were finally free. The first year of the Hasmonaean era, 143/2 BC, marks the beginning of the independent Jewish state and the realisation at last of the dream which Judas Maccabaeus had had of an autonomous homeland for his people.

With Jewish support Demetrius II was now in a strong enough position to have crushed Diodotus. Yet instead of removing him when he had the chance, he allowed events in the East to distract his attention. The ongoing tussle for the kingship had encouraged the ambitious Parthian monarch Mithradates I to venture down from the Iranian plateau and expand westwards into lands previously held by the Syrians. In 141 BC he invaded Babylonia and occupied Seleucia-on-the-Tigris, the original Seleucid capital founded (c. 305 BC) by Seleucus I just south of modern Baghdad. Now 20 years old and with his head stuffed full of schemes every bit as grandiose as any his father had ever had, Demetrius II lost no time in responding to the appeals for aid which came flooding in from the Greek settlers in that part of his realm. Rather than concentrate upon disposing of the pretender, as he should have done, he turned eastwards. In his youthful optimism he apparently hoped not only to recover the lost provinces but also to raise new resources there to assist him in the fight against Diodotus.

By this stage Cleopatra Thea had borne Demetrius II three children – a daughter Laodice and two sons Seleucus (later Seleucus

V) and Antiochus (later Antiochus VIII). She and they were left at Seleucia-in-Pieria on the coast under the protection of the king's general Aeschrion while Demetrius II gathered his forces and set out for the East. At first all went well. Wherever he appeared there was a general rising in support of him and in a series of early victories he defeated Mithradates' generals and drove them back one by one. But his bold plans came to nothing. The following year he was defeated and captured (139 BC). His army melted away and Demetrius II himself was paraded in public through the cities which the Parthians had won, an object lesson to their Greek inhabitants of the futility of resistance (Justin 36.1.5–6). In time Mithradates had him conveyed to one of his favourite royal residences and, although he kept him under guard, he treated his royal captive with all the honour due to his rank, even giving him his own daughter Rhodogune as wife.[5]

By an unexpected twist of fate therefore Diodotus found himself king by default, but instead of capitalising on his opportunity by instituting a policy of reconciliation he succeeded only in antagonising those who had previously favoured him. At the same time the news of Demetrius II's capture by the Parthians had reached his younger brother Antiochus Sidetes, who was then in Rhodes. He quickly gathered together a fleet and a force of mercenaries with the intention of crossing to the mainland to continue the struggle against Diodotus. But Diodotus' hold upon the coastal cities was so strong that none of them dared to admit him. Finally, to secure her own position and ensure the continuation of Ptolemaic influence in Syrian affairs, Cleopatra Thea took matters into her own hands. She invited Antiochus to come to Seleucia-in-Pieria to marry her and accede to the kingship. According to Josephus (*Jewish Ant.* 13.222) her invitation was partly on the advice of her counsellors, partly out of fear that Seleucia itself might soon be betrayed to Diodotus. That would have meant expulsion or even death for her children, if not herself, and she had already invested too much time and effort in the Seleucid dynasty to allow that to happen.

Cleopatra Thea's third marriage, at the age of about 27 and again to a husband younger than she was,[6] took place in the spring of 138 BC along with Antiochus' coronation as Antiochus VII Euergetes. It did not take her new husband long to defeat Diodotus and drive him first out of Upper Syria and then out of Dora in Coele Syria. The pretender finally ended up in his home town of

Apamea where he was captured after a siege and constrained to commit suicide (late 138 BC).[7] Antiochus VII, who soon proved himself a much more practical ruler than his brother had been, was now able to set about the mammoth task of trying to restore some semblance of order to a country which by this stage had been racked by almost a decade of civil unrest.

One of his first undertakings was to bring the recently independent state of Judaea back into the Seleucid fold. An initial attempt made while he was still engaged in the pursuit of Diodotus had ended disastrously with the rout of his general Cendebaeus by Simon's sons (1 Maccabees 15.38–41, 16.1–10; Josephus, *Jewish Ant.* 13.225–7) but a later invasion by a strong army led by the king himself (135/4 BC) was more successful. After ravaging Judaea, Antiochus VII blockaded the Jewish leader John Hyrcanus in Jerusalem. There followed a lengthy siege, during which Antiochus VII acted with the utmost chivalry, before Hyrcanus finally surrendered on terms.

The walls of Jerusalem were to be demolished (Hyrcanus would have them rebuilt after his conqueror's death) but the Jews managed to avoid the imposition of another Seleucid garrison by handing over hostages, including Hyrcanus' own brother, and paying an indemnity of 500 talents of silver (Josephus, *Jewish Ant.* 13.236–48). As the Jews themselves recognised, the Syrian monarch had been firm but fair, and it is testimony to his statesmanlike qualities and his sensitivity towards Jewish religious customs that it is the Jews who are said to have given him the name Eusebes (Pious) (Josephus, *Jewish Ant.* 13.244). Although there is no evidence for it, one cannot help wondering whether Antiochus VII's conciliatory attitude was influenced either directly by Cleopatra Thea or indirectly by a knowledge of the benefits his mother-in-law Cleopatra II had gained by cultivating the loyalty of the Jewish communities in Egypt.

Once the reorganisation of Coele Syria and the other western provinces was sufficiently advanced, Antiochus VII turned his attention to the East. In Hyrcania his brother Demetrius II still languished in captivity at the court of the Parthian king. Conditions had become less pleasant for him after the death of Mithradates I and the accession of his son Phraates II (138/7 BC) but after two unsuccessful attempts at escape he had reluctantly come to terms with his lot. He had a Parthian wife, the princess Rhodogune, by whom he had Parthian children. He had also grown a beard after the style of a Parthian prince and had adopted Parthian dress. In short, Demetrius II had gone native and when he finally did get back home he would not appeal at all to his ex-wife.

In 130 BC Antiochus VII set out with a powerful army said to have numbered 80,000 attended by 300,000 camp followers (Justin 38.10.2), intending to drive the Parthians out of Babylonia and compel his brother's release.[8] After three battles he had won back the country and had the enemy on the back foot, in retreat towards Iran. Men were beginning to call him 'the Great', like his ancestor and namesake Antiochus III who had originally retaken Parthia and Bactria by force of arms (212–205 BC). But the long, cold inland winter would prove his undoing.

At the end of the campaign season the Seleucid troops were divided up and quartered in several of the liberated cities but, as the months dragged on, the burden of feeding such a multitude together with all their camp followers became increasingly onerous. Phraates II had sent ambassadors to try to negotiate terms and they quickly became aware of the resentment which was building up locally and reported it back to their king. The negotiations themselves soon stalled for Antiochus VII would not budge from his stated position. His brother must be freed, the Parthians must relinquish all territory outside their homeland, and they must return to paying tribute to the Seleucids. Phraates II prepared to renew the war but, hopeful of making trouble for his enemy back home, he secretly let Demetrius II go. The ex-king set off westwards with an escort intended to keep him from contacting his brother.

When the spring of 129 BC at last arrived, Phraates II's agents did not find it hard to stir up the local populations against the Seleucid soldiers who had been billeted on them. Unfit and disorganised after months of indolence in their winter quarters, the troops proved an easy prey when their hosts turned on them. Antiochus VII hurried out with his royal guard to assist the nearest group and found himself confronted by the main Parthian army led by the king himself. Against advice he refused to retire and gave battle. The Parthians withdrew into the hills and Antiochus VII and his men followed them up a narrow gully. A general panic ensued when the enemy turned on them and they found themselves trapped. Deserted by his men, Antiochus VII met his death in true Macedonian fashion, with his sword in his hand. Impulsive and courageous, a lover of drinking and fighting, yet with many fine qualities as a leader, he was the last great king of his line. The words said to have been spoken over him by Phraates II make a fitting epitaph for him:

It is boldness and strong drink, Antiochus, which have been your undoing. For you expected to drink down the kingdom of Arsaces in great cupfuls.

(Athenaeus 10.439e)

Such was the end of Cleopatra Thea's third and best husband. As a result of the king's death the great Seleucid army was totally routed. Many were slain and even more captured, including Seleucus, the young son of Antiochus VII and Cleopatra Thea,[9] who would be brought up as a prince at the Parthian court, and his half-sister Laodice, the queen's daughter by Demetrius II, whose beauty won her a place in Phraates II's harem (Justin 38.10.10).

Immediately after his great victory the Parthian king regretted that he had ever let Demetrius II go and he made every effort to get him back. Perhaps he hoped that he might be able to make a lightning strike against Syria itself before a new government could be set in place. But he was too late. A mutiny had already broken out among a troop of Scythian mercenaries whom he had recruited against the Syrians but now refused to pay on the grounds that they were no longer needed, and they had begun ravaging Parthian territory. The following year (128 BC), when he tried to press his Seleucid captives into service against them, they made common cause with the Scythians and in the ensuing battle Phraates II himself was killed (Justin 42.1).

Meanwhile Demetrius II had got away. He arrived back home in Antioch at the same time as the news of the disaster in the East. We can imagine what his reception was like. The Antiochenes had been particularly hard hit by the destruction of Antiochus VII's army. There was hardly a single family which had not lost a son or a husband and for days the streets rang with the sound of lamentation. In the midst of all this the man whom the army had set out to rescue, but whom no one in Antioch ever expected or wanted to see again, turned up as large as life and twice as ugly and proceeded to reinstate himself as their king. But if the general population was aghast at the prospect of being ruled again by a monarch who had already once decimated their city, Cleopatra Thea must have been even more horror-struck.

Here was a man she had not seen for over 12 years. When he had first set out to recover the lost eastern provinces of the Seleucid empire, Demetrius II had been little more than a boy. The coins of the time show him fresh-faced and clean-shaven, a handsome youth with the diadem of Macedonian kingship tied round a neat pudding-basin haircut. The coins issued after his return, on the other hand, portray a haggard-looking middle-aged man with long curling hair and a full beard in the style of his captor Mithradates I.[10] The man who had come back to reclaim his kingdom and his conjugal rights looks for all the world like an elderly hippy 20 years too late for Woodstock.

Cleopatra Thea's first reaction was to send away her second son by Antiochus VII to a place of safety as quickly as she possibly could. Also called Antiochus, he would be brought up at Cyzicus at the far end of Asia Minor under the watchful eye of her loyal eunuch Craterus.[11] His mother was no doubt well aware that, had Demetrius II found him in the palace, he would have had him murdered to ensure a clear way to the succession for his own two sons Seleucus (V) and Antiochus (VIII). As matters turned out, in time they would both get to wear the crown but before that there would be many other complications to worry about.

At the same time as Demetrius II was settling back into Syria, down in Egypt the power struggle between Ptolemy VIII and Cleopatra II, which had been joined in 132/1 BC, was reaching a climax. Although he had been forced to flee to Cyprus with his younger wife Cleopatra III and their children, Ptolemy VIII had nevertheless won his way back and by 129 BC he had regained the Egyptian countryside and had Cleopatra II penned up in Alexandria. It was now her turn to flee into exile and she took herself off to Syria to appeal for help to Demetrius II (128 BC). As the husband once again of Cleopatra Thea, he was once again her son-in-law too.

The country was still reeling from the loss of Antiochus VII's great army and the last thing it needed at this stage was another war. Even so Demetrius II, ever one for grandiose schemes, could not resist Cleopatra II's offer to make him king of Egypt should he succeed in restoring her to her kingdom.[12] He marched southwards with his forces, but Ptolemy VIII was aware of what was going on and he was blocked at Pelusium. What is more, the moment he was out of the way, Antioch arose in revolt behind him (not entirely spontaneously, no doubt). It did not take long for the insurrection to spread and soon even his own forces were infected with the spirit of rebellion (Justin 39.1.2–3). Demetrius II was forced to beat a hasty retreat in order to pacify his own kingdom.

Never one to miss a trick, Ptolemy VIII then pressed his advantage home by adopting the same stratagem which his brother Ptolemy VI had used so successfully in promoting Alexander Balas. He found himself a pretender to the Seleucid throne and sent an Egyptian force to set him up as king in Antioch as Alexander II Zabinas. The story was put about that Zabinas was an adopted son of Alexander Balas but many remained sceptical.[13] The nickname Zabinas, meaning 'the bought one', which the Syrians gave him reflects the alternative tradition that, far from being of royal blood (even by adoption), Alexander II was actually of servile origin, the love-child of a slave mother and a Greek trader from Egypt called Protarchus (Justin 39.1.4). Despite this, many of the Seleucid cities rallied to his cause and Demetrius II soon found himself back in virtually the same situation he had been in 17 years earlier during the time of the pretender Diodotus Tryphon.

Cleopatra Thea was in Ptolemais at the time when the decisive battle between Demetrius II and Zabinas took place near Damascus in 127/6 BC. The king was soundly beaten and he was forced to retreat towards the coast. Ptolemais remained one of the few coastal cities which he still controlled in Phoenicia, but when he tried to take refuge there his wife ordered the city gates to be shut in his face. According to Appian (*Syr.* 68) Cleopatra Thea's action was motivated by sexual jealousy because of his marriage to the Parthian princess Rhodogune. That hardly seems very convincing when during his enforced absence she had married his brother and borne him four children. It is far more likely that it was the prospect of being able to rule at last in her own right which was driving her. By this time she must have been heartily sick of having to play second fiddle to someone who had already had one attempt at being king, had failed miserably at it, and looked set to fail again.

Shut out of Ptolemais, Demetrius II was reduced almost to the status of an outlaw in his own land. In desperation he took ship for Tyre, intending to seek sanctuary there in the great temple of Heracles Melkart, but when he landed he was seized and later killed, perhaps after being tortured (126/5 BC). The immediate orders for his arrest had come from the city's governor but there is a strong suspicion that their ultimate source was queen Cleopatra Thea herself.[14]

It was only a matter of months before she struck again. When the news reached him of his father's death, Seleucus, the elder of her sons by Demetrius II, declared himself king in his father's place as Seleucus V. But Cleopatra Thea had him murdered, either because he had taken the royal diadem against her express orders (Justin 39.1.9, Livy, *Per.* 60) or out of fear that he might attempt to avenge the death of his father (Appian, *Syr.* 69). Appian adds the gory and probably untrue detail that it was the queen herself who shot him dead with an arrow.

After having been passed round like a parcel for so many years, Cleopatra Thea was at last determined to control her own destiny. Indeed it is possible that in Phoenicia at least she may have succeeded in reigning as sole monarch for a brief period in 126/5 BC. Zabinas still ruled in Antioch and would remain king there until 123 BC, but there is an issue of silver tetradrachms from the mint at Sykaminos, just south of Ptolemais, which bears the portrait of Cleopatra Thea alone on the obverse and on the reverse a cornucopia surrounded by the inscription 'Queen Cleopatra Thea Eueteria (Goddess of plenty)'.[15] Although heavily idealised, it shows a handsome and powerful-looking woman in early middle age, with the characteristic heavy jowls of the Ptolemaic royal family. It is a face full of imperious strength, with a nose remarkably like that of her father Ptolemy VI[16] and the determined look of one set on having her own way at last.

Cleopatra Thea's assumption of the kingship in her own name was an unprecedented act. While it may have been acceptable within a single city like Ptolemais, the rule of a sole female was as unpalatable to the majority of the inhabitants of Seleucid Syria as it was to the native population of Ptolemaic Egypt, but for different reasons. In ancient Egyptian belief the male potency of the god-king was thought essential to ensure the annual return of the Nile flood and the maintenance of world order in the ongoing struggle against the ever-present forces of chaos. Consequently the Egyptian king's temporal role as leader of the army in battle was only a comparatively minor part of his wider duties as cosmic warrior responsible for the survival of truth, justice, and existence itself, which in the context of the Nile valley depended ultimately upon his powers as a 'rainmaker' king. In Seleucid Syria on the other hand it was the king's military leadership and his personal prowess in battle which were of prime importance. The continued domination of such a vast and diverse empire by a small Greek-speaking minority whose presence was concentrated in a handful of cities rested upon their ability to preserve the strength of the Macedonian military tradition which they had inherited from Alexander the Great. The Seleucid king had to be first in battle and the personal involvement of both Demetrius II and Antiochus VII in their respective Parthian campaigns had been part of that tradition. This was something that Cleopatra Thea alone could not give her people.

It is not known how long she managed to reign alone but before many months had passed she is found associated on the coins with Antiochus, her second son by Demetrius II, who was then about 16 years old. Antiochus had been sent to Athens to be educated at the time of his father's return from Parthia (Appian, *Syr.* 68) and he was now recalled and crowned Antiochus VIII Epiphanes Philometor Callinicus (Manifest, mother loving, and illustrious in victory). Despite his impressive title he is most usually known by his nickname Grypus, meaning 'hook-nosed', and although he might have loved his mother, she kept the young king firmly in his place. Their coins always show her in the foreground to emphasise her prominence and Grypus' subordination to her.

In view of the continuing war with Zabinas there was no doubt immense public pressure put on Cleopatra Thea to associate her son with her in the kingship. Furthermore by 124 BC Cleopatra II had returned to Egypt and been reconciled with her brother Ptolemy VIII, which would have cleared the way for the Egyptian king to abandon Zabinas and throw his weight behind the legitimate claimants to the throne. It is impossible to say whether Cleopatra Thea's acceptance of Grypus as co-ruler was a cause or a consequence of the alliance which Ptolemy VIII now made with the Seleucids but we can see that alliance being sealed and strengthened by the marriage of his second daughter Tryphaena to Grypus. Indeed Grypus' recall, his marriage to Tryphaena and the institution of the joint rule all look to be part of a package deal which Cleopatra Thea had managed to negotiate with her brother in exchange for Egyptian aid against Zabinas.[17]

With Ptolemy VIII's help it was not long before the tide began to turn against the pretender. In 123 BC Zabinas was defeated in battle and forced back to Antioch. The progressive desertion of one city after another had left him strapped for cash and in order to pay his troops he began stripping the city's temples of their golden images. He got as far as taking the golden Victory off the hand of the statue of Zeus, joking as he did so that Zeus had given him victory (Justin 39.2.5). But a few days later, when he tried to remove the statue of Zeus himself, the Antiochenes decided that enough was enough. They rose against him and drove him out. Abandoned by his followers and captured by brigands, Zabinas was delivered up to Grypus, who forced him to drink poison.

After Zabinas' demise, Grypus began to find his mother's overbearing nature more and more difficult to tolerate. He felt that it was he, not Cleopatra Thea, who had disposed of the pretender. Furthermore he had now reached the age of maturity and had a queen of his own who ensured his links to the Ptolemaic house. By rights Cleopatra Thea should have stepped aside as queen regent and let him rule alone with Tryphaena by his side. But she had no more intention of going gracefully than her sister Cleopatra III would have in a similar situation in Egypt a few years later. Not only was she ready to hang on, but she was also determined to keep the upper hand, whatever it cost her.

A couple of years later (121/0 BC) Grypus came in hot and exhausted one day from a hunting expedition. Cleopatra Thea kindly offered him a cool drink lovingly prepared with her own hand. Her son immediately suspected the worst and in an excess of politeness insisted that she have the first drink. After vainly protesting, she realised she had been betrayed and took the drink. It was of course poisoned and, in the ultimate irony, she died by the potion she had herself prepared. At least that is the way that Justin (39.2.7–8) tells the story. But since it is always the survivor and never the victim who controls the media it is legitimate to raise a query.

One of Grypus' hobbies, to which he was able to devote himself more fully once his mother was out of the way, was a study of different poisons, including snake venom, and their antidotes. In fact he composed a series of learned verses on just that topic.[18] What is more, he had already poisoned his enemy Zabinas and he would also use poison later in an unsuccessful attempt to dispose of his half-brother Antiochus IX Cyzicenus. Who then had mixed the cup that Cleopatra Thea drank? It is not too difficult to believe that she might have planned to murder him. After all, she had already had his brother Seleucus V murdered. But was she really hoist by her own petard in such a horrible way? From the proud and wilful face on the coin portraits one would like to think that, had she decided to get rid of Grypus, Cleopatra Thea would have made a better job of it than this.

While she arguably deserved her death for her obstinacy in holding on to power at whatever cost, Cleopatra Thea's strong-minded character nevertheless shines out like a beacon in the sea of weak and worthless royal males who surrounded her for much of her lifetime. Whatever yardstick they are measured by, the achievements of her last years were quite extraordinary. Before taking Grypus as her co-ruler, she had ruled briefly in her own right and issued coinage with her own name and image, the first and only Seleucid queen ever to do so. Even after the joint rule had been established, she had continued to take precedence. The coins of Cleopatra Thea and Antiochus VIII Grypus regularly bear her head in profile in the foreground with her son's behind hers and on the reverse the legend 'Queen Cleopatra and King Antiochus', in that order. Again this is unprecedented. Demetrius I had struck tetradrachms with the head of his sister and queen Laodice behind his own and Cleopatra Thea herself had already appeared in the foreground with her first husband behind her in the copper coinage of Alexander Balas.[19] But no other Seleucid queen is ever named on the coinage. We cannot help wondering whether her younger sister Cleopatra III ever saw any of these coins and how far sibling rivalry might have played a part in her decision to put herself first in the official titulature in Egypt when she began to rule there with her sons in 116 BC.

13

THE SELEUCID CONNECTION (3)

Cleopatra Selene and the Last of the Seleucids

Throughout her lifetime Cleopatra Thea had been as closely bound up with other royalty as any queen in history, including Queen Victoria. As Bellinger put it, it was her good fortune to be 'the daughter of a king, the sister of two kings, the wife of three, and the mother of four'.[1] Admittedly some of them did not survive for very long. Her brothers Ptolemy Eupator and Ptolemy VII enjoyed only brief periods of co-regency with their father and mother respectively, while her child by Alexander Balas, Antiochus VI Dionysus, lasted for less than three years (145–142 BC) as the puppet of Diodotus Tryphon. She herself later did away with another child when Seleucus V, her elder son by Demetrius II, had the effrontery to set himself up as king against her wishes (126/5 BC). Nevertheless her two offspring who did manage to last the distance, Antiochus VIII Grypus and Antiochus IX Cyzicenus, would come to dominate the next generation of the Seleucid dynasty.

In their turn their children, many born from dynastic marriages contracted with the three daughters of her sister Cleopatra III, would provide the royal house with its final generation of kings. The result was that the dynastic plans to join the Egyptian and Syrian royal families which had been set in motion back in the time of Antiochus the Great, when Cleopatra I had been married to Ptolemy V, would at last bear a belated and shrivelled fruit. In 75 BC two young Seleucid princes journeyed to Rome, where they petitioned the senate to recognise them as the legitimate kings of Syria and also grant them the throne of Egypt. Their claim to Syria was based upon the fact that they were the grandchildren of Cyzicenus, who had been one of Cleopatra Thea's sons by her third husband Antiochus VII. Their claim to Egypt, which the senate did not even deign to pronounce upon, rested on the lineage of their mother. She was Cleopatra Selene, the youngest of the three daughters of Ptolemy VIII and Cleopatra III and, if anything, her links with royalty were even more extensive than her aunt's had been.

It has already been related how the terms of Ptolemy VIII's will left Cleopatra III with the right to rule Egypt with whichever of her two sons she chose, and how she punished Ptolemy IX, who had been forced on her by public pressure, by obliging him to put away his sister–wife Cleopatra IV in favour of his more tractable younger sister Cleopatra Selene. At that time (116/5 BC) Antiochus VIII Grypus was sole king of Syria where he ruled with Cleopatra III's approval and support and her eldest daughter Tryphaena as his queen. Casting about for a means of avenging herself on her mother and regaining her position at the Ptolemaic court, the divorced princess fled to her exiled brother Ptolemy X in Cyprus and then crossed to Syria, when she found that he could not or would not support her.

There she offered herself and the backing of her army to her cousin, Grypus' half-brother Antiochus IX Cyzicenus. Her intentions seem to have been to get her own back on her mother by undermining Cleopatra III's vassal and son-in-law Grypus and eventually to make her way back to Egypt via Syria. Cyzicenus rose to the bait (there may already have been some hostile acts, including an attempt by Grypus to poison him) and in 114/3 BC there began a civil war from which the Seleucid dynasty would never recover.

The details of the war do not concern us here. Its early stages saw the two sisters Cleopatra IV and Tryphaena set at each other with an implacable hatred which culminated in Cleopatra IV's sacrilegious murder on the orders of Tryphaena in 112 BC after Grypus had taken Antioch, followed by the pay-back killing of Tryphaena when her brother-in-law recaptured the city the next year. After that the civil war dragged on for a further eight years during which time neither side was able to gain the upper hand. According to Josephus (*Jewish Ant.* 13.327) the rival kings were like two punch-drunk boxers who had exhausted their strength but were too embarrassed to retire from the ring. Instead they preferred to let the contest drag on as they clung to each other, gasping for breath.

The feud between the rivals naturally provided a heaven-sent opportunity for many of the cities which were nominally in their power to reassert their independence. But this left them vulnerable to the growing military expansionism of the Hasmonaean Jewish state.[2] For example, when John Hyrcanus besieged the great city of Samaria in 108 BC Cyzicenus was unable to relieve it even though he was theoretically in control of that whole region. Even after he had been reinforced by 6,000 Egyptian troops sent to him by Ptolemy IX (against the wishes of his mother Cleopatra III), he was unable to raise the siege and later in the year Samaria was taken by the Jews and utterly erased from the map.

In 103 BC hostilities were renewed between Cyzicenus and Grypus but by then they were both so weakened by their efforts that when the Greek cities in Palestine found themselves attacked by the new Jewish leader Alexander Jannaeus, they ignored both Seleucids in favour of a direct appeal to Ptolemy IX. He was then in exile in Cyprus, having been driven out by Cleopatra III and replaced by his younger brother, and he immediately saw in the call for help which came to him from the people of Ptolemais a splendid chance to get back to Egypt via Syria. As if the long-suffering Syrians did not have enough problems of their own with the rivalry of Grypus and Cyzicenus, the dynastic squabbles of the Ptolemaic house now spilled over on to their land as Cleopatra III and Ptolemy X reacted by invading Phoenicia to bring support to Jannaeus and block Ptolemy IX's attempt to enter Egypt along the southern coast.

At that stage Cleopatra III was perhaps not fully aware how exhausted the Seleucids were by their own struggles, nor could she know that they would keep well away from any involvement in her war against her elder son. Initially fearing that a renewal of the alliance between Ptolemy IX and Cyzicenus might lead to a combined attack on Egypt, she therefore sought to neutralise the latter's influence by lending her support to Grypus. By 103 BC Grypus' earlier lavishness had long ago exhausted his treasury and Cleopatra III accordingly supplied him with the forces which he could no longer afford from his own resources. At the same time she tied him even more closely to her cause by sending him her daughter Cleopatra Selene to marry (Justin 39.4.4).

Cleopatra Selene had been left behind in Alexandria by Ptolemy IX when he had been forced to flee to Cyprus. This was her first connection with the Seleucid house. Born between 140 and 135

BC, she was between about 32 and 37 years old by this time while her new husband was several years her senior (Josephus, *Jewish Ant.* 13.365). She may already have had two children by Ptolemy IX,[3] while Grypus had five sons and a daughter from his earlier marriage to her sister Tryphaena. In time all of his offspring would become kings and queens.[4] Although Cleopatra Selene would later prove herself still fertile, the marriage did not last long enough for the couple to add to this impressive total of royalty.

In 96 BC Grypus was murdered by his chief of staff Heracleon of Beroea, an ambitious disciplinarian who saw himself as kingly material. All that is known about this unpleasant martinet are the details of the spartan commissariat which he enforced on the troops under his command:

> He instituted messes for the soldiers, lying on the bare ground under the open sky in divisions of 1,000. Their food was a large loaf of bread and a piece of meat, their drink was ordinary wine diluted with water. Men with swords acted as waiters,[5] and silence was strictly enforced.
>
> (Poseidonius FGH 87 F 24)

Dinner under Heracleon's regime must have been a strange and unwelcome event after the wonderful noisy feasts which the soldiers had enjoyed under the reign of Grypus, and it was perhaps because of his overzealous insistence on discipline that Cleopatra Selene realised that he would never be acceptable to the Syrians as king. At any rate she immediately crossed over to the opposition. Fleeing from the palace, she gave herself to Cyzicenus who was once more in control of Antioch.

This was her second Seleucid connection. Meanwhile Grypus' eldest son Seleucus, who would succeed him as Seleucus VI Epiphanes Nicator, was raising an army in Cilicia in preparation for an attempt to win back his father's throne. Under the circumstances the most that Heracleon could do was to carve out a small fiefdom for himself in north-eastern Syria, centred on his home town of Beroea, and we hear no more of him. Seleucus for his part soon turned out to be a vigorous and skilful leader and it was not long before one city after another came over to him as he advanced southwards with his army. In 95 BC Cyzicenus marched out from Antioch to meet him but he was defeated in a pitched battle and met his end, either by execution after being captured (Josephus, *Jewish Ant.* 13.366) or by committing suicide before he could be taken alive (Eusebius 1.260). Cleopatra Selene was once more left a widow.

Despite his success, Seleucus VI was not destined to last long as king. When news had reached him in Cyprus of the marriage of his sister and ex-wife Cleopatra Selene to his one-time ally Cyzicenus, Ptolemy IX had been afraid that this new alliance would make her more likely to take sides against him with their brother Ptolemy X. He had therefore brought Grypus' third son Demetrius over from Cnidos and set him up in Damascus as king Demetrius III. But not only did Seleucus VI have to worry about the claims of his own brother, backed by the exiled Egyptian king. He also had Cyzicenus' son and heir against him. The latter had entered into an agreement with the independent coastal city of Arados, where he had himself crowned as Antiochus X Eusebes Philopator (Pious, father loving).

To lend credence to his claim and, more importantly, assure himself of continuing support from Ptolemy X, Eusebes also took over his father's widow. As well as being his ex-stepmother and aunt, Cleopatra Selene was also the niece of his maternal grandmother Cleopatra Thea. There must have been a considerable difference in their ages for she was now between 40 and 45 years old while her husband, who was Cyzicenus' son by an unknown first wife, was probably little more than 20. A little anecdote told by Appian (*Syr.* 69) to the effect that the Syrians probably gave him the title Eusebes as a joke because of his filial piety in wedding and bedding the woman who had been the wife of both his uncle and his father may reflect the malevolent wagging of contemporary tongues. So too may another story told about him by Appian, that although the Syrians believed it was his piety which protected him from a plot hatched against him by his cousin and rival Seleucus VI, it was a call-girl who had fallen in love with his beauty who actually saved him.

Even so, despite the known difference in their ages and the likelihood of some extramarital distraction, Eusebes had two sons by Cleopatra Selene and it was these two who turned up in Rome 20 years later, claiming the kingship of both Syria and Egypt. Our sources only name one of them. As Antiochus XIII Asiaticus he would be the last king of the Seleucids, in opposition to another claimant called Philip II Philoromaeus, who was the grandson of Grypus and thus the last representative of the rival line of descent. By that stage the feud between the half-brothers, which had originated in Cleopatra Thea's marriage first to Demetrius II and then to Antiochus VII, had descended from their sons to their sons' sons. No doubt the process would have continued *ad infinitum*, but by now the kingdom had been destroyed and in 64 BC it would be made into a Roman province by Pompey and put under the direct rule of a governor appointed by the senate. By that time too the Syrians were so fed up with the Seleucids that the citizens of Antioch are said to have given Pompey a large bribe to refuse Antiochus XIII's request to confirm him as king (Eusebius 1.261–2).

Once he had the support of his new wife Cleopatra Selene and her Ptolemaic connections behind him, Antiochus X Eusebes lost no time in taking the fight to Seleucus VI whose stiff-necked and violent manner had quickly made him unpopular with the Antiochenes. He finally drove him out of Syria back to Cilicia, where Seleucus VI's efforts to exact money from the inhabitants of the Greek city of Mopsuestia ended in a riot. The rioters set fire to the palace and the king was burned to death (95 BC).[6] But that was not the end of the feuding for the cudgels had also been taken up by Seleucus VI's twin brothers Philip I and Antiochus XI. The latter managed to supplant Eusebes in Antioch for a period, but Eusebes counterattacked and in the ensuing rout Antiochus XI was drowned in the Orontes. On his death his twin assumed sole power. This was perhaps a slight improvement in so far as it meant that for a while Syria had only three rather than four rival kings vying with each other for control of the kingdom.

Eusebes, however, had a more serious problem to worry about than the dynastic claims of his cousins. After he had secured his country's eastern borders against the threat of incursions by the fierce nomadic tribes from beyond the Oxus river, the Parthian king Mithradates II the Great (124/3–87 BC) had been able to resume the policy of westward expansion initiated by Mithradates I and Phraates II back in the time of Demetrius II and Antiochus VII. Well aware of the threat which this posed, Eusebes responded to a request for aid from an Arab queen called Laodice whose tribe was coming under Parthian pressure and in 89 or 88 BC he fell fighting bravely in battle against the Parthians, like his grandfather Antiochus VII before him.[7]

After four marriages Cleopatra Selene was once again left a widow and so she would remain. Perhaps already resident in Ptolemais, she would bide her time until the right moment came to push the claims of her sons. Before that though there would be another falling out among the surviving sons of Grypus. First, war broke out between Philip I and Demetrius III. In *c.* 88 BC Philip was besieged in Beroea but the tables were turned and the besieger became the besieged when Philip's ally Straton called in Parthian assistance. Demetrius III was forced to surrender and he ended his days in honourable captivity at the Parthian court (Josephus, *Jewish Ant.* 13.384–6). Finally Antiochus XII, the youngest of the five sons of Grypus and the only one yet to become involved in the contest for the kingship, had himself crowned in Damascus as successor to Demetrius III and threw his hat into the ring (87/6 BC). Although he was not unchallenged by his brother Philip, he ruled there for three years before he was killed campaigning against the Nabataean Arabs and Damascus elected to become part of the growing Nabataean empire.

By this stage all the different ethnic groups which had once formed part of the mighty Seleucid empire were waxing fat as a result of the disorder brought about by the incessant feuding between the rival kings. Yet Jews, Parthians, and Arabs were not the only ones to benefit from the kingdom's descent into chaos. On Philip I's death (84/3 BC) it was not his minders, the Parthians, who assumed control of Syria but Tigranes, king of Armenia. Tigranes had begun his career as a vassal of the Parthians, who had put him on the throne of Armenia, and he had then managed to take advantage of dynastic rivalries within the Parthian royal house to extend his power both eastwards into the upper Tigris region, where he founded a great capital city named Tigranocerta after himself, and westwards into Syria and Cilicia.

Although many in the West welcomed his arrival as a respite from yet another weary round of civil war, their number did not include either the promoters of Philip I's young son, also called Philip, or Cleopatra Selene who now put in her bid for the Seleucid throne in the name of her elder son Antiochus XIII. Exactly where the queen's stronghold was at this period is unknown. Tigranes' governor held Antioch and the plains of Cilicia but since the Armenian king had no fleet the coastal cities always remained outside his control, however energetically he tried to expand his influence. At the time when Pompey refused to give Antiochus XIII back his kingdom, he would claim that he had 'lain in hiding in a corner of Cilicia' throughout all of Tigranes' reign (Justin 40.2.3). Yet in Cicero's account of their trip to Rome in 75 BC it is implied that the young prince and his brother had come from Syria as well as returning there (Cicero, *Against Verres II*. 4.61–8). The boys and their mother are therefore perhaps more likely to have been based in one of the southern coastal cities, such as Ptolemais or Seleucia-in-Pieria.[8]

It is at Ptolemais where we last hear of Cleopatra Selene. For the first few years after his accession Tigranes was more interested in strengthening his power in the East than he was in either Cilicia or Syria, and it was not until late in his reign that he began to undertake the conquest of Coele Syria. By the end of 72 BC he was in control of Damascus, which he had won back from the Nabataeans, and was poised to invade Judaea with a huge army (Josephus, *Jewish Ant*. 13.419). In alarm the Jewish queen Alexandra, the widow of Alexander Jannaeus, sent envoys to try to buy him off. They met up with Tigranes at Ptolemais, which he was preparing to put under siege since Cleopatra Selene had prevailed upon its inhabitants to shut the city's gates against him.

Having accepted the Jewish envoys' homage and the presents which they had brought and encouraged them to hope for a favourable response, Tigranes was able to press home the siege of Ptolemais confident in the knowledge that he would no longer need to use force to win over Judaea. The city finally fell in 69 BC and Cleopatra Selene was taken captive. But her son Antiochus XIII eluded his grasp. Perhaps he was already further north in Asia Minor, from where he would later get his nickname Asiaticus.[9] The queen, however, was deported to Seleucia-on-the-Tigris and finally put to death. Tigranes knew that, if he allowed her to live, she might still prove a formidable opponent since the Romans, having recognised her son's claim to the Seleucid throne, would be likely to support her too.

It is a great pity that so little is known about Cleopatra Selene beyond the bare details of her four marriages. The few facts there are about her life are enough to suggest that her later alliances at least were the result of some definite policy which she herself may have initiated in a bid to draw the Seleucid and Ptolemaic houses together through intermarriage rather than by war and conquest. Of course she personally had little say either in her first marriage and divorce from her brother Ptolemy IX or her second to Grypus. Both were part of her mother Cleopatra III's machinations against Ptolemy IX. But the speed and decisiveness with which she abandoned the usurper Heracleon after Grypus' murder and attached herself to Cyzicenus (96 BC) looks like a calculated attempt to consolidate Ptolemaic control over that side of the Seleucid dynasty. So too does her last marriage to Cyzicenus' son Antiochus X Eusebes, and it is arguably the culmination of this policy rather than mere political opportunism which led her to send her sons off to Rome in 75 BC to petition for the crowns of both Syria and Egypt.

Although they were rivals for the kingship, her second and third husbands, the half-brothers Grypus and Cyzicenus, were both fully Seleucid on the male side for their fathers Demetrius II and Antiochus VII were both sons of Demetrius I.[10] At the same time they could be said to be half Ptolemaic already on their mother's side since they were both the children of Cleopatra Thea. By marrying them Cleopatra Selene was therefore strengthening her family's hold upon both branches of the Seleucid line in a manner which also drew together both branches of the Ptolemaic line back to the time of the great Cleopatra I 'the Syrian', with whom the Seleucid connection had originated. As the children of her aunt Cleopatra Thea, Grypus and Cyzicenus represented the line of descent from the 'good king' Ptolemy VI and Cleopatra II (both offspring of Ptolemy V and Cleopatra I) while she herself as the daughter of Ptolemy VIII (the third child of Ptolemy V and Cleopatra I) and his niece Cleopatra III stood in a direct relationship to the currently dominant line of the Ptolemaic house. In a way therefore Cleopatra Selene was in a much stronger position to bring about a union of Egypt and Syria than Cleopatra Thea had been a generation earlier for within Egypt the male line descending from Cleopatra Thea's parents had already failed with the premature death of Ptolemy Eupator and the murder of Ptolemy VII. At the same time the line of Ptolemy VIII and Cleopatra III was also starting to run exceedingly thin on the male side since Cleopatra Selene's younger brother Ptolemy X had left only a single son while the elder, Ptolemy IX, had only two illegitimate sons by a concubine.

The option of unification through force had been tried often enough in the past but it had always failed. By this time too both royal families must have realised that Rome would never countenance a union of the whole of the East through conquest. A ruler strong enough to achieve that would have posed an unacceptable threat. But unification through intermarriage would not seem nearly so threatening as, say, Demetrius II's attack on Egypt in 127 BC or Cleopatra III's incursion into Syria in 103 BC. This is how Cleopatra Selene might have thought. Unfortunately though her plans came to nothing. She had not reckoned with the continuation of the feud between Grypus and Cyzicenus into the next generation or the emergence in the region of dynamic warlords like Tigranes of Armenia and Mithradates of Pontus. Nor could she have foreseen the Romans' growing awareness of the East and its riches as during the first century BC political power in the Republic became ever more dependent upon the possession of vast amounts of wealth.

14

THE TWILIGHT OF THE PTOLEMIES

Cleopatra Berenice III, Cleopatra V Tryphaena

Cleopatra Selene's first Syrian marriage to Antiochus VIII Grypus in 103 BC served its purpose well. Any inclination which the rival Seleucid king Antiochus IX Cyzicenus might have felt to support his former ally Ptolemy IX in his attempt to regain his kingdom was firmly nipped in the bud. When Cleopatra III and Ptolemy X arrived in Syria ready to block Ptolemy IX's advance on Egypt, neither king showed the slightest desire to tangle with their army, which in any case was far larger and better equipped than anything either of them could have fielded by that time.

As we saw, Ptolemy IX's efforts to invade Egypt came to nothing and he was forced to return to his place of exile in Cyprus. But Cleopatra III's triumph was short-lived. Soon after her return to Alexandria she was displaced by her younger son and co-ruler, probably some time in September 101 BC.[1] Thereafter Ptolemy X ruled in his own right, with his niece Berenice as his queen. She now took the dynastic name Cleopatra and is henceforth known as Cleopatra Berenice III. Although in reality she was Ptolemy X's niece, in the demotic titulature the royal couple are described as 'Pharaoh Ptolemy known as Alexander, the mother loving god, and queen Berenice his sister, his wife, the mother loving gods, the saviour gods'.[2]

Ptolemy X continued to rule Egypt for the first decade of the new century. Every day he grew more and more like his father Ptolemy VIII – continuously sozzled, normally incapable of walking unaided because of his immense bulk, but none the less able to show an amazing agility when it came to performing obscene dances of a certain type, at which he was an acknowledged expert (Poseidonius, FGH 87 F 26). The Alexandrians grew more and more disgusted with him and in 89 BC the army and the citizen body combined to throw him out. He withdrew to Syria where he took advantage of the good offices of his sister Cleopatra Selene and her latest husband Antiochus X Eusebes to raise a mercenary army.

Backed by these troops he returned to Egypt and re-entered the capital, but to pay them off he had to melt down the gold coffin which held the mummified body of his mighty namesake Alexander the Great, who had lain in state in the royal mausoleum in Alexandria ever since Ptolemy I had hijacked his body over two centuries before. Although the coffin was later replaced with one of crystal (Strabo 17.794C), or perhaps more accurately alabaster, the cavalier treatment he had meted out to their city's famous founder was the last straw as far as the Alexandrians were concerned and they promptly drove Ptolemy X out again. His brother Ptolemy IX, who may already have been back in Egypt with an army awaiting their uprising,[3] was reinstated as king (89/8 BC) and Ptolemy X was forced to flee the country. He escaped to Lycia, intending to cross from there to Cyprus, but he was cornered while attempting to make the crossing and defeated and killed in a naval battle.

By this time Ptolemy IX had run out of sisters to serve as his consort and so for this second period of his kingship from 88 to 80 BC we find his daughter Cleopatra Berenice III as his queen. Such a degree of incest was not unknown in the pharaonic period. In the New Kingdom, for example, both Akhenaten and Ramses the Great took their own daughters to wife. But this is the only marriage of this type in the Ptolemaic dynasty. No doubt Ptolemy IX's decision was motivated primarily by political considerations. According to Cicero (fr.9 Müller) Cleopatra Berenice was extremely popular with the Alexandrians and Ptolemy IX desperately needed their support in the face of a renewed outbreak of Egyptian nationalism centred on the Thebaid. The native rebellion, which had begun under Ptolemy X, took three years to suppress and ended with the almost total destruction of Thebes by the Ptolemaic army (Pausanias 1.9.3). Although the city survived as a religious centre, it would never fully recover its former glory.

He would also have needed a queen beside him when he was crowned a second time in a native Egyptian coronation at Memphis (before 1 November 88 BC[4]). At that same time he may also have celebrated the ancient Egyptian *Heb Sed* (jubilee festival), when after 30 years in office the pharaoh's kingly powers were magically renewed in a series of secret rituals before the gods of Egypt. Although he had been driven out in 107 BC and had spent most of his life in exile from Egypt, Ptolemy IX dated the years of his kingship from his accession as king of Cyprus in June 116 BC so that his recall by the Alexandrians early in 88 BC actually took place in his 29th regnal year, making him eligible for magical rejuvenation almost immediately.

Ptolemy IX is said to have had two sons by his previous marriage to his second sister–wife Cleopatra Selene (Justin 39.4.1), but if these offspring ever existed (which has been doubted) they had probably died at an early age.[5] Consequently on his death in 80 BC at the age of 62 Ptolemy IX's only legitimate child to survive him was his daughter and widow Cleopatra Berenice III. She now enjoyed a brief period of rule as sole monarch (March–August 80 BC) before the Romans, who for some years had not been overly concerned with Ptolemaic affairs, suddenly decided to intervene and give her a new consort.

At this time the only legitimate male descendant of the Ptolemaic line was a young man called Alexander, after his father. He was the son of Ptolemy X Alexander I, the rival younger brother who had been driven out finally and killed in the sea battle in 88 BC. While there has never been any doubt that Ptolemy X was his father, a great deal of uncertainty remains about the identity of his mother. The Egyptian word for 'son', *šr*, can also be used to mean 'stepson'. Therefore a small group of demotic texts which refer to Ptolemy X and Cleopatra Berenice ruling in the first year of their joint reign (101/0 BC) with 'her *šr* Alexander' has given rise to a view that Alexander II may have been the child of Cleopatra Berenice as well as her uncle–husband Ptolemy X.[6] The usual interpretation, however, is that *šr* should be taken to mean 'stepson' here, making Alexander II the offspring of Ptolemy X by an earlier legal wife. But who that wife may have been remains a complete mystery. A remote possibility is that she may have been Cleopatra IV, Ptolemy IX's first sister–wife, if she had been married to her younger brother in Cyprus for a short time after her divorce and before she went on to Syria in 115 BC to become the wife of Antiochus IX Cyzicenus, but there is no hard evidence to support this hypothesis.

Alexander II was among Cleopatra III's grandchildren whom she had deposited as a precautionary measure, along with her treasure, in the sanctuary of Asclepius on Cos before she had set off for Syria with her army in 103 BC. He had remained on Cos for most of his father's reign, perhaps because his stepmother Cleopatra Berenice had not wanted him in Alexandria,[7] and he was still there in 88 BC when the island was overrun by Mithradates VI of Pontus in the course of his invasion of Greece. The Coans were obliged to hand over to him both the treasure and the children and Alexander was subsequently brought up as a royal hostage at the Pontic court. But in 84 BC he managed to escape to the camp of the Roman dictator Sulla, who had been given the command against Mithradates, and he went back to Rome in his entourage.

It was this young man, now in his mid-twenties, whom Sulla sent to Alexandria to be consort to his cousin queen Cleopatra Berenice III and to be crowned king of Egypt as Ptolemy XI Alexander II. Although Cleopatra Berenice was already queen in her own right, Sulla's move was justifiable in so far as the experience of both Cleopatra II and Cleopatra III had shown that the rule of a sole female was too alien to the native tradition to be acceptable to the Egyptian priesthoods and the native population of the country, however popular the queen was personally with the Greek-speaking Alexandrians. But in his reluctance to have Cleopatra Berenice as his wife, perhaps because she expected him to be the junior partner and play second fiddle to her,[8] the new king lost no time in murdering her. In revenge the Alexandrians then dragged him off to the gymnasium and murdered him. His reign had lasted only 19 days, his marriage slightly less.

To replace him the Alexandrians found two sons of their previous king Ptolemy IX by a concubine. One was made ruler of Cyprus, the other king of Egypt as Ptolemy XII. His title initially was Ptolemy XII Theos Philopator Philadelphus (The father loving, brother loving god), to which was later added the surname Neos Dionysos (The young [or 'new'] Dionysus). But the Alexandrians, who would soon come to regret the new king with whom they had saddled themselves, most usually called him by his nickname Auletes (The flute player). According to Cicero (*De leg. agr.* 2.16.42) Ptolemy XII had been in Syria at the time of his predecessor's murder in mid–80 BC. He acceded to the throne some time between June and September that year and arrived in Alexandria later in the year. To legitimise his position, the new ruler needed a wife, also of the royal line. Luckily there was a suitable candidate to hand in another illegitimate child of Ptolemy IX, called Cleopatra Tryphaena, and the pair were married by January 79 BC.

Cleopatra V Tryphaena is a shadowy figure and it is uncertain whether she was Ptolemy XII's full sister or the child of a different mother. The title Theoi Philopatores and Philadelphi (The father loving and brother/sister loving gods) which the couple took on their marriage has sometimes been thought to indicate that they were full brother and sister.[9] So too has the occurrence of the word 'sister' in the titulature of Cleopatra Tryphaena herself. Yet neither of these titles has much value as evidence when we remember that only a generation earlier Cleopatra Berenice III had been called the 'sister' of Ptolemy X when the relationship was in fact that of uncle and niece. Furthermore in 80 BC the new royal couple would have been obliged to emphasise the closeness of their relationship (as well as their love for their father) in order to play down the fact that neither of them was of full Ptolemaic blood.

An equally interesting problem is why Ptolemy XII and his brother the last king of Cyprus, who was also called Ptolemy, should have been living in Syria at the time that they were invited to Egypt by the Alexandrians. One obvious solution is to suppose that they may have been among the young royals whom Cleopatra III had lodged for safety on Cos in 103 BC and who had subsequently been taken hostage by Mithradates VI. Although Ptolemy XI Alexander II had managed to get away to Sulla, we know that Mithradates still had at least two princes left in his grasp. Appian (*Mithr.* 111) records that he betrothed two of his daughters to 'the kings of Egypt and Cyprus' with the intention of making a dynastic alliance with the Ptolemaic house. Yet the plan never came to fruition for the princesses still languished in Pontus, apparently unmarried, at the time of their father's death in 63 BC.

Perhaps Ptolemy XII and his brother had managed to get to Syria after it had passed into the possession of Mithradates' son-in-law and ally Tigranes, the king of Armenia. If that is so, what is to prevent us identifying them with the two legitimate sons of Ptolemy IX and his second wife Cleopatra Selene, who had been born before the king was expelled by his mother Cleopatra III in 107 BC and left in her care when Cleopatra Selene was sent off to Syria to marry Antiochus VIII Grypus? Unfortunately the difficulty with this identification is twofold. First there is the strength of the tradition that Ptolemy XII was illegitimate. Not only does this survive in three separate authors (Cicero, *De leg. agr.* 2.16.42, Justin 39. prol., Pausanias 1.9.3), the first of whom was contemporary with the events he was describing, but the tradition also gains independent support from the claim to the kingship of Egypt which the two Seleucid sons of Cleopatra Selene and Antiochus X Eusebes would lay before the Roman senate in 75 BC.

It goes without saying that the Seleucid princes are hardly likely to have made such a claim without some grounds for doing so. Those grounds are most likely to have been their mother's belief that, even though they were Seleucid on their father's side, they were never the less royal on both sides. What is more, their descent from a full Ptolemaic princess made them purer in blood and more 'Ptolemaic' than Ptolemy XII and his brother could ever be as the children of a concubine. Second, there is the objection that Cicero refers to Ptolemy XII as a 'boy' (*De rege Alex.* fr. 9.2), which is a word he is hardly likely to have used had Ptolemy XII been born before 107 BC. In short, although the suggestion has been made that Cicero could have been using 'boy' rather as a term of contempt,[10] the weight of evidence that Ptolemy XII was a bastard son of Ptolemy IX (as therefore was his younger brother, too) is really too overwhelming to be set aside without good reason.[11]

Whatever the exact details of their parentage, both kings ruled only on the sufferance of Rome. Part of the kingdom of the Ptolemies had already been whittled away in the previous generation when Ptolemy VIII's bastard son Ptolemy Apion, who had been made king of Cyrene under his father's will, had bequeathed his inheritance to the Roman people when he died in 96 BC. By 80 BC popular belief in Rome had it that there existed a similar testament made by 'the king of Alexandria' (Cicero, *De leg. agr.* 1.1) which effectively meant that the Romans could also annex Egypt and Cyprus, too, whenever they chose to do so. Whether such a testament actually existed and, if so, whether it was Ptolemy X's, deposited with the Romans as collateral for the funds they had given him to finance his attempted return to Alexandria in 88 BC, or a will drawn up by his son Ptolemy XI as the price which Sulla had exacted in return for setting him up as king in 80 BC, are vexed questions which have been much discussed.[12] Thankfully they need not concern us. Regardless of the will's origins or its legality, the political reality was that it was Roman backing which kept Ptolemy XII on his throne and everyone knew it, particularly the Alexandrians. At the same time the existence of the will (or the strong conviction that it existed, which amounted to the same thing) meant that while the senate was prepared to support Ptolemy XII unofficially, it was naturally loath to recognise his title as true king of Egypt.[13]

In this uneasy situation Ptolemy XII had no choice, if he wanted to stay on his throne, but to do whatever he thought would best please the Romans and to resort to large-scale bribery in an attempt to win the senate's favour. As Will has noted,[14] the best argument there is for the authenticity of the will is the 20 or so years and the huge amount of money and effort which Ptolemy XII was prepared to devote to making sure that its provisions would never be executed. Indeed the whole history of Ptolemy XII's reign is the story of his struggle for recognition by the Romans and the Alexandrians' growing shame and anger as they watched his self-abasement and felt his hand digging ever deeper into their own pockets in search of the gold for which everybody who was anyone in Roman politics had such an insatiable craving.

In 63 BC the people of Alexandria had to look on in helpless rage as their despicable king provided a force of 8,000 cavalry to assist Pompey in the subjugation of Judaea, and feasted hundreds of the top Roman brass at Egyptian expense while they proceeded to occupy an area which had once belonged to the Ptolemies themselves (Pliny 33.136). In fact, if Appian (*Mithr.* 114) is to be believed, even at this time Alexandria was already seething with revolt and Ptolemy XII even tried to call in the Roman general and his army to assist him in quelling his own subjects. For reasons of his own Pompey refused, fortunately for them because the danger of this course was what might happen to king and country alike if the Romans were ever given even the slightest excuse for war against them. The Alexandrians had already seen Syria reduced to a Roman province (64 BC) and along with their hatred of the Romans and their contempt for Ptolemy XII's subservience to them went a healthy dread that, once a Roman army entered Egypt on whatever pretext, it might never leave.

So tense was Alexandria during these years that even an apparently trivial matter could provoke a major diplomatic incident. The mood of the city, simultaneously fearful and resentful, is admirably caught by the historian Diodorus, who happened to be in the country at the time and witnessed a lynching:

Once when king Ptolemy had not yet been granted the status
of Friend [sc. of the Roman People] and the populace was
avidly currying the favour of the legates then in the country
from Italy and was eager to give no ground for complaint
or pretext for war out of their fear [of Rome], one of the
Romans killed a cat. The mob made a rush at his house and
neither the officials sent by the king to beg for his release
nor the fear which everyone felt for Rome proved powerful
enough to save him from their vengeance, even though what
he had done was an accident. And I am not relating this
from hearsay but it is something I saw with my own eyes
during my visit to Egypt.

(Diodorus 1.83.8–9)

That was in 60 BC. Matters came to a head the following year when
Julius Caesar was consul. Although Caesar was generally believed
to be in favour of Egypt's annexation, Ptolemy XII managed to
buy him off with 6,000 silver talents, a huge sum which represented
half a year's revenue for the whole country. In return Caesar
rammed through a law giving the king the recognition for which
he had sought so desperately and so long, and granting him the
coveted status of 'friend and ally of the Roman people'. But since
the Romans now regarded Cyprus as a separate state from Egypt,
it turned out that Egypt was all that Ptolemy XII's immense bribe
had bought him. The next year Publius Clodius, Caesar's tame
tribune of the plebs, brought forward a bill to make Cyprus a
Roman province. In exchange for his kingdom, Ptolemy XII's
younger brother Ptolemy of Cyprus was offered the prestigious
office of high priest of Aphrodite at Paphos but he chose instead
to die with honour by committing suicide. His treasure was ship-
ped to Rome and the island became a Roman possession.

Whether or not Ptolemy XII had thought he was buying title
to Cyprus as well as to Egypt we do not know, but certainly the
Alexandrians were surprised and outraged by the Roman decision.
They insisted that their worthless king should demand the return
of the island or else renounce his friendship with the Romans.
Never had feelings against Rome run so high and Ptolemy XII
found himself faced with a strong and organised opposition from
all sections of the community. Unable to win them over by per-
suasion or compel them by force to withdraw their demands, he
was forced to leave Alexandria (summer 58 BC) and make for

Rome to appeal for military aid to secure his position. He left his family behind in the city, no doubt to hold the fort, and in his absence the Alexandrians set up his eldest daughter Berenice IV as their ruler along with a 'Cleopatra Tryphaena' as her associate. The latter died after a year, leaving Berenice IV as sole ruler, a position she would hold until her father's restoration in 55 BC.

Who was this 'Cleopatra Tryphaena' who was co-ruler of Egypt in 58/7 BC? That there was a period of joint rule by two women is confirmed by a papyrus which refers to 'the queens' (BGU VIII 1762.3–4) but they are not named in the papyrus. Porphyry (FGH 260 F 2 (14)), who is our only literary source for the existence of the joint reign, makes her a daughter of Ptolemy XII rather than his wife Cleopatra V Tryphaena. Historians therefore sometimes distinguish two Cleopatra Tryphaenas, with the younger one being numbered Cleopatra VI Tryphaena. Yet the evidence for her existence is somewhat nebulous. There are some indications that Ptolemy XII's wife Cleopatra V Tryphaena may have died as early as 69/8 BC. For example, her name disappears from the monuments and papyri around this time and in 68 BC we find a dedication made on behalf of the king alone when we would normally expect such an inscription to name and honour both king and queen. On the other hand, when the Horus temple at Edfu was finally completed in December 57 BC, her name could still be written alongside Ptolemy XII's on the lintel above the great doors of cedar and bronze which hung in the entrance pylon. As Bevan says,[15] had the queen died almost 12 years earlier it would be very surprising if the priests had yet to discover the fact of her death.

Furthermore the geographer Strabo (17.796C), who visited Egypt soon after it became a Roman province in 30 BC and whose information about the country is usually very reliable, tells us that Ptolemy XII had only three daughters and that it was the eldest of these whom the Alexandrians made queen.[16] By them he presumably means Berenice IV, Cleopatra VII who would be left as next in line when their father had Berenice IV put to death after his restoration in 55 BC, and Arsinoe, who was only about 15 or 16 when she was taken to Rome as a captive by Julius Caesar after the Alexandrine War and forced to walk in chains in his triumphal procession (46 BC). Here at least there is no room for a daughter called Cleopatra Tryphaena.

As the evidence is so unclear, it is perhaps worthwhile trying to go beyond it by reminding ourselves what sort of expectations the

Egyptians held about the institution of kingship itself and considering how a joint rule of mother and elder daughter might have fitted in with such expectations, compared to a rule by two sisters. Time after time throughout Ptolemaic history the reactions of the native population of Egypt when they were confronted by a woman attempting to rule in her own right had made it quite clear that the notion of a female ruler without a male counterpart was totally alien to the native tradition,[17] however powerful or popular the individual in question. Indeed it would not be very long before Berenice IV too would be forced to take a male consort. As the career of even the great Cleopatra VII demonstrates,[18] the tradition of kingship in Egypt demanded that, as well as an Isis as sister, wife, and mother, there should always be a Horus alongside her as both her child and her lover in order for chaos to be kept at bay, truth and justice to flourish, and the land's fertility to be assured for the coming year.

Given these constraints it is very difficult to see how a joint rule of two sisters could be assimilated to such a world view. On the other hand, a co-regency of a mother and her eldest daughter can be more easily accommodated by supposing that the mother is there as queen regent, serving either until a consort can be found for her daughter or one of her own sons becomes old enough to take his place in the male–female equation which always lay at the heart of the ancient Egyptian ideal of kingship. Accordingly it seems better to argue that, while Porphyry is essentially correct in recording a joint rule of Cleopatra Tryphaena and Berenice IV, he has made a mistake in making this Cleopatra a daughter of Ptolemy XII rather than his wife. This is Ptolemy XII's half-sister and queen, Cleopatra V Tryphaena, who was still alive in 57 BC as the Edfu inscription shows, acting as senior partner in the co-regency in her husband's absence. There is no Cleopatra VI Tryphaena, no unknown younger daughter serving as junior partner in a joint rule by two sisters, an arrangement which would be quite unique and otherwise unparalleled in the history of ancient Egypt.

After a year as regent Cleopatra V Tryphaena died, leaving her eldest daughter Berenice IV as sole ruler. In 57 BC neither of her brothers was yet old enough to be associated in the kingship with her for Ptolemy XIII (as he would later be) was no more than 3 or 4 years old while his brother, later Ptolemy XIV, was younger still. This is why ever since they had forced her father out the previous summer the Alexandrians had been preoccupied with finding a husband for her to be their king. In view of the connections already existing between the two royal houses, their thoughts naturally enough turned first of all towards the remnants of the Seleucid dynasty and their initial approach was to the younger son of Antiochus X Eusebes and Cleopatra Selene. His name is not recorded but he was one of the two princes whom Cleopatra Selene had sent to Rome in 75 BC to petition the senate for the throne of Egypt as well as Syria.

For one marvellous moment therefore it looked as though Cleopatra Selene's dynastic plans to join the two families together might at last come to pass, Roman obstructionism notwithstanding. But while the Alexandrian envoys were still dickering about the terms of the marriage, the young man contracted a serious illness and died. The Alexandrians then approached one of the only survivors of the other branch of the Seleucid royal family, descended from the union of Antiochus VIII Grypus with Cleopatra Selene's elder sister Tryphaena. Philip II, who was their grandson, had been the last monarch of an independent Syria (65–64 BC) before Pompey had expelled him and made the country into a Roman province. However the proposed match was blocked by Aulus Gabinius, who was then proconsul of Syria, on the grounds that it would be against the interests of Rome.

While all this frantic husband-hunting was taking place, Ptolemy XII was still in Rome pursuing the case for his restoration. Our sources make no mention of him in connection with these two unsuccessful attempts to find a consort for his daughter. Nevertheless it is almost impossible not to suspect him of some clandestine involvement, particularly since we know that during this same period he successfully used a combination of murder, threats, and bribery to block an embassy which the Alexandrians had sent to Rome to argue against his restoration to the throne. Furthermore it cannot be entirely coincidental that when he did return to Egypt in 55 BC his restoration would be accomplished by the self-same Gabinius and his army, and that Gabinius personally received a bribe of 10,000 talents for his assistance in the matter.

When their second attempt to find a Seleucid prince for Berenice IV to marry broke down, the queen's advisers in growing desperation cast their net yet wider. Eventually they came up with an illegitimate Syrian princeling called Seleucus, whom the Alexandrian public with their characteristic penchant for catchy nicknames immediately christened Kybiosaktes (Seller of salt-fish). But Berenice found his crassness appalling (or was it perhaps his smell?) and unlike her subjects she was not prepared to make a joke of it. Within the first week of their marriage she had him strangled, thereby beating the family record set by Ptolemy XI Alexander II when he had murdered her great aunt and namesake Cleopatra Berenice III within three weeks of their wedding day in 80 BC.

The Ptolemaic courtiers now began to look beyond the Seleucids to other likely royal houses in Asia Minor. At last they found someone suitable for their queen in the person of Archelaus, who claimed to be a son of Mithradates the Great of Pontus but was probably the offspring of Mithradates' general Archelaus. A friend of Mark Antony, Archelaus had been appointed high priest of the temple of the Great Mother at Comana in Syria but he now bribed Gabinius to let him go to Egypt and in March/April 56 BC he arrived in Alexandria to marry Berenice IV and become her king. Although their joint reign spanned two regnal years, it actually lasted barely a year by the calendar. In spring 55 BC Gabinius, with instructions from Pompey and his huge bribe from Ptolemy XII, illegally brought his army out of Syria, without authorisation from the senate, and marched down into Egypt to put Ptolemy XII back on the throne.

Gabinius' cavalry was led by Mark Antony, who distinguished himself by his chivalrous conduct during the campaign and perhaps had his first glimpse at this time of the 14-year-old princess who, unbeknown to them both, held his destiny in her hands (Appian, B.C. 5.8). The 'war' was soon over. Although Archelaus resisted, his Alexandrian troops mutinied and he fell in battle. Once restored, Ptolemy XII lost no time in disposing of the daughter who had usurped his crown and avenging himself upon the Alexandrians who had aided and abetted her. The murder of Berenice IV still left him with two girls and two boys. Cleopatra was the eldest, her sister Arsinoe was several years younger, and his two sons, both called Ptolemy, were about 6 and 4 years old respectively. Thus it was that on the death of Ptolemy XII in 51 BC it was Cleopatra who inherited the kingdom as Cleopatra VII with her elder brother Ptolemy XIII as her king and co-ruler, in accordance with the terms of her father's will.

15

CLEOPATRA VII'S SUICIDE

Although this book is not about the most famous Cleopatra of them all, but about her less well-known namesakes, it would obviously be quite unacceptable to pass over Cleopatra VII in complete silence. Every year countless books and articles are written in many languages about her life, her achievements, and her posthumous reputation and it would be pointless to try to compete with them in just a single chapter. So I have chosen to concentrate instead upon what is undoubtedly the best-known incident of her full and varied life – the way in which she left it.

Whether it is from the movies, or Shakespeare's *Antony and Cleopatra*, or one of the many popular accounts of the queen and her doomed liaison with Mark Antony, we all know how Cleopatra VII committed suicide. Her death by the bite of an asp has become a part of popular mythology. Along with the assassination on the Ides of March 44 BC of Julius Caesar (her earlier lover and the father of her child Caesarion) it is one of the most famous events in the whole history of the ancient world. But how much (or how little) do we know about what really happened? Did she die of snakebite and, if so, was her chosen method of suicide intended to have any symbolic meaning? And did she kill herself entirely of her own volition, or was she skilfully manoeuvred into committing suicide by her enemy Octavian for political reasons of his own?

First, the events of Cleopatra's last days. In the absence of any contemporary evidence Plutarch's *Life of Antony* remains our most important source, although it has to be treated with extreme care as a carefully crafted piece of literature rather than a straightforward historical account.[1] He tells us how, after he had taken Pelusium by storm, Octavian arrived on the outskirts of Alexandria in late

July 30 BC and encamped near the hippodrome just outside the Canopic gate on the city's eastern edge. Antony sallied out against his advance cavalry and drove them back to their camp, but that was to be the limit of his success. After his attempts to win over Octavian's troops by bribery had failed and Octavian himself had refused a challenge to single combat, Antony determined to stake all on one last battle the following day.

Although Octavian later made a great deal of it, celebrating the day of the battle (1 August by the current Roman calendar, equivalent to 3 August by our Julian calendar[2]) as a public holiday and renaming the month itself August after his later title as the emperor Augustus, the battle for Alexandria was very much an anti-climax. In the morning Antony led his troops out towards the hippodrome and watched as the Egyptian fleet sailed out eastwards to engage Octavian's galleys. When they got near enough, the Egyptian crews raised their oars in salute and went over to the enemy and seeing this Antony's cavalry also deserted. His infantry was defeated and Antony was forced to retire, crying out in his rage and frustration that Cleopatra had betrayed him. Later that day Octavian was able to enter the city without further opposition.

After the battle Cleopatra barricaded herself into the mausoleum which she had constructed for herself in the inner city.[3] She had with her only her hairdresser Eiras, her lady-in-waiting Charmion, and perhaps an unnamed eunuch, added by Dio (51.10.6) who is our other major source for these events. From there she sent a message to Antony, which apparently said (or which he misunderstood to say) that she was dead. Believing the news, Antony ordered his slave Eros to kill him too, but Eros turned the sword upon himself. Antony was forced to stab himself. As he lay bleeding, Cleopatra's secretary Diomedes arrived with orders to bring him to her. Antony was carried in the arms of his servants to the sealed doors of her tomb, where Cleopatra and her women let down ropes and hauled him up to an upper storey. There he finally lost consciousness and died in her arms, after advising her to put her trust in Proculeius, who was one of Octavian's staff.

News of Antony's death was quickly brought to Octavian and Proculeius arrived soon afterwards. His orders were above all to take Cleopatra alive, if he could, and prevent her setting fire to her treasure which she had with her in the mausoleum. Proculeius spoke to her through a grating in the door and tried to cheer her up. He then retired but soon returned, accompanied by Cornelius

187

Gallus, a friend of the poet Virgil and the leader of the rest of Octavian's forces which had come by sea along the Libyan coast. While Gallus kept the queen talking, Proculeius and two servants climbed up a ladder to the back window through which Antony had been taken in and came down the stairs behind her. One of her women cried out a warning and Cleopatra tried to stab herself with a dagger which she was wearing but Proculeius was too quick for her. He disarmed her and also searched her to see whether she had any poison concealed about her, before putting her under the guard of a freedman called Epaphroditus who was given strict orders to keep her alive.

Cleopatra's capture meant also the capture of her treasure and it may have been that rather than the queen herself which was uppermost in Octavian's mind at this stage. Cleopatra's treasure was the last great hoard left intact in the East.[4] As such it represented Octavian's only chance to satisfy his veterans' increasingly strident demands for their back pay and severance benefits. He had already been faced with growing discontent among his troops on his return to Italy after the battle of Actium (September 31 BC) and Cleopatra's threat to incinerate her treasure along with herself on her funeral pyre had therefore been a serious matter. As it was, when news reached Rome of his seizure of the treasure, interest rates immediately plummeted from 12 per cent to 4 per cent and Octavian could breathe more freely again.

Soon after her capture Octavian permitted Cleopatra to leave the mausoleum to attend to the last rites for Antony. In the excess of her grief (her breasts are said to have been inflamed and ulcerated from beating them) she succumbed to a fever and determined to put an end to her life by refusing food. At this point Octavian had her taken to the palace. A physician called Olympus, who attended her there, recorded in an account which he later wrote of these events but which is unfortunately lost,[5] that he was willing to assist her in her plan, but Octavian became suspicious and by threatening the lives of her children prevailed upon her to allow herself to be nursed back to health.

While she was recovering, the queen was visited by Octavian himself, probably on 8 (our 10) August. It has sometimes been doubted that this visit ever took place[6], but the existence of two different versions of the meeting suggests that, although many of the details may have been fictionalised, the interview did indeed occur. In fact it would seem very strange had Octavian not wanted to see his royal captive face-to-face at some stage. Plutarch's account of their meeting (*Antony* 83) begins on a note of pathos with the queen lying in the most miserable conditions and in a very sorry state both physically and mentally. But in the course of the interview flashes of her earlier fiery spirit are seen returning as she leaps up to beat and abuse a servant who had been unwise enough to reveal to Octavian that she had been trying to keep back some of her treasure.[7] Her changed attitude is sufficient to convince Octavian that her will to live is still intact and, having promised to treat her well, he departs 'thinking he had deceived her, but rather he was the one deceived' (*Antony* 83.7).

In Dio (51.12–13) on the other hand it is Cleopatra who is made to initiate the interview. Here she is presented as the archetypal *femme fatale*. Reclining on her couch in a most becoming mourning garb, she regales Octavian with snippets from the love letters once sent to her by his adoptive father Julius Caesar and tries to use on him the same feminine wiles which she had employed so successfully on Caesar and Antony. As a man Octavian is not insensible to her charms, but manfully he pretends that he is.[8] Her failure to win him over makes Cleopatra fall back into despondency once more but Dio's Octavian also tries to cheer her up by promising to treat her well. But his hidden intention is to keep her alive for his triumph. Suspecting some ulterior motive, here too Cleopatra feigns a change of heart and so deceives her captor.

Although these accounts differ radically in detail, the bottom line common to them both is Octavian's unspoken determination to do whatever may be necessary to keep the queen alive so that she can be taken back to Rome to adorn his triumphal procession. Opposed to this is Cleopatra's even stronger determination to avoid that final humiliation at all costs, a point which emerges strongly also from other references to the queen's suicide.[9] In both Plutarch and Dio it is she who is the deceiver and Octavian who is the one deceived.

At this point Plutarch and Dio diverge. Dio's Cleopatra, having not only deceived Octavian but also successfully fooled Epaphroditus and his assistants into relaxing their guard, proceeds directly to her suicide. Plutarch (*Antony* 84) on the other hand interposes two further incidents – the arrival of a secret message from a member of Octavian's staff, a young man called Cornelius Dolabella, and a final visit by the queen to Antony's tomb. No other source records either of these events and although a second visit to the grave site soon after interment would be quite in keeping with the extended nature of ancient Greek burial practice, Cleopatra's soliloquy over Antony's ashes clearly owes more to the ritual laments of tragedy than to historical reality.[10] Although the visit itself is quite likely, the authenticity of the details is therefore rightly queried. Dolabella's message, however, is another matter. Dolabella, who is described as a young aide-de-camp who was on friendly terms with the queen and to whom she had therefore appealed for information, secretly let her know that Octavian was preparing to march his army back to Syria and that he had decided to ship her and her children off to Rome within three days.

Aware that her time was limited and that the humiliation of the triumph was inevitable, as was the Roman annexation of Egypt, Cleopatra now made her final preparations for death. After visiting Antony's tomb, she bathed, dressed herself in her royal finery and regalia, and had a last banquet set before her. A countryman who arrived carrying a basket of extra large and fine figs was consequently admitted by her guards without raising any suspicions. After dining, the queen gave a sealed tablet, already written upon, to her warder Epaphroditus with orders to take it to Octavian. Then having dismissed all her servants except Eiras and Charmion, she closed the doors.

As soon as Octavian received the tablet and read her request to be buried next to Antony, he guessed what had happened. Although his retainers lost no time in getting to the palace, they were already too late. They came upon Cleopatra's guards still unaware that anything was amiss, but when the doors were opened they found her already dead, lying upon a golden couch in her full regalia. Eiras lay dying at her feet and Charmion, who was also close to death, was attempting to arrange the diadem upon the queen's brow. 'Is it well done?' one of the guards angrily asked her and with her last words Charmion managed to reply:

> It is well done and fitting for a Princess
> Descended of so many royal Kings.
> (Shakespeare, *Antony and Cleopatra*,
> Act 5 Scene 2)[11]

Having wound his readers up to such a marvellous finale, at this point Plutarch does a sort of Jekyll and Hyde act. In an abrupt and disconcerting change of character he exchanges the bow tie and velvet smoking jacket of the literary historian for the lab coat of the criminal pathologist and embarks upon a scientific discussion of the exact cause of Cleopatra's death. From this, as also from Dio's (51.14) account, it very quickly emerges that no one had any sure knowledge of the exact manner in which the queen had died.

The only marks upon Cleopatra's body were said to have been two slight puncture marks upon her arm (Plutarch, *Antony* 86.5, Dio 51.14.1). Hence the immediate suspicion that she had been bitten by a snake which she had deliberately arranged to have brought in for that purpose in the basket of figs. Other variants had it concealed in a water pot (recorded by both Plutarch and Dio) or a bouquet of flowers (Dio only) but the snake itself was never found, although some claimed to have seen traces of it on the seaward side of the chamber where the windows lay. On the other hand there were those who claimed that Cleopatra had a hollow comb (Plutarch) or hairpin (Dio) smeared with poison which she had hidden in her hair and that this is what she had pricked herself with.

How credible then is the theory of Cleopatra's death by snakebite? Plutarch had carefully prepared earlier for the story of the asp by recounting the experiments Cleopatra had made on venomous animals during the preceding winter in an effort to find a painless poison (*Antony* 71.6–8) as well as by introducing the arrival of the countryman with the basket of figs at the appropriate point in his narrative. Yet it is significant that when it finally comes to the crunch he himself is unwilling to accept the story which he has just told so masterfully. Indeed these same two versions, snakebite and poison, also occur in one of the earliest references which there is to Cleopatra's suicide (Strabo 17.795C) and since its writer, the geographer Strabo, was in Egypt only a few years after the event (25 BC – c. 19 BC) it seems likely that both theories must still have been in circulation in Alexandria at that stage. There may therefore have been genuine doubt among the Alexandrians about how their queen had killed herself. On the other hand there are indications that Octavian may have encouraged the dissemination of the snakebite theory as the authoritative version and this is probably why this is the version which appears in the earliest Roman sources, albeit in a garbled form.

On learning of Cleopatra's death, Octavian is said to have tried various drugs and also summoned a group of snakebite experts called the Psylli to suck the poison out of the wound in an effort to revive her,[12] and according to Plutarch he himself seemed to believe the snakebite story. As a result an image of Cleopatra with the asp clinging to her was later carried in the procession at his triumph and this no doubt explains why the Roman poets Virgil, Propertius, and Horace, who were probably among the immense crowd which witnessed Octavian's triumph at Rome, all speak of her death by snakebite.[13] Along with Strabo these three writers are also nearest in time to the event itself so that it has often been thought significant that they all mention more than one serpent. The most likely explanation, however, is that the statue which they saw carried in the procession depicted Cleopatra grasping, or encircled by two snakes. However close they may have been to the emperor, it is only a remote possibility that any of these poets had access to an independent source which recorded that the queen had used two snakes rather than one for her suicide.

Since none of our ancient sources are able or willing to do so, it seems impossible for us to choose between the alternative theories of poison or snakebite. Nevertheless it is perhaps worthwhile underlining the practical difficulties which would have been associated with the latter, particularly if more than one snake had been used. The Egyptian cobra, which is generally believed to be the type of snake most likely to have been used by Cleopatra,[14] is about 2 m long. It would certainly be possible to introduce a single snake of that size hidden in a container of some type. But it would become increasingly difficult if more than one were required, either for symbolic reasons or to make sure that there was enough venom to be effective. As the cobra discharges most of its venom at the first bite, one snake could not be relied upon to kill more than a single person. So if Eiras and Charmion had also committed suicide by the same method, we are faced with a minimum of three snakes, or possibly four if Cleopatra herself had required two. While the introduction of one snake is perhaps credible, the mind soon begins to boggle at this Medusa-like proliferation of reptiles.[15]

Assuming, however, that Cleopatra did die by snakebite, was her chosen method of death intended to be symbolic in any way, as has often been argued? Again there are difficulties. First and most obviously, if Cleopatra had intended to make a symbolic statement by her death, then arguably either she or her women would have taken at least some measures to ensure that the symbol itself had not slithered out of the window before it could be seen and its significance could be appreciated fully. Second, ancient

Egyptian iconography is so replete with serpents of every description, both good and bad, that it is difficult to determine exactly what Cleopatra may have meant hers to symbolise.

It was originally argued that Cleopatra's asp was the uraeus, the emblem of the ancient pharaohs, which stood upon the royal crown and dealt death and destruction to the king's enemies. Sacred to Re, its bite conferred immortality upon the queen when she turned it upon herself.[16] Cleopatra, however, did not need immortality for as a living goddess and a divine ruler she was already immortal. In its origins too the snake is more likely to represent Wadjet, the cobra goddess of Lower Egypt, rather than the sun god.[17] As such it often appears in association with Nekhbet, the vulture goddess of Upper Egypt, to symbolise the pharaoh's kingship over the Two Lands of Egypt, or twinned as the double uraeus, either encircling the winged solar disk or on the royal crowns.[18] Yet Isis too could manifest herself in a serpentine form as Isis Thermoutharion, either alone or in association with the equally serpentine Agathus Daemon (Good Spirit), the patron god and protector of Alexandria. So did Cleopatra die as pharaoh of Egypt, or in her divine persona as Isis, or as Isis and Alexandria combined?

Perhaps there is no need to decide between these competing claims because perhaps no symbolism ever existed. Behind all these theories of a symbolic suicide is the unspoken assumption that when Cleopatra died as the last ruler of a great line of kings, she was presenting herself as the last of the Ptolemies or even as the last of the pharaohs of Egypt. Yet it is just as likely that if she saw any symbolism in her death, she saw herself as the last of the line descending from Alexander the Great. The diadem which the dying Charmion was weakly trying to arrange on the queen's temples when the guards burst in was not necessarily one of the elaborate composite Greco-Egyptian crowns sported by the later Ptolemies. Although we can never know for sure, it is just as likely to have been the plain cloth headband of Macedonian kingship, which her ancestor Ptolemy I had adopted as the successor of Alexander and which she herself is often portrayed wearing on her coinage. Certainly the ambitions of world domination which Cleopatra and Mark Antony shared and the actions which arose from those ambitions had a lot more to do with the emulation of Alexander the Great and the reconstruction of an empire uniting East and West than with any notions of ancient Egyptian kingship.

Finally there is the question of the extent of Octavian's own involvement in Cleopatra's suicide. The extreme view, which was expressed as early as the 1880s, that Octavian had the queen murdered and that the whole story of her suicide is accordingly nothing more than a hoax has long since been discredited.[19] But the suggestion that even so he may have manoeuvred Cleopatra into taking her own life in order to get rid of someone who had the potential to be a major source of embarrassment to him politically seems to have achieved almost the status of an orthodoxy thanks to its adoption by Sir William Tarn in his account of the period in the *Cambridge Ancient History*.[20]

With slight variations,[21] the argument goes that despite his own desire to parade her as his captive and the Roman public's desire to see her thus humiliated, Octavian realised that it would be far too dangerous to let Cleopatra live and to take her to Rome. Her appearance there in public might give the lie to all his careful propaganda aimed at presenting her as Rome's greatest and most dangerous enemy since Hannibal. It might serve to remind the populace of earlier and happier times when she and Octavian's adoptive father Julius Caesar had been lovers and he had dedicated a statue of her in the temple of Venus Genetrix. A riot might break out among the devotees of Isis in the capital if they regarded Cleopatra as the living incarnation of their goddess, as she claimed to be. Or there might be a widespread revulsion of public feeling in her favour such as there had been in 46 BC when her sister Arsinoe had been led in chains (perhaps at Cleopatra's own insistence) in Julius Caesar's triumph celebrating his victory in the Alexandrine War.

Consequently Octavian deliberately made it easy for the queen to kill herself. Instead of having her guarded properly with Roman troops, he craftily left her in the care of her own servants, supervised only by his freedman Epaphroditus who if necessary could have been disowned or disposed of much more easily than a high-ranking Roman officer. He had also learnt earlier from Proculeius of her determination never to be led in his triumph and by working upon this and her concerns for the survival and succession of her children he systematically reduced her to such a state of despair that suicide seemed to be the only way out left for her.

While it is credible that Octavian may have been influenced by considerations of what might happen if Cleopatra appeared in Rome or worries about what to do with her after the triumph, it is not so easy to believe that even someone as devious as he was would have hit upon such a convoluted scheme for disposing of an enemy. Although it is an argument from silence, it is significant that none of our ancient sources shows any trace of scepticism about her death. They may disagree about how she committed suicide but the fact of her suicide seems never to have been questioned, even in the outpouring of malicious gossip which attended the emperor's death (Tacitus, *Annals* 1.10). Furthermore the charge that she was not kept under proper guard is not difficult to refute. Although a prisoner, Cleopatra deserved a certain consideration and privacy on several counts – as a head of state, as a woman, and as an invalid. To imply therefore that she should have been kept under strict military supervision at all times is unrealistic, to say the least.

An equally telling argument against any covert involvement on Octavian's part is the fact that Cleopatra is said to have made at least two earlier attempts to take her life (Plutarch, *Antony* 79.3–4, 82.3–4). She had tried to stab herself when Proculeius had first taken her captive within the mausoleum. Then when she fell sick of a fever after the burial of Antony, she had determined to starve herself to death. In both cases those attempts were foiled. Admittedly if Octavian had been concerned to appear totally innocent of her death, it would have looked highly suspicious had she died at the hands of Proculeius in the initial scuffle at the mausoleum. But why did he dissuade her from taking her life on the second occasion by threatening the lives of her children? At that point she was already perilously close to death from sickness and grief. There was a Greek doctor Olympus at hand ready to assist her and he would have been just as disposable as any of Octavian's own freedmen had Octavian wanted to use him as a 'cut-out'. Yet Octavian nevertheless perversely continued to make every effort to keep her alive.

Furthermore the story of her last days as it is told by both Plutarch and Dio is hardly flattering to Octavian.[22] Despite his best efforts, Octavian is shown as being thoroughly duped and finally outwitted by Cleopatra. Once the Alexandrians learnt of it, her survival against all odds after the city's capture can only have added to her heroic stature and it is just possible that Octavian may have emphasised his role in keeping her alive in an attempt to diminish that stature. But the fact that in the end he could not keep her alive, however much he may have wanted her for his triumph, does so little for his image that it is hard to believe that this can be the way in which he wanted himself presented – a clever, calculating, and supremely successful Roman general foiled at the last by a foreigner and a woman. The story that we have of her death from the fatal bite of a deadly snake smuggled in somehow or other, or a less dignified end from an unknown poison concealed with the cunning of an oriental sorceress where even the most clever of males would never think to look, and of the vain efforts later made to revive her, might be the best that Octavian's propaganda could salvage at the time from what was ultimately Cleopatra's triumph and not his. To assert against all the ancient evidence that he was the deceiver and she was the deceived rather than vice versa detracts from the glory of Cleopatra's last victory without adding anything of substance to her opponent's. Whether it was snakebite or poison that she died by, when she died was Cleopatra's decision, not Octavian's. Regardless of the details, popular mythology is surely correct in recognising and honouring that truth.

16

THE END OF THE LINE
Cleopatra Selene of Mauretania

Cleopatra VII was 39 years old when she died. She had been queen of Egypt for 22 of those years. It is often said that when she committed suicide, probably on 12 August 30 BC by our Julian calendar,[1] she was the last of the Ptolemies. In one sense that is true for, regardless of the provisions of any will which might have been made by Ptolemy X or Ptolemy XI, after Antony had been deserted by the Egyptian fleet and defeated in the battle outside Alexandria on 3 August 30 BC, Egypt was Octavian's by right of conquest. But since he did not formally annex the country until 31 August, it is sometimes believed that during the short period after Cleopatra's death her children enjoyed an 18-day reign as her heirs and successors.[2] So in another sense they too could be said to have been the last of the Ptolemies.

Cleopatra VII had four children. Although he had been only 3 years old at the time, in the days of crisis after the assassination of Julius Caesar in 44 BC she had associated the eldest, Caesarion, who was Caesar's reputed son, as her co-ruler as Ptolemy XV Caesar – after she had first murdered her younger brother and then consort Ptolemy XIV to clear the way to the succession for him. Ten years later (34 BC) in a magnificent ceremony known as the Donations which was held in the gymnasium in Alexandria before Antony and Cleopatra (as Isis) seated respectively on gold and silver thrones, Antony had recognised him as Caesar's legitimate son by his Macedonian marriage to Cleopatra (and therefore by implication superior to Octavian, who was only an adopted son) and declared him King of Kings alongside his mother who was hailed as Queen of Kings. Their own three children, the twins Alexander Helios (Sun) and Cleopatra Selene (Moon) who had been born in 40 BC and the toddler Ptolemy Philadelphus (born 36 BC), who were seated below their parents on lower thrones beside Caesarion, were also given kingdoms and titles at the same time.[3]

In the winter of 31/0 BC as part of the preparations in expectation of Octavian's final onslaught another ceremony was held to celebrate the coming of age of both Caesarion and Antyllus, Antony's own son and heir by his third wife Fulvia (Plutarch, *Antony* 71.3, Dio 51.6.1–2). This rite of passage – Caesarion, aged 16, being enrolled into the Alexandrian ephebate and the 14-year-old Antyllus taking the *toga virilis* of Roman manhood – was primarily a political act which was intended to designate the boys as the replacement leadership should anything happen to their parents. But as adults it exposed them to a much greater potential danger and, having realised this, Cleopatra decided to send Caesarion away. He was despatched to safety accompanied by his tutor Rhodon, and with part of Cleopatra's treasure they set off up the Nile to Coptos from where they would cross to the Red Sea coast to take ship for India.

At the time just after Antony's death, when Octavian had prevailed upon the queen to give up her self-imposed hunger strike by threatening her children's lives, Antyllus had already been betrayed by his tutor Theodorus and put to death on Octavian's orders (Plutarch, *Antony* 81.1–3). The same fate soon befell Caesarion too. Shortly after his mother's suicide he was either overtaken and killed while still *en route* to India (Dio 51.15.5) or lured back to Alexandria by his tutor with the false promise that Octavian had invited him to succeed as king of Egypt (Plutarch, *Antony* 81.4) and subsequently executed there.

It is understandable that Octavian should be loath to leave the sons and heirs of his enemies alive, particularly since they were now both adults. But Cleopatra's children by Antony fared better, as did his other children by his other wives. After they had walked in Octavian's triumphal procession (29 BC) in company with a statue of their mother with the asp (or asps) shown battening upon her, Alexander Helios, Cleopatra Selene, and Ptolemy Philadelphus were given over to Octavia, Antony's fourth wife, who brought them up with her own children. We hear no more of Alexander or Ptolemy. They may have survived to live out lives of quiet decency or harmless flamboyance, as so many modern ex-royals have done, for Dio (51.15.6) says that the emperor granted their lives to Cleopatra Selene on the occasion of her marriage. As for Cleopatra Selene, when she came of age, she was married by

Augustus to a Numidian prince Juba II, a learned young man who had been brought up in Italy where he had given himself over to historical research.

The couple shared in common the fact that as children they had both graced Roman triumphs for as a boy Juba had walked in the procession of 46 BC which celebrated Julius Caesar's African victories over his father Juba I, who had been true to his loyalty to Pompey and given military support to Scipio, the Pompeian commander in Africa. He had subsequently remained in Italy where he was granted Roman citizenship and as Gaius Julius Juba he is found accompanying the emperor Augustus on a number of his campaigns. Augustus seems to have taken a great liking to him for in 25 BC, only eight years after its annexation by the Romans, he was given the client kingdom of Mauretania, roughly equivalent to modern Morocco, to rule over.

Juba II's marriage to Cleopatra Selene is dated to *c.* 20 BC by the commencement of their joint coinage, which shows 'Rex Juba' on one face of the coin with the inscription in Latin and 'Basilissa (queen) Cleopatra', often in her divine persona as Isis, on the other with the inscription in Greek. The coin portraits are too stylised to be entirely reliable. Nevertheless they can be trusted to reproduce the main facial features of their subjects. In the case of the queen they suggest that Cleopatra Selene had inherited her mother's strong prominent nose but leave us with the impression that she was probably prettier than Cleopatra VII, all of whose portraits flatly contradict the popular belief that she must have been a great beauty.

An epigram in the Greek Anthology, written by a contemporary poet called Crinagoras who was closely associated with the household of Octavia and also wrote epigrams for her daughter Antonia, Cleopatra Selene's half-sister, is believed to commemorate their union. Crinagoras shows more enthusiasm than geographical knowledge in making the Nile the boundary between Egypt and Morocco but the poem is nevertheless a nice compliment to the newly weds:

> Great neighbouring lands of the world, which the Nile's
> Waters swollen from black Ethiopia separate,
> You both have common kings by marriage,
> Making of Egypt and Libya a single race.

May the children born of these lords hold from
Their parents in turn firm sway over both lands.
          (Crinagoras, 25 Gow-Page = *Anth.Pal.* 9.235)

Ten years had elapsed by this time since the defeat and suicide
of the young bride's mother Cleopatra VII. Old wounds had been
given a chance to heal and, far from playing down her ancestry
after her marriage, Cleopatra Selene seems to have been almost at
pains to emphasise it. Although many coins reflect her name by
the device of a sickle moon, others also emphasise her identity as
Isis and show such typically Egyptian devices as the Nile crocodile.
Indeed one early type goes so far as to mention her descent,[4] and
so when a son was born it is hardly surprising to find that he was
called Ptolemy.

Her husband, who traced his own descent from Heracles, was
much taken up with promoting the further hellenisation and now
the romanisation of his kingdom as well as with the pursuit of his
voluminous researches and the care of his extensive art collection.
He renamed Iol, his capital, Caesarea in honour of his patron
Caesar Augustus, had the theatre remodelled by an architect perhaps imported from Rome, and reorganised the royal Mauretanian
guard along the lines of a Roman force.[5] But while the king's
administrative and academic pursuits may have meant that in the
emperor's eyes he was politically harmless, they did not mean that
Juba II was entirely insensible to life's other pleasures. Many of
the king's scholarly writings were of a geographical nature and it
may have been in the course of a research trip undertaken to gather
material for them that he picked up his second wife Glaphyra at
the court of her father king Archelaus of Cappadocia.

Glaphyra seems to have been something of a troublemaker. Her
first marriage had been to Herod's son Alexander who apparently
doted upon her (Josephus, *Jewish Ant.* 16.10.7). But she was hated
at the Jewish court because of her open boasting that Herod's
wives and daughters were not as high born as she was. The Jewish
women had their revenge, however, by falsely accusing her of an
affair with her father-in-law, and after Herod had killed Alexander
for conspiring against him (7 BC) she was given her dowry and
sent back to her father. It was there that Josephus says Juba II
met and married her. This second marriage must have taken place
sometime between the death of her first husband Alexander in 7

BC and Glaphyra's third marriage, which may have been as soon as 4 BC or as late as AD 6–7.[6]

It used to be assumed that Cleopatra Selene was already dead by this stage and that Juba II was therefore a widower, but the evidence of numerous Mauretanian coins with the head of the queen and securely datable to AD 11–17 suggests that this second marriage was no more than a brief and uncharacteristic interlude in Juba II's otherwise blameless life. It is unlikely that coins with Cleopatra Selene's name and title would continue to have been struck for so many years after her death. The most likely explanation therefore is that Juba II probably soon grew tired of Glaphyra (who then became the wife of her former brother-in-law Archelaus after he had divorced his wife Mariamne in her favour, much to the horror of his fellow Jews) and that he must have remarried Cleopatra Selene after he had returned to Mauretania.

If this is the case, then it is probable that Cleopatra Selene acted as regent during her husband's absence and that at least some of the coins which she issued in her sole name date from this time. Exactly when she died is unknown, although it is most likely to have been in the same period of c. AD 11–17. Another epigram by Crinagoras associates her death with an eclipse of the moon but in the light of the coin evidence its previous identification with an eclipse which took place on 22 March 5 BC is no longer tenable.[7] Indeed it may well be the case that Crinagoras is simply imitating the poetical conceit of an earlier epigrammatist in speaking of the fading of the moon's light at the passing of the queen who had been named after her:[8]

> When she rose the moon herself grew dark,
> Veiling her grief in night, for she saw
> Her lovely namesake Selene bereft of life
> And going down to gloomy Hades.
> With her she had shared her light's beauty,
> And with her death she mingled her own darkness.
>   (Crinagoras, 18 Gow-Page = *Anth.Pal.* 7.633)

Her son Ptolemy was probably Cleopatra Selene's only child.[9] He succeeded to the throne after the death of his father (c. AD 23) and reigned until AD 40, when he was summoned from his kingdom and put to death by the emperor Caligula. Why Caligula should have done this remains a mystery. Suetonius (*Gaius* 35.2) says that it was because Ptolemy had offended him by appearing at a public spectacle dressed in a robe of a more splendid purple than the emperor's own. This does not sound too implausible given Caligula's notoriously touchy nature. Furthermore Ptolemy's father Juba II had apparently been responsible for establishing a settlement for the manufacture of sea purple on the island of Mogador just offshore from the modern town of Essaouira on Morocco's Atlantic coast,[10] so Ptolemy might have been promoting his country's products in the same way that members of the British royal family, for example, feel obliged to serve as clothes horses for London fashion designers. Yet for a variety of reasons scholars have felt unable to accept what Suetonius says and have offered a number of other explanations instead.

One theory which has been put forward is that Ptolemy was wearing his purple garment as a high priest of Isis and that Caligula therefore had him done away with because as the son of Cleopatra Selene he saw in him an unacceptable competitor for the favours of a goddess to whom he himself was particularly devoted.[11] Another is that the emperor may have suspected him of complicity in the recent conspiracy of Gaetulicus.[12] Yet a third is that Ptolemy's murder may have had some connection with a family quarrel for he was distantly related to the emperor on his mother's side since his grandfather Mark Antony was Caligula's great-grand-father. Perhaps more believable merely because it is so mundane is Balsdon's earlier suggestion that Caligula wanted to convert Mauretania into a Roman province simply because it was adminis-tratively convenient to do so, although if he is right Caligula really deserves more that the slight slap on the wrist which is all that the author rather indulgently gives him for his criminal murder of such an elderly and inoffensive vassal.[13]

As so often, what it comes down to is that we simply do not have enough evidence to say why the king was put to death. What we do know, however, is that since Ptolemy left no recorded descendants, this truly was the end of the line. There were of course still Ptolemies and Cleopatras in plenty for by this time the names had become widespread throughout the hellenistic world. They would endure for centuries to come – the name Cleopatra surviving, of course, into our own time. But as far as the line of the Ptolemaic kings was concerned, Ptolemy of Mauret-ania really was the last of the Ptolemies in the fullest and most final sense of the term just as his mother Cleopatra Selene had been the last of the royal Cleopatras.

APPENDIX 1: WHO'S WHO AMONG THE PTOLEMIES

To save space and avoid confusion, in the text the Ptolemies and their wives are referred to by name and number only, rather than as often happens, by name, number, title, and/or nickname or a combination of several of these elements. The summary below, which is based in the main upon Peremans and Van't Dack (1968), brings all that information together, along with the most essential dates and relationships (although some of the dates still remain uncertain). The main source of confusion with the dynasty is that the system of numeration tends to be different in older works after Ptolemy VI Philometor since his son Ptolemy VII Neos Philopator, who reigned with his mother Cleopatra II for only a brief period in 145 BC before he was murdered by his uncle Ptolemy VIII Euergetes II, is not included in the series as a separate king. Thus in, for example, Bevan (1927), Ptolemy VIII Euergetes II is called Ptolemy VII Euergetes II, Ptolemy IX is Ptolemy VIII and so on. The dates of each Ptolemy's reign are given first, after his name and title(s).

PTOLEMY I SOTER (SAVIOUR)
323 (as satrap, king from 305)–282 BC

Born c. 367/6 BC, the son of the Macedonian general Lagus and Arsinoe, who was perhaps a concubine of Philip II of Macedon. Alexander the Great's general from 336 BC and satrap of Egypt from 323 BC, he declared himself king from November 305 BC. He occupied Coele Syria after 301 BC, and later Cyprus, the Aegean islands and southern Asia Minor. Founded the Alexandrian Museum and Library and established the worship of Sarapis. Died between January and summer 282 BC.

PTOLEMY II PHILADELPHUS (SISTER LOVING)
282–246 BC; co-regent with Ptolemy I from late December 285 BC

Born 308 BC, the son of Ptolemy I and his third wife Berenice I. Married 1) Arsinoe I, daughter of Lysimachus (*c.* 289/8 BC), 2) his own elder sister Arsinoe II (*c.* 279–274 BC) whom he took as co-ruler. Retained control of Coele Syria in the First Syrian War (274–271 BC) but lost territory to Antiochus II in the Second Syrian War (260–253? BC). A notable patron of the arts and literature, he also established the Ptolemaic ruler cult (he and Arsinoe II were both proclaimed gods in 272/1 BC). Died late January 246 BC.

PTOLEMY III EUERGETES I (BENEFACTOR)
246–222 BC

Born *c.* 284 BC, the oldest son of Ptolemy II and Arsinoe I. Married Berenice II, daughter of Magas of Cyrene (247 BC), hence acquiring Cyrenaica for Egypt. Invaded Syria in reprisal for the murder of his sister Berenice, wife of Antiochus II (Third Syrian (Laodicean) War, 246–241 BC). Began construction of the Horus temple at Edfu in 237 BC to conciliate the native priesthoods after a native Egyptian uprising. Died between October and December 222 BC.

PTOLEMY IV PHILOPATOR (FATHER LOVING)
222–205 BC

Born *c.* 244? BC, son of Ptolemy III and Berenice II. Married his full sister Arsinoe III (217 BC). Challenged by Antiochus III the Great (Fourth Syrian War, 221–217 BC) but defeated him at Raphia on 22 June 217 BC with the aid of 20,000 native Egyptian troops and thus regained Coele Syria. Upper Egypt seceded late in his reign and was ruled by native Nubian kings from 207 to 187 BC. His death in ?October/November 205 BC was perhaps concealed until the following summer.

PTOLEMY V EPIPHANES EUCHARISTOS (THE MANIFEST, BENEFICENT (GOD))
summer/early September 204–180 BC

Born 9 October 210 BC, the only son of Ptolemy IV and Arsinoe III. Became king under the regency of his ministers Sosibius and Agathocles. The Fifth Syrian War (202–200 BC) ended in an Egyptian defeat at Panium (200 BC) and the loss of Coele Syria and most Egyptian possessions in Asia Minor and the Aegean. Married Cleopatra I 'the Syrian', daughter of Antiochus III and his queen Laodice, as part of the peace settlement (winter 194/3 BC). Regained Upper Egypt in 187/6 BC and the Delta in 184/3 BC. Died in September/October 180 BC.

PTOLEMY VI PHILOMETOR (MOTHER LOVING)
September/October 180–145 BC (except for autumn 164 to May 163 BC)

Born 186 BC, elder son of Ptolemy V and Cleopatra I. Ruled under his mother's regency until her death in 176 BC, when he took the title Philometor. Married his elder sister Cleopatra II (April/October 176 BC). When Antiochus IV invaded Egypt in 170 BC his sister–wife and younger brother Ptolemy VIII were associated with him as co-rulers (170/69–164/3 BC). He was expelled by Ptolemy VIII in autumn 164 BC but reinstated in 163 BC on appeal to Rome. In the later part of his reign he attempted to re-establish Egyptian power in western Asia by dynastic marriages of his daughter Cleopatra Thea to the rival Seleucid princes Alexander Balas and Demetrius II. Successfully invaded Syria and invited by the Antiochenes to become king of Asia, but declined. Died in spring/summer 145 BC of wounds after battling the forces of Balas on the plain of Antioch.

PTOLEMY EUPATOR (BORN OF A NOBLE FATHER)
co-regent with Ptolemy VI, 152 BC

Born 163 BC, the elder son of Ptolemy VI and Cleopatra II. Co-regent with his father, 152 BC, and king or governor of Cyprus. Died young, probably in late August 152 BC.

PTOLEMY VII NEOS PHILOPATOR (NEW, FATHER LOVING)
145/4 BC

Born *c.* 162 BC, second son of Ptolemy VI and Cleopatra II. Made co-regent with his father in spring/summer 145 BC and ruled briefly with his mother after his father's death. Murdered by his uncle Ptolemy VIII after his return in August/September 145 BC.

PTOLEMY VIII EUERGETES II PHYSCON (BENEFACTOR, POT BELLY)
co-ruler with Ptolemy VI and Cleopatra II, 170/69–164/3 BC; sole king in association with Cleopatra II, autumn 164 to May 163 BC; king of Cyrene, 163–145 BC; king of Egypt, late summer 145–116 BC

Born *c.* 182/1? BC, younger son of Ptolemy V and Cleopatra I. Also known as Tryphon (The Magnificent), although he is most usually known by his nickname Physcon. Married 1) his sister Cleopatra II on his return from exile in 145 BC, 2) her daughter Cleopatra III (May 141 to June 140 BC) after the birth of Ptolemy IX, without divorcing Cleopatra II. Subsequently ruled with one or both wives. When he died in June 116 BC he left Egypt to Cleopatra III to rule with whichever of their two sons she chose.

PTOLEMY MEMPHITES
perhaps co-regent 131 BC

Born 144/3 BC, son of Ptolemy VIII and Cleopatra II. Put to death by his father in 131 BC.

(Late 132–130 BC. Revolution of Cleopatra II)

PTOLEMY APION

Born after *c.* 154? BC, illegitimate son of Ptolemy VIII and his concubine Eirene. On his father's death (116 BC) he was given Cyprus and ruled it as king to 96 BC, when he left it to the Roman people on his death.

(116–101 BC. Reign of Cleopatra III in association variously with her sons Ptolemy IX and Ptolemy X)

PTOLEMY IX PHILOMETOR SOTER II LATHYRUS (MOTHER LOVING, SAVIOUR, CHICKPEA)
116–107 BC and 88–80 BC; king of Cyprus, 105–88 BC

Born 18 February 142 BC, elder son of Ptolemy VIII and Cleopatra III. Also nicknamed Physcon, like his father, but most usually known by his other nickname Lathyrus. Associated as co-ruler with his mother in accordance with his father's will but against her wishes, he was twice replaced by his younger brother Ptolemy X (110/9 BC and March–May 108 BC) before his definite expulsion in autumn 107 BC. After his attempt to regain Egypt via Syria was thwarted by his mother and brother (103–101 BC), he returned to Cyprus. Recalled after his brother's expulsion and death, he ruled until his death in March 80 BC. A native revolt against him ended in the sack of Thebes.

PTOLEMY X ALEXANDER I
107–88 BC; king of Cyprus, 114/3–107 BC

Born c. 140 BC, second son of Ptolemy VIII and Cleopatra III. Nicknamed 'Kokke's child' and Pareisaktos (one secretly brought in, 'the ring-in') but not usually referred to by these names. Taken by his mother Cleopatra III as her first choice for co-ruler in 116 BC but not accepted by the Alexandrians. Twice recalled as co-ruler for short periods before Ptolemy IX's final expulsion in 107 BC (see under Ptolemy IX) and ruled jointly with Cleopatra III until she died, or he murdered her, in late 101 BC. Married his niece Cleopatra Berenice III as his consort (101 BC). Expelled by the Alexandrians again, he died in a naval battle while attempting to cross to Cyprus (March 88 BC).

(88–80 BC. Second period of rule of Ptolemy IX associated with his daughter Cleopatra Berenice III)

(March–September 80 BC. Reign of Cleopatra Berenice III, last 19 days in association with Ptolemy XI)

PTOLEMY XI ALEXANDER II
June 80 BC

Born *c.* 105 BC, son of Ptolemy X and an unknown first wife. Taken as hostage from Cos by Mithradates (88 BC), he escaped to Sulla's camp (84 BC) and accompanied him to Rome. In 80 BC Sulla married him to his cousin and stepmother Cleopatra Berenice III and made him co-ruler with her. Having murdered her within three weeks, he was killed in his turn by the Alexandrians after a reign of 18 or 19 days.

PTOLEMY XII NEOS DIONYSUS PHILOPATOR PHILADELPHUS AULETES (THE NEW DIONYSUS, FATHER LOVING, SISTER LOVING, THE FLUTE PLAYER)
June/July 80 to September 58 BC; April 55–51 BC

Born 98–95 or 115–107 BC, the illegitimate son of Ptolemy IX and a concubine. Best known by his nickname Auletes. Married his half-sister Cleopatra V Tryphaena (by January 79 BC). Called to the kingship by the Alexandrians but forced out by them after the Roman annexation of Cyprus. Restored by Aulus Gabinius, proconsul of Syria, on Pompey's orders (55 BC). Died February/March 51 BC.

PTOLEMY OF CYPRUS
king of Cyprus 80–59/8 BC

Younger brother of Ptolemy XII. Last Ptolemaic king of Cyprus, he committed suicide when the island was annexed and made into a Roman province.

(58/7 BC. Joint reign of Cleopatra V Tryphaena and her daughter Berenice IV)

(57 BC to April 55 BC. Reign of Berenice IV, later in association with 1) Seleucus Kybiosaktes, 2) Archelaus)

(Spring/summer 51 to 12 August 30 BC. Reign of Cleopatra VII in association with 1) Ptolemy XIII, 2) Ptolemy XIV, 3) Caesarion)

PTOLEMY XIII
? March/April 51 to early January 47 BC

Born *c.* 61 BC, elder son of Ptolemy XII and Cleopatra V Try-phaena. Co-regent briefly with his father, then with his elder sister and wife Cleopatra VII, but attempted to expel her. Drowned in the Nile after being defeated by Cleopatra VII and Julius Caesar in the Alexandrine War.

PTOLEMY XIV PHILOPATOR (FATHER LOVING)
47–44 BC

Born *c.* 59/8 BC, younger son of Ptolemy XII. Made provisional ruler of Cyprus with his sister Arsinoe by Julius Caesar (48 BC). Married to Cleopatra VII after his brother's death and made her co-ruler by Caesar, but murdered by her in ?August 44 BC.

PTOLEMY XV CAESAR PHILOPATOR PHILOMETOR
(FATHER LOVING, MOTHER LOVING)
44 BC to 30 August 30 BC

Born 47 BC, illegitimate son of Cleopatra VII and Julius Caesar. Most usually known as Caesarion, which is what the literary sources call him. After the murder of Ptolemy XIV Cleopatra VII temporarily associated him with her (42–41 BC) and he was made her co-ruler from 36 BC. Put to death on Octavian's orders after death of Cleopatra VII.

PTOLEMY PHILADELPHUS (BROTHER LOVING)

Born 36 BC, illegitimate son of Cleopatra VII and Mark Antony. Proclaimed king of Phoenicia, Syria, Cilicia and all the countries between the Euphrates and the Hellespont (34 BC). Taken to Rome by Octavian in 30 BC.

PTOLEMY OF MAURETANIA
c. AD 23–40

Born c. 19–18 BC, only son of Juba II, client king of Mauretania, and Cleopatra Selene, Cleopatra VII's daughter by Mark Antony. Succeeded his father in c. AD 23. Put to death by the emperor Caligula in AD 40.

APPENDIX 2:
GENEALOGICAL TABLES

Table 1 shows the wives and children of Philip II of Macedon.

Tables 2 and 3 show the connections which were progressively established as a result of dynastic marriages between the Ptolemaic and Seleucid houses in the later stages of their history.

1 Philip II's wives and children

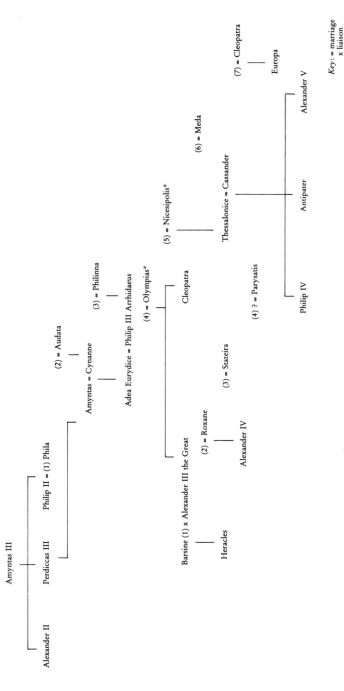

Key: = marriage
x liaison

*According to Satyrus, Olympias was Philip's fifth wife, Nicesipolis his fourth

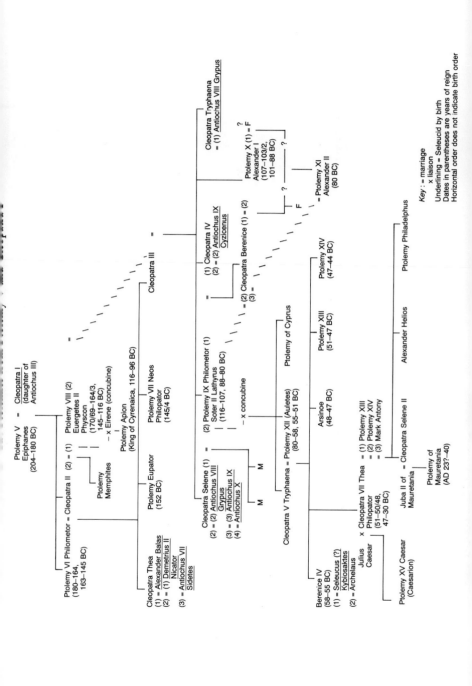

Ptolemy V = Cleopatra I
Epiphanes   (daughter of
(204–180 BC)   Antiochus III)

Ptolemy VI Philometor = Cleopatra II (2) = (1)   Ptolemy VIII
(180–164,   Euergetes II
163–145 BC)   Physcon
                                                   (170/69–164/3,
                                                   145–116 BC)
                          Ptolemy   – x Eirene (concubine)
                          Memphites
                                                   Ptolemy Apion
                                                   (King of Cyrenaica, 116–96 BC)

Ptolemy Eupator   Ptolemy VII Neos   Cleopatra III   =
(152 BC)   Philopator
                         (145/4 BC)

Cleopatra Thea   Cleopatra Tryphaena
(1) = Alexander Balas   = (1) Antiochus VIII Grypus
(2) = (1) Demetrius II
         Nicator
(3) = Antiochus VII   (1) Cleopatra IV   Ptolemy X (1) =   ?
      Sidetes   (2) = (2) Antiochus IX Alexander I   ? F
                                                 Cyzicenus   (107–103/2,
                                                               101–88 BC)
Cleopatra Selene (1) =
(2) = (2) Antiochus VIII   (2) Ptolemy IX Philometor (1)   = (2) Cleopatra Berenice (1) = (2)   ?
          Grypus   Soter II Lathyrus   (3) =   ? F
(3) = (3) Antiochus IX   (116–107, 88–80 BC)   = Ptolemy XI
          Cyzicenus   Alexander II
(4) = (4) Antiochus X   – x concubine   (80 BC)

                                    M
                        M   Ptolemy of Cyprus
                    M

Cleopatra V Tryphaena = Ptolemy XII (Auletes)
                        (80–58, 55–51 BC)

Berenice IV   Arsinoe   Ptolemy XIII   Ptolemy XIV
(58–55 BC)   (48–47 BC)   (51–47 BC)   (47–44 BC)
(1) = Seleucus (?)
      Kybiosaktes
(2) = Archelaus

Julius   x Cleopatra VII Thea   = (1) Ptolemy XIII
Caesar   Philopator   = (2) Ptolemy XIV   Alexander Helios   Ptolemy Philadelphus
            (51–50/48,   = (3) Mark Antony
            47–30 BC)

Ptolemy XV Caesar   Juba II of = Cleopatra Selene II
(Caesarion)   Mauretania

                         Ptolemy of
                         Mauretania
                         (AD 23?–40)

Key : = marriage
      x liaison
Underlining = Seleucid by birth
Dates in parentheses are years of reign
Horizontal order does not indicate birth order

3 The Seleucids from Antiochus III and Laodice

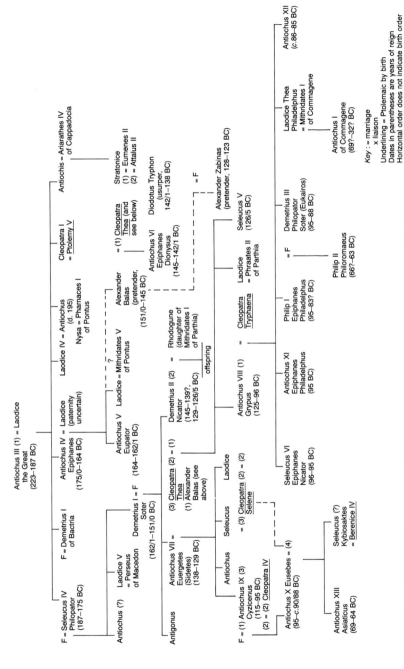

Key: = : marriage
x : liaison
Underlining = Ptolemaic by birth
Dates in parentheses are years of reign
Horizontal order does not indicate birth order

NOTES

1 FROM MYTH TO LEGEND: THE EARLIEST CLEOPATRAS

1 Gomme and Sandbach, 1973: 133.
2 Henderson, 1975: 134–5.
3 Articles on the mythological Cleopatras (Kleopatra 1–10) are by Eitrem, 1921: 732–4, those on the historical Cleopatras by Stähelin, 1921: 734–89 (Kleopatra 11–29: Kleopatra 29 is a doublet of no. 10), and Stein, 1921: 789. Stähelin, 1924: 912 adds another minor historical Cleopatra.
4 For the mythological Cleopatras see also Roscher, 1894: 1223–4 s.v. Kleopatra.
5 On the variants of the Cleopatra myth see Pearson, 1917: II 311–15.
6 For what follows I have relied mainly on Hammond and Griffith, 1979 and Borza, 1990.
7 Hammond and Griffith, 1979: 99.
8 Borza, 1990: 82–3, 110–13 rejects the whole story of the Macedonian link with the Temenidae as a fifth-century invention of Alexander I, designed to ingratiate himself with the mainland Greeks.
9 The list survives only in fragmentary form on a papyrus (P.Oxy. XXVII 2465 fr. 1, col. ii), although variant versions are cited by other writers.
10 Hammond and Griffith, 1979: 13.

2 CLEOPATRA, PERDICCAS II, AND ARCHELAUS

1 The Briges were the ancestors of the Phrygians of north-western Asia Minor, whither they seem to have migrated c. 800 BC: see Hammond, 1972: 410–14. This was well before the arrival of Perdiccas and his brothers. It was not the Briges whom the Macedonians dispossessed but the Bottiaeans (Thucydides 2.99.3). The confusion has arisen out of the fact that Midas is so common as a Phrygian dynastic name that it has attached itself to the later ruler of an area once dominated by the founders of the Phrygian state.

2 Borza, 1990: 84.
3 The date of Alexander I's death is calculated as *c.* 452 BC by Hammond and Griffith, 1979: 103–4.
4 For the view that the division of the kingdom between Perdiccas and his brothers Alcetas and Philip was intended by Alexander see Cole, 1974: 55–7, followed by Borza, 1990: 135. Hammond and Griffith, 1979: 115 regard it as the accidental outcome of Alexander's sudden and perhaps violent death. Alexander must have been at least 60, perhaps older at the time of his demise. It is difficult to believe that he would not have made some arrangements regarding the succession but only too easy to believe that they were disregarded after his death.
5 '[Plato's] representation is too baroque to have been entirely fabricated': Greenwalt, 1989: 23.
6 For what follows I have mainly followed Greenwalt, 1989. The problem of what rules governed the Macedonian royal succession and how closely they were followed has been much discussed; see Hatzopoulos, 1986 and Prestianni Giallombardo, 1977. Greenwalt's explanation seems to me the most cogent, although even he does not give sufficient weight to what could be called the principle of 'open slather'. It was entirely in keeping with the traditions of the Argeads that the race seems often to have gone to the strongest.
7 See Hammond and Griffith, 1979: 699–701.
8 IG I³ 89.
9 Hammond and Griffith, 1979: 136.
10 See Hammond and Griffith, 1979: 169, n.2, Borza, 1990: 178.
11 Hammond and Griffith, 1979: 169, n.2.
12 Greenwalt, 1989.
13 Greenwalt, 1988b.
14 For a brief summary of the early history of the Lyncestae see Hammond and Griffith, 1979: 14–17.
15 For references see Borza, 1990: 153, n.56.
16 Borza, 1990: 154, n.58.
17 Greenwalt, 1988a: 37.

3 PHILIP II'S LAST WIFE

1 Or perhaps his excerptor. The fragment of Satyrus is quoted by Athenaeus 13. 557b–e. It is unclear whether these words form part of Satyrus' original account or are a précis by Athenaeus. The passage is discussed by Tronson, 1984.
2 After the death of Alexander the Great in 323 BC Arrhidaeus eventually became king for a brief period as Philip III or Philip Arrhidaeus, in a co-regency with Alexander's posthumous son. But at that stage the Argeads were desperately scraping the bottom of the dynastic barrel. The nature of Arrhidaeus' incapacity is discussed by Greenwalt, 1984: 74–6.
3 For the date see the arguments of Heckel, 1981: 54–5.

NOTES

4 See Borza, 1983, who discusses the role of the symposium at Alexander's court.
5 Carney, 1992: 176–7.
6 Kate Mortensen has reminded me that the marriage of Amyntas, Philip's nephew, to Cynanne, Philip's daughter by his second wife Audata, is also thought to have taken place in this period. If that is so, then Alexander would really have felt hemmed in.
7 It is also difficult to deny that in this part of the *Life of Alexander*, which deals with the boyhood of Alexander, Plutarch is giving a strictly chronological account of events.

4   A DOUBLE MYSTERY

1 Diodorus 16.93–4, Justin 9.6.4–7.14, Aristotle, *Politics* 1311b.2. The fragmentary P. Oxy. XV 1798 (=FGH 148 F 1) adds little.
2 The date is based upon the fact that Diodorus (16.93.6) connects the rape with an Illyrian war and the last Illyrian war mentioned by him (16.69.7) is datable to 344 BC. For persuasive arguments that the rape should rather be dated between 338/7 BC and spring 336 BC see Fears, 1975: 120–3.
3 Develin, 1981: 98–9, Heckel, 1981: 57.
4 Perhaps in June 336 BC, although the exact date is uncertain.
5 Hammond and Griffith, 1979: 484.
6 Both Develin, 1981: 98, and Ellis, 1981: 128–9 reject the notion of Persian involvement in the murder of Philip but offer no arguments for disbelieving it.
7 For the latter view see Ellis, 1981: 122.
8 Lehmann, 1980: 527–31.
9 First mentioned in Lane Fox, 1980: 80–4.
10 Thus Borza, 1990: 266.
11 Musgrave, 1991: 7, n.21.
12 For views about the number (and sex) of Cleopatra's children, see Musgrave, 1991: 7, nn.23, 24. Ancient 'evidence' for the existence of a son as well as a daughter depends upon Pausanias 8.7.7 and Justin 11.2.3.
13 Xirotiris and Langenscheidt, 1981: 142ff. See most recently Musgrave, 1991: 3, who favours 'the upper end of the range, say, 45–50'.
14 Details in Carney, 1991: 18.

5   ALEXANDER'S SISTER

1 Kingsley, 1986: 169–70.
2 Hammond, 1980: 472–3.
3 Livy 8.24.17 speaks of the mutilated corpse of Alexander of Epirus being returned home to 'his wife Cleopatra and his sister Olympias', but that may imply only that Olympias was temporarily present as a mourner.
4 Hammond, 1980: 475.

5 Suidas s.v. 'Leonnatos'.
6 Carney, 1988: 399.
7 Details in Diodorus 18.33–6.
8 Hornblower, 1981: 162.
9 'Tiring of her semi-captivity in Sardis': Macurdy, 1932: 47.

6 FROM AEGAE TO ALEXANDRIA

1 Errington, 1974: 20–37.
2 For details of Macedonian history during the Antigonid period see, in ascending order of comprehensiveness, Green, 1990: passim, Errington, 1990: 162–217, Hammond and Walbank, 1988: 259–569. For Roman–Macedonian relations, see Gruen, 1984: passim, Hammond and Walbank, 1988: 391ff.
3 Walbank, 1957–79: I 564–5.
4 The account is preserved in Athenaeus 5.196a–203b. On the procession see Rice, 1983 although, following Fraser, 1972: I 231–2, she does not accept the view that the procession is that of the Ptolemaieia of 271/0 bc.
5 Walbank, 1957–79: II 523, 546.
6 Gruen, 1984: 673–5.
7 Gruen, 1984: 679.
8 Gruen, 1984: 681–2.

7 THE SELEUCID CONNECTION (1): CLEOPATRA I

1 OGIS I 90. For an excellent up-to-date translation of the Rosetta Stone and a discussion of its historical significance see Quirke and Andrews, 1988.
2 Holleaux, 1942: 339–55.
3 Walbank, 1957–79: III 356, Gruen, 1984: 684, n.63.
4 Green, 1990: 350.
5 Details in Richter, 1965: III 265, and see also Boussac, 1989. It is clear too from the gold octodrachm that the identifications by Thompson, 1973: 92–3 of several of the faience portrait figures from Ptolemaic Egypt as representations of Cleopatra I must now be abandoned.
6 Illustrated in Richter, 1984: 234, figs 210 and 212.
7 Smith, 1988: 75–6.
8 Eddy, 1961: 300.
9 The first royal marriage between brother and sister had been that of Ptolemy II and Arsinoe II, hence their title Philadelphus (Brother/sister loving). But Ptolemy III was the product of the king's earlier union with Arsinoe I, the daughter of Lysimachus.
10 Pestman, 1967: 15.
11 Pestman, 1967: 46.
12 Mitford, 1957: 180–1.
13 Rostovtzeff, 1941: 712–19.

14 Evidence for April in Samuel, 1962: 140, for July in Pestman et al., 1977: no.9, note a.
15 Pestman, 1967: 142–3.

8 CLEOPATRA II AND PTOLEMY VI

1 Although it remains unsure whether Cleopatra II was the eldest.
2 Pestman, 1967: 46–7.
3 Bevan, 1927: 283.
4 Macurdy, 1932: 148. For an attempt to give a less biased view of Eulaeus and Lenaeus see Mørkholm, 1961.
5 Habicht, 1989: 343–6, gives a judicious summary of the war from Antiochus IV's viewpoint.
6 Carney, 1987: 434.
7 Gruen, 1984: 650–1.
8 Gruen, 1984: 652.
9 Fraser, 1972: I 119, II 211, n.212.
10 Walbank, 1957–79: III 322.
11 Porphyry FGH 260 F 49 A–B.
12 On their background see Mørkholm, 1961: 39–41.
13 Ray, 1976: 26 (Text 3.9–10 verso).
14 Translated by J. D. Ray.
15 Ray, 1976: 33 (Text 5.2,5), 124–5.
16 Samuel, 1962: 142–3.
17 Pestman, 1967: 50.
18 Macurdy, 1932: 150–1.
19 Schürer, 1973: I 169.
20 Josephus in fact contradicts himself from one account to another; for details see Tcherikover, 1959: 276–7.
21 The colony still existed in Roman times when it was known as 'the Jewish camp'. In 48 BC the Jews there were still numerous enough to present an obstacle to the army of Mithradates and Antipater on its way from Palestine to support Julius Caesar; for details see Tcherikover, 1959: 278–9, Schürer, 1973: III.i 48.

9 CLEOPATRA II AND PTOLEMY VIII

1 For evidence of Jewish settlement elsewhere in the Delta at this period see Schürer, 1973: III.i 47–9, Kasher, 1985: 106–35. For the status of Jewish military colonists in Ptolemaic Egypt see Kasher, 1985: 38–63.
2 Ptolemy VI's case was helped by the fact that he now had the redoubtable figure of Cato the Censor speaking up for him in the senate; see Astin, 1978: 270–1. Cato was a politician whom only the foolhardy would cross.
3 Eupator is first attested as co-ruler between 4 April and 31 August 152 BC in both Greek and demotic texts: see Schubert, 1992: 120 and n.6. He was not yet co-ruler on 3 February that year and he was perhaps already dead by the end of August.

4 Walbank, 1957–79: III 546–7.
5 For variant views see Gruen, 1984: 710, n.183.
6 An amnesty decree issued by Ptolemy VIII in Cyprus in December/January 145/4 BC partly survives on an inscription (SEG XII 548) in the National Museum, Nicosia.
7 Lanciers, 1988: 422–3.
8 For discussion of the version in 3 Maccabees see Schürer, 1973: III.i 537–41.
9 Probably 140–138 BC; see Astin, 1959.
10 The garment Ptolemy VIII is described as wearing, a *chitoniskos*, would have come only to the knees, the sleeves only to the elbows, on a man of normal size.
11 Macurdy, 1932: 156.
12 Menecles of Barce FGH 270 F 9.
13 For the relationship between Ptolemy Memphites' birth and Ptolemy VIII's Egyptian coronation see Thompson, 1988: 152.
14 Pestman, 1967: 54–7.
15 Ptolemy IX's birthdate is fixed by its coincidence with that of a new Apis bull, born on 18 February 142 BC; Mooren, 1988: 438.
16 Valerius Maximus 9.2.5. An earlier date is suggested for the atrocity by Fraser, 1972: II 166, n.325.
17 Not all the Cyrenaeans had been in favour of Ptolemy VIII when he was foisted on them as 'king' in 163 BC. Ptolemy VI had been able to counter his brother's first attempt on Cyprus (162 BC) by fomenting a rebellion against him in Cyrene, and it was only with difficulty that Ptolemy VIII had kept control of the city (Polybius 31.18).
18 Assuming the coincidence between the birth of the Apis bull and Cleopatra III's son Ptolemy IX is correct, Cleopatra III must have been at least a year beyond puberty in 142 BC. Her date of birth is usually given as 160–155 BC, making her somewhere between 12 and 17 years old at the time of her impregnation.
19 See Pestman, in press: 86. I am indebted to Professor Pestman for kindly providing me with a copy of this reference. Following Boswinkel and Pestman, 1982: 64–7, the date of the marriage used to be put in late 140 or early 139 BC. Its exact date is unimportant (although we should like to know whether by that time Cleopatra III was already pregnant again with Ptolemy X). What is significant is that it took place only after the birth of Ptolemy IX.
20 P. dém. Berl. 3113, quoted by Boswinkel and Pestman, 1982: 65.
21 For the date of P.Amh. II 45 see Pestman, 1985: 24, n.2.
22 P. dém. Berl. 3090+91, quoted by Boswinkel and Pestman, 1982: 65.
23 Pestman, 1967: 56–60.
24 Will, 1979–82: II 428.
25 Otto and Bengtson, 1938: 47–8. Their argument relies heavily on the fact that it was in 132 BC that Ptolemy VIII first took the title Tryphon (The Magnificent), but this need not be connected with any Syrian ambitions.
26 Pestman, 1967: 64, Samuel, 1962: 147–9.

10 CLEOPATRA II, CLEOPATRA III, AND PTOLEMY VIII

1 On the question of the will see Chapter 14.
2 Macurdy, 1932: 161.
3 Otto and Bengtson, 1938: 30.
4 Boswinkel and Pestman, 1982: 66, n.4, Rowell, 1990: 77.
5 On the date of Cleopatra III's birth see Chapter 9, n.18.
6 Perhaps even the previous year (Pestman, 1967: 148), but see also Boswinkel and Pestman, 1982: 65.
7 See Chapter 9.
8 See Thompson, 1988: 290, Appendix D.
9 For further details see Thompson, 1988: 194.
10 For references see Thompson, 1988: 290.
11 Mooren, 1988: 442.
12 See Chapter 9, n. 19.
13 Otto and Bengtson, 1938: 45ff.
14 A demotic text, P.BM 10384, suggests that Cleopatra II had already broken with her brother by 11 November 132 BC; see Mooren, 1988: 436, n.10.
15 See Samuel, 1962: 145–6.
16 In P.Amh. II 44 of 138/7 BC.
17 For a full listing see Clarysse and Van der Veken, 1983.
18 Pestman, 1967: 146–7.
19 Otto and Bengtson, 1938: 88–9.
20 Most recently by Cauville and Devauchelle, 1984: 48–50. For a rebuttal see Mooren, 1988: 443–4, n.58.
21 P. Köln II 81.
22 We know of the nickname Kokke only indirectly because her younger son Ptolemy X was called 'Kokke's child' (Strabo 17.797C, *Chronicon Paschale* p.347 Bonn). The Greek word *kokkos* means 'scarlet' but it is unclear in what way Cleopatra III was scarlet. Hesychius gives 'vagina' as a slang meaning and Green, 1990: 877, n.4 therefore suggests that she may have been known as Cleopatra the Cunt.

11 CLEOPATRA III AND HER CHILDREN

1 For full listing see Thompson, 1989: 699, n.17.
2 Pestman, 1967: 152.
3 Once in late 110 to early 109 BC for a period of about three months, and again for an even shorter period between March and May 108 BC; see Otto and Bengtson, 1938: 162–73, Samuel, 1962: 150.
4 Boswinkel and Pestman, 1982: 67–9.
5 Cleopatra III may have already been associated with Aphrodite on Cyprus itself from before 131 BC if the doubtful restoration originally proposed for OGIS I 159.3–4 as 'High Priest of Paphian Aphrodite and Cleopatra the goddess' is accepted.
6 Pestman, 1967: 155.

7 Yet the 'saviour' title (Soter/Soteira) was not dropped elsewhere. To give a semblance of continuity it was retained in the royal protocol. Ptolemy X took his brother's titles Philometor Soter while Cleopatra III herself kept the same titles as before but sometimes added Thea Euergetis, which she had borne during her marriage to Ptolemy VIII Euergetes; see Pestman, 1967: 69–70.
8 For Ptolemy IX in Cyprus see Mitford, 1959: 104, 127–8.
9 Van't Dack et al., 1989: 39–49.
10 For references see Van't Dack et al., 1989: 126, n.59.
11 According to the editor the meaning of the term translated as 'high ground' is apparently far from clear. It might mean a hill or patch of scrub adjacent to Ptolemais, where the invasion force was encamped, rather than a high point within the city itself.
12 Or 'a company of men to go to the town'.
13 Van't Dack et al., 1989: 75–7, 110.
14 Van't Dack et al., 1989: 77ff.
15 Bevan, 1927: 331, Macurdy, 1932: 168.
16 Van't Dack et al., 1989: 123 and n.48.
17 P. Adl.Gr. 11 and 12. See the discussion of Samuel, 1962: 152 and Pestman, 1967: 72.
18 Justin 39.4.5–6, Pausanias 1.9.3, Poseidonius FGH 87 F 26.
19 Although the king probably associated someone else with him to fulfil the religious duties of the office.
20 Koenen, 1970: 84.
21 Calderini, 1972–87: III,2. 124–5 s.v. Kleopatra.
22 The Street of Cleopatra Aphrodite is last attested in 44 BC (P.Oxy. XIV 1629.7).
23 Arsinoe, Oxyrhynchus, Schedia, and Kom Truga (Delta region); see Ronchi, 1974–7: III 582–4.
24 See Rowell, 1990: 217–18, 225–32.
25 Derchain, 1971: 49, n.4 and pl. 14.
26 Troy, 1986: 179.
27 Otto and Bengtson, 1938: 74, n.1 give full references to Cleopatra VII as Isis and Aphrodite. For her recognition as 'the female Horus' see Troy, 1986: 179–97.

12 THE SELEUCID CONNECTION (2): CLEOPATRA THEA AND HER HUSBANDS

1 For a summary acount of Seleucid history from the accession of Alexander Balas to the death of Antiochus VII see Habicht, 1989: 361–73.
2 Bevan, 1927: 304, quoting Mahaffy.
3 See Chapter 9.
4 See also Josephus, *Jewish Ant.* 13.135–42, Diodorus 33.4, and the useful summary account by Downey, 1961: 122–3.
5 For a summary account see Bivar, 1983: 34–5.
6 Antiochus VII was about 21 in 138 BC.
7 Fischer, 1972: 212–13.

8 For Antiochus VII's Parthian campaign see Fischer, 1970.
9 Not to be confused with Demetrius II's and Cleopatra Thea's son of the same name, who would be king briefly as Seleucus V in 126/5 BC before his murder by his mother.
10 See Richter, 1984: figs 239 and 240 and cf. fig. 261 (Mithradates I).
11 Hence Antiochus IX's nickname Cyzicenus, just as his father Antiochus VII had been called Sidetes from his rearing at Side.
12 Grainger, 1990: 164, n.131 has suggested that, after his years as prisoner of the Parthians, Demetrius II had come to realise that only a union of Syria and Egypt could ensure their survival. His involvement was therefore the result of a deliberate policy. This hardly seems to fit with his earlier actions.
13 Eusebius, *Chron.* 1.257–8. Justin 39.1.4–5 makes Antiochus VII his father. Green, 1990: 876, n.124 suggests that Zabinas may have told both stories at different times but the name Alexander, which was not used as a Seleucid dynastic name (except for Alexander Balas whose parentage was also doubtful), is enough to make one suspect that Justin is simply wrong.
14 Appian, *Syr.* 68, Livy, *Periocha* 60. Grainger, 1991: 135–6 doubts any involvement of Cleopatra Thea in Demetrius II's death, ascribing it to the Tyrian governor who was the king's own appointee.
15 Gardner, 1878: 85, pl. 23.1.
16 Although the similarity is more marked on the later coins of her joint reign with Antiochus VIII Grypus.
17 Otto and Bengtson, 1938: 104, Bellinger, 1949: 65, n.28.
18 Remnants in the medical writer Galen (Kühn) 14, p. 185.
19 Gardner, 1878: 50, pl. 15.1 and 2 (Demetrius I and Laodice), 57, pl. 17.6 and Richter, 1984: fig. 238 (Balas and Cleopatra Thea), and see Houghton, 1988.

13   THE SELEUCID CONNECTION (3): CLEOPATRA SELENE AND THE LAST OF THE SELEUCIDS

1 Bellinger, 1949: 58.
2 For a partisan account of the relationship between the Jews and the independent Greek cities in this period see Kasher, 1990: 120–70.
3 For Cleopatra Selene's children see Chapter 14.
4 Grypus' five sons all became kings of Syria, often in opposition to each other, while his daughter Laodice became the queen of Mithradates I of Commagene.
5 Rather than slave girls perhaps?
6 Josephus, *Jewish Ant.* 13.368. Variant traditions are discussed by Bellinger, 1949: 74, n.70.
7 There are various traditions about Eusebes' death. I have followed the account of Josephus, *Jewish Ant.* 13.371, as Bellinger, 1949: 75, who discusses the variants.
8 As suggested by Bevan, 1902: II 263.
9 Bellinger, 1949: 82.

10 And grandsons of Seleucus IV, who was one of Cleopatra I's brothers.

14 THE TWILIGHT OF THE PTOLEMIES: CLEOPATRA BERENICE III, CLEOPATRA V TRYPHAENA

1 For Cleopatra III's death see Chapter 11.

2 Pestman, 1967: 72. Earlier texts also call Cleopatra Berenice III 'Cleopatra surnamed Berenice' and after 91/0 BC she is simply called 'queen Cleopatra'.

3 Samuel, 1965: 376–85, and most recently Van't Dack et al., 1989: 136–50.

4 Van't Dack et al., 1989: 150.

5 The evidence for the existence of Ptolemy IX's two sons is fully discussed by Otto and Bengtson, 1938: 117, n.1. They are not included by Sullivan, 1990 in his Ptolemaic stemma. If they did exist and were among the grandchildren of Cleopatra III sent to Cos for safekeeping in 103 BC and later captured by Mithradates VI in 88 BC, their presence as hostages at the Pontic court may explain Ptolemy IX's refusal in 87/6 BC to provide Lucullus with a fleet against Mithradates, as Will, 1979–82: II 518 suggests. Indeed they may have been put to death by Mithradates later.

6 Pestman, 1967: 72, 76. For the demotic texts see Van't Dack et al., 1989: 152.

7 It may be significant that Alexander II is mentioned only in texts of 101/0 BC, while queen Cleopatra Berenice only figures rarely in texts of 98–96 BC and never in 96/5 and 95/4 BC; see Pestman, 1967: 72.

8 Fraser, 1972: 124 thinks that it may have been Cleopatra Berenice's age which Ptolemy XI found objectionable (she had been born c. 120 BC, Alexander II c. 105 BC). But there may already have been some friction between them: see n.7.

9 For example by Macurdy, 1932: 176, Sullivan, 1990: 92.

10 For example by Sullivan, 1990: 92.

11 See the discussion of Olshausen, 1963: 30–1, n.39.

12 Summary and bibliography in Van't Dack et al., 1989: 156–61.

13 The refusal of the Roman senate to recognise Ptolemy XII seems to me adequate explanation for the deferral of his native-style coronation until March 76 BC, when it finally took place in Alexandria, without the need for the elaborate theory of Sullivan, 1990: 93–5 that the Memphite high priest Petubastis may have aspired to control part of Egypt during Ptolemy XII's early years as a consequence of his (supposed) relationship to the royal family. To argue that because Petubastis' mother was called Berenice she was an otherwise unattested sister of Ptolemy XI overlooks the fact that many of the wives of these priests are called Berenice or Arsinoe (listing in Thompson, 1988: 132–3, n.124). Their names reflect the importance of the royal cult of Berenice and Arsinoe at Memphis, not their holders' parentage or even their ethnicity.

14 Will, 1979–82: II 520.

15 Bevan, 1927: 354–5.

16 The number is confirmed by Strabo's statement later in the same chapter that on his demise Ptolemy XII left two sons and two daughters, of whom the eldest was Cleopatra VII.

17 So too was the notion of a king ruling without a queen – hence Ptolemy IX's marriage to his own daughter Cleopatra Berenice III.

18 Cleopatra VII was associated with the elder of her two young brothers, Ptolemy XIII, for the first four years of her reign. After his death Ptolemy XIV, who was still younger, became her co-ruler, and after Cleopatra murdered him in her Year 8, his Year 4, in late summer/autumn 44 BC she took her son Caesarion as co-ruler; see Skeat, 1969: 41–2.

15 CLEOPATRA VII'S SUICIDE

1 Pelling, 1988: 10–18, 26–36.

2 For the chronology of Cleopatra's last days in so far as it can be determined see Skeat, 1953.

3 For the location of the mausoleum see Fraser, 1972: II 33–4, n.81.

4 Tarn, 1934: 107–8.

5 See Pelling, 1988: 313.

6 Tarn, 1934: 110, Johnson, 1967: 394.

7 Cleopatra's excuse, that she had wished to keep some items back for presents for Octavian's wife Livia and sister Octavia also occurs in a slightly different form in Dio 51.13.3.

8 Florus 2.21.9–10, drawing upon the same tradition (perhaps Octavian's own memoirs), makes Octavian even more of a good boy scout: 'the chastity of the princeps was too much for her'.

9 Livy, *Periocha* 133, Velleius Paterculus 2.87.1.

10 Pelling, 1988: 317–18.

11 Shakespeare's words are here taken almost exactly word for word from Plutarch, *Antony* 85.8.

12 Dio 51.14.4. The Psylli are also mentioned by Suetonius, *Augustus* 17.4.

13 Virgil, *Aeneid* 8.697, Propertius 3.11.53–4, Horace, *Odes* 1.37.26–8.

14 Griffiths, 1961: 113, n.2.

15 Thus Griffiths, 1961: 118, n.9, after arguing for the symbolic use of two snakes by Cleopatra, still has only three cobras to kill all three women.

16 For this summary of the view of Spiegelberg I have relied on Griffiths, 1961: 113–16.

17 Griffiths, 1961: 113.

18 For example, all three versions of the uraeus occur on the artefacts from Tutankhamun's tomb.

19 See Bevan, 1927: 382, n.2.

20 Tarn, 1934: 109–10. The theory originated with Groag, 1914: 65–6.

21 Johnson, 1967: 394 and Grant, 1972: 225 both doubt the story of Octavian's visit to the queen and Grant suggests that Dolabella was

acting as Octavian's agent when he brought her the information that she and her children were to be sent to Rome within three days.
22 Pelling, 1988: 319.

16   THE END OF THE LINE: CLEOPATRA SELENE OF MAURETANIA

1 For the chronology of Cleopatra VII's last days in so far as it can be determined see Skeat, 1953.
2 For the 18-day reign see Clement of Alexandria, *Stromateis* 21.129.1 f.
3 Alexander Helios, who was dressed in Persian regalia, was made king of Armenia, Parthia, and Media. The 2-year-old Ptolemy Philadelphus, who wore Macedonian dress, was granted Syria, Cilicia, and control over all lands west of the Euphrates as far as the Hellespont, and Cleopatra Selene was given Cyrenaica and Libya: Plutarch, *Antony* 54.4–9, Dio 49.41, and see Pelling, 1988: 249–50.
4 Mazard, 1981.
5 See Braund, 1984.
6 See Gow and Page, 1968: II 225–6.
7 See Macurdy, 1932: 228.
8 Gow and Page, 1968: II 226.
9 For arguments against accepting the existence of a daughter Drusilla see Macurdy, 1932: 225–6.
10 See Euzennat, 1976: 586.
11 Hofmann, 1959: 1780–3. See the contrary arguments of Faur, 1973: 249–53.
12 Fishwick, 1971: 467–73, Fishwick and Shaw, 1976: 491–4.
13 Balsdon, 1934: 192–3. Ptolemy was probably almost 60 years old by this time.

SELECT BIBLIOGRAPHY

Journal titles are abbreviated according to *L'Année Philologique*, editions of papyri according to Oates, J., Bagnall, R. and Willis, W. (1992) *Checklist of Greek and Latin Papyri, Ostraca and Tablets*, 4th edn, Atlanta: Scholars Press. *RE* denotes *Paulys Real-Encyclopädie der classischen Altertumswissenschaft*, ed. Wissowa, G. and Kroll, W., Stuttgart: J. B. Metzler.

Astin, A. E. (1959) 'Diodorus and the date of the embassy to the East of Scipio Aemilianus', *CPh* 54: 221–7.

—— (1978) *Cato the Censor*, Oxford: Clarendon Press.

Balsdon, J. P. V. D. (1934) *The Emperor Gaius*, Oxford: Clarendon Press.

Bellinger, A. R. (1949) 'The end of the Seleucids', *Transactions of the Connecticut Academy of Arts and Sciences* 38: 51–102.

Bevan, E. (1902) *The House of Seleucus*, London: Edward Arnold.

—— (1927) *A History of Egypt under the Ptolemaic Dynasty*, London: Methuen.

Bivar, A. D. H. (1983) 'The political history of Iran under the Arsacids', in *Cambridge History of Iran. Volume 3(1)*, ed. Yarshater, E., Cambridge: Cambridge University Press.

Borza, E. N. (1983) 'The symposium at Alexander's court', *Ancient Macedonia* 3: 45–55.

—— (1990) *In the Shadow of Olympus. The Emergence of Macedon*, Princeton: Princeton University Press.

Boswinkel, E. and Pestman, P. W. (1982) *Les Archives Privées de Dionysios, Fils de Kephalas (P.L.Bat.22)*, Leiden: Brill.

Boussac, M. -F. (1989) 'Cachets de la collection Benaki', *BCH* 113: 325–34.

Braund, D. C. (1984) 'North African rulers and the Roman military paradigm', *Hermes* 112: 255–6.

Calderini, A. (1972–87) *Dizionario dei nomi geografici e topografici dell'Egitto greco-romano*, Milan: Cisalpino-Goliardica.

Carney, E. D. (1987) 'The reappearance of royal sibling marriage in Ptolemaic Egypt', *PP* 237: 420–39.

—— (1988) 'The sisters of Alexander the Great: royal relicts', *Historia* 37: 385–404.

—— (1991) 'The female burial in the antechamber of Tomb II at Vergina', *Ancient World* 22.2: 17–26.

—— (1992) 'The politics of polygamy: Olympias, Alexander and the murder of Philip II', *Historia* 41: 169–89.

Cauville, S. and Devauchelle, D. (1984) 'Le temple d'Edfou: Etapes de la construction. Nouvelles données historiques', *RevEg.* 35: 31–55.

Clarysse, W. and Van der Veken, G. (1983) *The Eponymous Priests of Ptolemaic Egypt (P.L.Bat. 24)*, Leiden: Brill.

Cole, J. W. (1974) 'Perdiccas and Athens', *Phoenix* 28: 55–72.

Derchain, P. (1971) *El Kab I. Les monuments religieux à l'entrée de l'Ouady Hellal*, Brussels: Fondation Egyptologique Reine Elizabeth.

Develin, R. (1981) 'The murder of Philip II', *Antichthon* 15: 86–99.

Downey, G. (1961) *A History of Antioch in Syria from Seleucus to the Arab Conquest*, Princeton: Princeton University Press.

Eddy, S. K. (1961) *The King is Dead*, Lincoln: University of Nebraska Press.

Eitrem, S. (1921) 'Kleopatra 1–10', *RE* 11.1: 732–4.

Ellis, J. R. (1981) 'The assassination of Philip II', in *Ancient Macedonian Studies in Honor of Charles F. Edson*, Thessaloniki: Institute for Balkan Studies.

Errington, R. M. (1974) 'Macedonian "Royal Style" and its historical significance', *JHS* 94: 20–37.

—— (1990) *A History of Macedonia*, Berkeley, Los Angeles, Oxford: University of California Press.

Euzennat, M. (1976) 'Mogador ("Cerne")', in *Princeton Encyclopedia of Classical Sites*, ed. Stillwell, R. et al., Princeton: Princeton University Press.

Faur, J.-C. (1973) 'Caligula et la Maurétanie: la fin de Ptolémée', *Klio* 55: 249–71.

Fears, J. R. (1975) 'Pausanias, the assassin of Philip II', *Athenaeum* 53: 111–35.

Fischer, T. (1970) *Untersuchungen zum Partherkrieg Antiochus' VII. im Rahmen der Seleukidengeschichte*, self-published dissertation, Munich and Tübingen.

—— (1972) 'Zu Tryphon', *Chiron* 2: 201–13.

Fishwick, D. (1971) 'The annexation of Mauretania', *Historia* 20: 467–87.

Fishwick, D. and Shaw, B. D. (1976) 'Ptolemy of Mauretania and the conspiracy of Gaetulicus', *Historia* 25: 491–4.

Fraser, P. M. (1972) *Ptolemaic Alexandria*, Oxford: Oxford University Press.

Gardner, P. (1878) *A Catalogue of Greek Coins in the British Museum. IV. The Seleucid Kings of Syria*, ed. Poole, R.S., London: Longmans.

Gomme, A. W. and Sandbach, F. H. (1973) *Menander. A Commentary*, Oxford: Oxford University Press.

Gow, A. S. F. and Page, D. L. (1968) *The Greek Anthology. The Garland of Philip*, Cambridge: Cambridge University Press.

Grainger, J. D. (1990) *The Cities of Seleucid Syria*, Oxford: Clarendon Press.

—— (1991) *Hellenistic Phoenicia*, Oxford: Clarendon Press.

Grant, M. (1972) *Cleopatra*, London: Weidenfeld & Nicolson.

Green, P. (1990) *Alexander to Actium. The Hellenistic Age*, London: Thames & Hudson.

Greenwalt, W. S. (1984) 'The search for Arrhidaeus', *Ancient World* 10: 69–77.

—— (1988a) 'Amyntas III and the political stability of Argead Macedonia', *Ancient World* 18: 35–44.

—— (1988b) 'The marriageability age at the Argead court: 360–317 BC', *CW* 82: 93–7.

—— (1989) 'Polygamy and succession in Argead Macedonia', *Arethusa* 22: 19–45.

Griffiths, J. G. (1961) 'The death of Cleopatra VII', *JEA* 47: 113–18.

Groag, E. (1914) 'Beiträge zur Geschichte des zweiten Triumvirats', *Klio* 14: 43–68.

Gruen, E. (1984) *The Hellenistic World and the Coming of Rome*, Berkeley, Los Angeles, London: University of California Press.

Habicht, C. (1989) 'The Seleucids and their rivals', in *Cambridge Ancient History. Volume 8*, ed. Astin, A. E. et al., 2nd edn, Cambridge: Cambridge University Press.

Hammond, N. (1972) *A History of Macedonia. I*, Oxford: Clarendon Press.

Hammond, N. and Griffith, G. (1979) *A History of Macedonia. II*, Oxford: Clarendon Press.

—— (1980) 'Some passages in Arrian concerning Alexander', *CQ* 30: 455–76.

Hammond, N. and Walbank, F. W. (1988) *A History of Macedonia. III*, Oxford: Clarendon Press.

Hatzopoulos, M. B. (1986) 'Succession and regency in classical Macedonia', *Ancient Macedonia* 4: 279–92.

Heckel, W. (1981) 'Philip and Olympias (337/6 BC)', in *Classical Contributions. Studies in Honour of M. F. McGregor*, ed. Shrimpton, G. S. and McCargar, D. J., Locust Valley, NY: J. J. Augustin.

Heinen, H. (1974) 'Les mariages de Ptolémée VIII Euergète et leur chronologie', *Akten XIII internationalen Papyrologenkongresses. Marburg/ Lahn 1971*, Munich: C. H. Beck Verlag.

Henderson, J. (1975) *The Maculate Muse*, New Haven and London: Yale University Press.

Hofmann, M. (1959) 'Ptolemaios von Mauretanien', *RE* 23.2: 1768–87.

Holleaux, M. (1942) *Etudes d'Epigraphie et d'Histoire Grecques. III. Lagides et Séleucides*, Paris: Boccard.

Hornblower, N. J. (1981) *Hieronymus of Cardia*, Oxford: Oxford University Press.

Houghton, A. (1988) 'The double portrait coins of Alexander I Balas and Cleopatra Thea', *SNR* 67: 85–93.

Johnson, W. R. (1967) 'A Quean, a great Queen? Cleopatra and the politics of misrepresentation', *Arion* 6: 387–402.

Kasher, A. (1985) *The Jews in Hellenistic and Roman Egypt*, Tübingen: J. C. B. Mohr (Paul Siebeck).

—— (1990) *Jews and Hellenistic Cities in Eretz-Israel*, Tübingen: J. C. B. Mohr (Paul Siebeck).

Kingsley, B. M. (1986) 'Harpalos in the Megarid (333–331 BC) and the grain shipments from Cyrene', *ZPE* 66: 165–77.

Koenen, L. (1970) 'Kleopatra III als Priesterin des Alexanderkultes', *ZPE* 5: 61–84.

Lanciers, E. (1988) 'Die Alleinherrschaft des Ptolemaios VIII', *Proc. XVIII International Congress of Papyrology. Athens 1986*, Athens: Greek Papyrological Society, 2: 405–33.

Lane Fox, R. (1980) *The Search for Alexander*, London: Allen Lane.

Lehmann, P. W. (1980) 'The so-called tomb of Philip II. A different interpretation', *AJA* 84: 527–31.

Macurdy, G. H. (1932) *Hellenistic Queens. A Study of Woman Power in Macedonia, Seleucid Syria, and Ptolemaic Egypt*, Baltimore: Johns Hopkins Press.

Mazard, J. (1981) 'Un denier inédit de Juba II et Cléopâtre-Séléné', *GNS* 31: 1–2.

Mitford, T. B. (1957) 'Ptolemy Macron', *Studi Calderini-Paribeni* 2: 163–87.

—— (1959) 'Helenos, governor of Cyprus', *JHS* 79: 94–131.

Mooren, L. (1988) 'The wives and children of Ptolemy VIII Euergetes II', *Proc. XVIII International Congress of Papyrology. Athens 1986*, Athens: Greek Papyrological Society, 2: 435–44.

Mørkholm, O. (1961) 'Eulaios and Lenaios', *ClMed* 22: 32–43.

—— (1966) *Antiochus IV of Syria*, Copenhagen: Gyldendal.

Musgrave, J. H. (1991) 'The human remains from Vergina Tombs I, II and III: an overview', *Ancient World* 22.2: 3–9.

Olshausen, E. (1963) *Rom und Ägypten von 116 bis 51 v. Chr.*, self-published dissertation, Erlangen and Nürnberg.

Otto, W. (1934) *Zur Geschichte der Zeit des 6. Ptolemäers*, Munich: Bayerischen Akademie der Wissenschaften.

Otto, W. and Bengtson, H. (1938) *Zur Geschichte des Niederganges des Ptolemäerreiches*, Munich: Bayerischen Akademie der Wissenschaften.

Pearson, A. C. (1917) *The Fragments of Sophocles. II*, Cambridge: Cambridge University Press.

Pelling, C. B. R. (ed.) (1988) *Plutarch. Life of Antony*, Cambridge: Cambridge University Press.

Peremans, W. and Van't Dack, E. (1968) *Prosopographia Ptolemaica VI*, Louvain: Publications Universitaires.

Pestman, P. W. (1967) *Chronologie Egyptienne d'après les Textes Démotiques (332 avant J.-C. – 453 après J. -C. (P.L.Bat. 15)*, Leiden: Brill.

—— (ed.) (1985) *Textes et Etudes de Papyrologie Grecque, Démotique et Copte (P.L.Bat. 23)*, Leiden: Brill.

—— (ed.) (in press) *The Archive of the Theban Choachytes (Second Century BC)*, Leiden: Brill.

Pestman, P. W. et al. (1977) *Recueil de Textes Démotiques et Bilingues*, Leiden: Brill.

Poole, R. S. (1883) *A Catalogue of Greek Coins in the British Museum. VII. The Ptolemies, Kings of Egypt*, London: Methuen.

Prestianni Giallombardo, A. M. (1977) ' "Diritto" matrimoniale ereditario e dinastico nella Macedonia di Filippo II', *Rivista Storica dell'Antichita* 6–7: 81–110.

Quaegebeur, J. (1978) 'Reines ptolémaïques et traditions égyptiennes', in *Das ptolemaïsche Ägypten*, ed. Maehler, H. and Strocka, V. M., Mainz am Rhein: Philipp von Zabern.

Quirke, S. and Andrews, C. (1988) *The Rosetta Stone: Facsimile Drawing with an Introduction and Translations*, London: British Museum Press.

Ray, J. D. (1976) *The Archive of Hor*, London: Egypt Exploration Society.

Rice, E. E. (1983) *The Grand Procession of Ptolemy Philadelphus*, Oxford: Oxford University Press.

Richter, G. M. A. (1965) *The Portraits of the Greeks*, London: Phaidon.

—— (1984) *The Portraits of the Greeks*, abridged and revised by R.R.R. Smith, Oxford: Phaidon.

Ronchi, G. (1974–7) *Lexicon Theonymon rerumque sacrarum et divinarum ad Aegyptum pertinentium*, Milan: Cisalpino-Goliardica.

Roscher, W. H. (ed.) (1890–4) *Ausführliches Lexikon der griechischen und römischen Mythologie*, Leipzig: B.G. Teubner Verlag.

Rostovtzeff, M. (1941) *A Social and Economic History of the Hellenistic World*, Oxford: Clarendon Press.

Rowell, S. M. (1990) *'Kleopatra III: A Revisionist View'*, unpublished MA(Hons) thesis, Macquarie University.

Samuel, A. E. (1962) *Ptolemaic Chronology*, Munich: C. H. Beck Verlag.

—— (1965) 'Year 27=30 and 88 BC', *CE* 80: 376–400.

Schubert, P. (1992) 'Une attestation de Ptolémée Eupator régnant?', *ZPE* 94: 119–22.

Schürer, E. (1973) *The History of the Jewish People in the Age of Jesus Christ (175 BC–AD 135)*, rev. edn by Vermes, G. and Millar, F., Edinburgh: T. & T. Clark.

Skeat, T. C. (1953) 'The last days of Cleopatra: a chronological problem', *JRS* 43: 98–100.

—— (1969) *The Reigns of the Ptolemies*, 2nd edn, Munich: C. H. Beck Verlag.

Smith, R. R. R. (1988) *Hellenistic Royal Portraits*, Oxford: Clarendon Press.

Stähelin, F. (1921) 'Kleopatra 11–29', *RE* 11.1: 734–89.

—— (1924) 'Kleopatra 22a', *RE* Supplementband 4: 912.

Stein, A. (1921) 'Kleopatra 30–33', *RE* 11.1: 789.

Sullivan, R. D. (1990) *Near Eastern Royalty and Rome, 100–30 BC*, Toronto: University of Toronto Press.

Tarn, W. W. (1934) 'The East against the West. Section vii. Alexandria', in *Cambridge Ancient History. Volume 10*, ed. Cook, S. A. et al., Cambridge: Cambridge University Press.

Tcherikover, V. (1959) *Hellenistic Civilization and the Jews*, Philadelphia: Jewish Publication Society of America.

Thompson, D. B. (1973) *Ptolemaic Oinochoai and Portraits in Faience*, Oxford: Clarendon Press.

Thompson, D. J. (1988) *Memphis under the Ptolemies*, Princeton: Princeton University Press.

—— (1989) 'Pausanias and protocol: the succession to Euergetes II', in *Egitto e Storia Antica dall'Ellenismo all'Età Araba*, ed. Criscuolo, L. and Geraci, G., Bologna: Editrice CLUEB.

Tronson, A. (1984) 'Satyrus the Peripatetic and the marriages of Philip II', *JHS* 104: 116–26.

Troy, L. (1986) *Patterns of Queenship in Ancient Egyptian Myth and History*, Uppsala: Boreas.

Van't Dack, E. et al. (1989) *The Judean–Syrian–Egyptian Conflict of 103–101 BC. A Multilingual Dossier concerning a 'War of Sceptres'*, Brussels: Koninklijke Academie.

Walbank, F. W. (1957–79) *A Historical Commentary on Polybius*, Oxford: Oxford University Press.

Will, E. (1979–82) *Histoire politique du monde hellénistique*, 2nd edn, Nancy: Presses Universitaires.

Xirotiris, N. I. and Langenscheidt, F. (1981) 'The cremation from the royal Macedonian Tombs at Vergina', *ArchEph*. 142–60.

INDEX

233